APPRECIATING
WHISKY

PHILLIP HILLS

HarperCollins*Publishers*

Phillip Hills is the founder of the Scotch Malt Whisky Society, through which he led the revolution in public understanding of malt whisky and created the market for specially bottled fine malts which all whisky companies now supply. He is the director of The Malt Masterclass, a company specialising in corporate tastings and classes. He is also the first (and only) holder since 1791 of a private licence to distill whisky, which he does for demonstration purposes using a copper pot-still.

HarperCollins Publishers
Westerhill Rd, Bishopbriggs, Glasgow G64 2QT Scotland

www.collins.co.uk

First published 2000
This edition 2002

Reprint 10 9 8 7 6 5 4 3 2 1 0

ISBN 0 00 714713 9

Illustration credits
Fiona Steel pp 18, 22, 86, all chemical diagrams; Graham Lees pp 42 (top), 43 (top), 105, 147, 148, 149, 189; The Macallan Distillers Ltd 78, 80, 87, 88, 90, 96, 97 (bottom), 99 (right), 102,110,111, 157; Seagram UK Ltd pp 43 (centre), 94, 95, 101; Morrison Bowmore pp 81 (left), 103, 107, 140, 153, 154; North British Distileries pp 114, 173, 174; Glenmorangie plc pp 82, 89, 13, 164, 167; Willian Grant & Sons pp 169, 172; Kintyre Photography pp 160, 161;Gordon & Macphail Ltd pp 178, 180; The Scotch Whisky Research Institute p 38; The Scotch Malt Whisky Society p 182; The Malt Masterclass p 185; Glenturret Distilleries p 89; PhotoDisc Inc. p 42; National Museums of Scotland p 170; M. Hedderwick p 37

Printed and bound in Singapore by Imago

Contents

INTRODUCTION

To appreciate a thing is to evaluate it, to know its worth. That is not the same as knowing its price. Any fool can find the price of something: it is what you must pay the owner to induce him to part with it. Worth is quite independent of price. Only if you know its worth, can you decide whether the price is right, so knowing the worth is logically prior to knowing the price. Appreciating whisky is about knowing the worth of whisky.

I must say that that the title wasn't my idea. For years, now, I have been saying things about whisky which some people seemed to find interesting and others offensive, and which my friends have urged me to write about, preferably in the form of a book. But the things I was saying were very different sorts of things (I am versatile in the matter of offence) and it was far from clear just how the book should be organised. I got as far as making a rather vague proposal to the publishers. They liked the proposal, but not my title (*How To Make Enemies With Scotch Whisky*). They suggested *Appreciating Whisky*. At first I thought it was a lousy title, but the more I thought about it, the more apparent it became that it comprehended most of the things I wanted to say.

Appreciating whisky involves enjoying it and knowing what it is you enjoy. Both parts are essential to appreciation. You can enjoy something without appreciating it: pigs appear to enjoy their swill, but we would not say that they were capable of appreciating it, for (we assume) they bring no intelligence or critical appraisal to their enjoyment. On the other hand, you can know a whole lot about something, but merely knowing it does not mean that you appreciate it. I once had an English professor who knew everything there was to know about Shakespeare except the delight. To appreciate, you have to value. Cromwell (I hope his shade will forgive my using his words in so banal a context) said his ideal soldier was 'a plain, russet-coated captain, who knows what he fights for, and loves what he knows.' 'Love' is maybe too strong a term to use of whisky – it is only liquor, after all – so I will employ the more mundane 'enjoy'. So long as you get the drift ...

I should make it clear at the outset that by speaking of love and knowledge of whisky, I have no wish to imply that appreciation is a rarefied matter, confined to a few cognoscenti, who are entitled to treat the rest of us as plebs because we don't have their acumen or their understanding. Anyone who has both love and knowledge is able to appreciate. My favourite example comes from Steinbeck's *Cannery Row*: it is not only entertaining, it is a perfectly accurate portrayal of appreciation. I will paraphrase.

Mack and the boys are bums who live in a converted barn on a vacant lot next to the canneries in Monterey. One of their number, Angel, has a part-time job as barman in La Ida's, a well-managed whorehouse and social service facility. Mac and the boys are perennially dry, since they lack the wherewithal to purchase liquor. Angel keeps a jug beneath the bar of La Ida's, which is known as the Wining Jug, into which is pitched anything anyone leaves in a glass. The resulting potation, while not refined, is at least varied, depending as it does on who leaves what in his glass. Every evening after Angel has returned from work, Mac and the boys sample the contents of the Wining Jug. This they do with great seriousness and gratitude. They sample, they savour, and they discuss. They remark on any unusual elements. They know how much wine has been ordered and how much beer; they catch the whiff of anything unusual in the mix. And as the jug goes down, they reminisce about previous wining jugs, about refined or exotic admixtures. They appreciate.

If this seems too fictional an account, I can tell you about my friend Jimmy the Fish. Tim Steward and I run a lot of whisky tastings. Few people who go to a whisky tasting drink all the whisky, and there is usually a lot left in the glasses. When we clear up afterwards, we generally tip the remains into a plastic water bottle and Tim gives the mixture, a litre at a time, to Jimmy. We have to ration it, otherwise Jimmy would kill himself, for he is fond of the stuff. It is, however, evident that his appreciation goes well beyond the mere alcoholic content, for he will often comment on the liquor, appraising its character at least as accurately as do the people who have inspected it in fancy nosing glasses.

Knowledge about whisky comes in two quite different forms: what we may call tacit and explicit knowledge. The latter comprises facts about whisky: its production, maturation and distribution; details of distilleries, who did what and when. The former is more personal: it consists of the recollection of experience, with reflection upon and appraisal of the same. For appreciation, this is much the more important of the two. I know people who are undoubtedly connoisseurs of fine whiskies, who have never read a book about whisky in their lives, nor would consider doing so; whose acquaintance with the sciences is slight but whose experience of drinking drams is long and deep, and who can refer present sensations to those of the past with apparently perfect recall.

In some ways these people are in an enviable position. Having been brought up in a Scottish society in which whisky drinking is an everyday and accepted activity, critical appraisal of their dram is as natural as assessing the weather. That happy state, however, is not available to most of us, and especially to the many people who come to Scotch whisky relatively late in life. The purpose of this book is to provide a shortcut, in the form of information and techniques by which one may acquire a due appreciation of Scotch whisky without spending a lifetime doing so. The book is also intended to give some guidance on how to go about acquiring the experiential basis for critical judgement.

It is tempting to describe the difference between the two sorts of knowledge of whisky as being that between objective and subjective knowledge – and by implication to disparage the latter. Between knowledge of facts about whisky – how it is made, what it is made from and so on – and subjective impressions, which cannot be verified or communicated concisely. It is a distinction which has been fundamental to Western thought since about the fifth century BC and in many ways has served us well. The whole of science, for example, is based on a canon of objectivity; it is an ideal which is embodied not only in the theory but in the mundane practice of scientific method. However, it is an ideal whose applicability to matters of private experience is fraught with problems. In what follows, I prefer to think in terms of tacit and explicit knowledge rather than subjective and objective. (This borrows from an interesting but deeply unfashionable philosopher who, however, seems to have had rather more in the way of actual experience of the world than is common among academic philosophers.)

The first part of the book consists of what you might call the objective facts about whisky. Some of these will be familiar to anyone who has read a bit about the subject; others hopefully will not. The problem about so-called objective facts is that they are infinite in number, and we have to decide which are and which are not relevant – and of course in deciding we must employ judgements as to value and relevance, so that our vaunted objectivity begins to wear a little thin. Besides, today's facts are yesterday's theories, and if we are to have a contemporary understanding of our subject, we must consider today's theories, which means addressing concepts as well as data.

Happily, there has never been a better time to do so, for in the last twenty or so years there have been great advances in our understanding of just about everything, and hence of whisky. One purpose of the present book is to bring together findings from a number of disciplines which pertain to an understanding of whisky, and to present them in a non-technical manner. So if you were rotten at chemistry at school, don't skip that section. Chemistry has moved on a lot from the stinky labs of your youth and so has chemistry teaching. Nobody need be without at least the elements. And you can't hope to understand good liquor unless you have them.

The same goes for the rest of the subjects covered. You may think you know about smell, having done it all your life, but the chances are, you don't, and if I do my job properly, you will find a whole world out there of which you were unaware. I know I did when first I came to read the contemporary literature. You may wonder why it is necessary to understand the metaphors of whisky language or the internal cultures of corporations in order to appreciate whisky. Well, we live in a world in which production is increasingly in the hands of international corporations and whisky is no exception. Most of what most people know about Scotch whisky is got from its advertising: values as well as facts. Most whisky brands are owned by very large corporations; whisky is marketed by the people who work for those corporations and the presentation of whisky is determined by the priorities of the people who market it, whose main aim is to further their careers within the organisation. What is said about whisky in the advertising is part of the same causal chain and, if in the advertisement, hyperbole verges on falsehood, we shouldn't be surprised. Only if you know the background and understand the language, are you likely to be able to unpick what is said about your drink and sort out the reality from the carefully-cultivated illusion.

The second part of the book is about tacit knowledge of whisky: getting to know the stuff on the basis of experience rather than book-larnin': actually addressing whisky, assessing it in the light of what we have learned in the first part. It should be clear that the two can't be separated entirely, and the one must inform the other. Part Two is not intended to be the sort of guide to whisky which tells you how many points out of ten a particular bottling gets. This is about doing it yourself. It's not about helping you to impress friends even more ignorant than yourself: it is, dear reader, about helping you climb by your own efforts from the slough of incomprehension into the dim light of understanding. And, believe me, the light is dim.

With any luck, though, it will allow you to see your way to having a lot of fun. Both whisky drinking and whisky tasting are very enjoyable things to do, and the more you know, the more you are likely to enjoy them both. This is not universally the case, for knowledge has disadvantages. You become much more clearly aware of what you do not like, and what before may have been a vague distaste will with knowledge become concentrated and active. But so do the pleasant sensations, and the trick, obviously, is to avoid the disagreeable – which, being equipped with your newfound knowledge, you are better able to do.

Having said all that, appreciating whisky is not just about taste. There are other forms of appreciation. I don't propose to deal with them, save in passing. Some I don't think worth more than a mention (collecting labels, for example), some because I disapprove of them (collecting whiskies), and others because they are too personal and therefore of little general interest. Perhaps I ought here to make clear my attitude to collectors of whiskies.

As far as I am concerned, whisky is for drinking. That is its sole *raison d'être*. You can do lots of things with it other than drinking it, but none of those things takes any cognizance of its reality as whisky. You could equally well do them with other things. You can – people do – collect almost anything. Collecting is a sort of idiocy, the collector seeking simply to aggregate a holding of whatever takes his or her fancy: Rembrandts, beer mats, furry toys, corkscrews, postage stamps, esoteric diseases. All that matters is getting more of the same.

This is of little consequence, save in two ways. First, by removing from circulation articles of a certain sort, it diminishes the diversity of our environment. Second, by encouraging competition among fellow-collectors, it creates a market in which values are unrelated to utility and thereby denies the things collected to people who value them for their original, proper purpose. These considerations manifestly apply to whisky. It is no longer possible to come across an unusual or old bottle of whisky in the normal course of one's drinking life: they have all been snapped up by collectors. The price of such whiskies relates only to their value to the collectors and not at all to people who want to put the stuff to its proper use by drinking it.

In the case of whisky there is additional cause for resentment. It is an objection on what you might call metaphysical grounds: the real value in whisky lies solely in its virtue as potation: it is well-named *spirit*, for the enjoyment of it is an immaterial thing. It is the antithesis of a collectable commodity, since enjoyment procures destruction. But collected, the value of whisky inheres solely in the fact that it is not to be drunk. An opened bottle is a bottle whose value to the collector is destroyed. A collector is the direct opposite of a drinker and the interests of collectors are inimical to those of drinkers. I was told the other day of a whisky bottling which had been bought in its entirety by an investor, solely on the ground of his expectation of its increase in market value. If all our liquor were so treated, we should have nothing to drink.

For, as they say, the avoidance of doubt, I should make it clear that I distinguish between a collection and a cellar. The individual who keeps a cellar is very different from a collector, for though bottles may be kept for a very long time indeed, the intention is that they should be opened. There can be some crossover between the two – we are none of us perfect – but on the whole they are quite distinct.

The market for Scotch whisky has changed greatly over the last ten years, especially as regards malt whiskies. Until the early 1980s, it was hard to find more than a few bottled malts in any bar, even in Scotland. For the malt whisky drinker, the problem was getting the stuff at all, and especially getting anything other than the principal brands, most of whose owners bottled their spirit at ten years old. Now an equal and opposite difficulty faces the newcomer to malt whiskies: there has been a huge proliferation of bottled malts and the problem is one of choice. And things are getting worse, as special bottlings – whether by the distillers or by independent bottlers – proliferate.

There is no simple way to guide you through this. You have to make the choice for yourself. But if you are to have the freedom to choose, you have to know what you are doing, which means not being dependent for information on the people who want to sell you the stuff. There is a good basic principle here: don't believe anything you are told by anyone who is trying to sell you anything. This is not to say that people selling whisky are all liars – they aren't – just that it is very hard to tell who is and who isn't. And because a company tells the truth about its product in one advert, you cannot assume it will do so in another. All it takes is a shift in staff or management or marketing policy and the presentation of the whisky will change. However, don't assume that a whisky is bad just because its promotion is mendacious and misleading. There is lots of really good whisky being promoted by means of horrible and completely irrelevant imagery. At the time of writing, Bowmore is the most obvious example: an excellent whisky with weird adverts aimed at one cannot imagine whom.

But why should anybody care? It's only drink, after all. Why make a fuss about it? What does it matter and who does it matter to? There are lots of books about whisky with pictures of distilleries and Highland glens and none of their authors seem to have suffered too much from angst. Well, it matters to the Scots, or some of them. Whisky, as Scotland's national drink, matters to the Scots much more than does, say, schnapps to the Germans or vodka to the Poles. It is part of their conception of who they are.

And the quality of our food and drink matters to people everywhere. There are forces at large in the world which, if we let them, will have us subsist only on whatever crap makes them profits. We shall eat and drink well only if we insist on our right to do so, and to know what it is that we consume, which brings me to a final, introductory point.

All knowledge involves criticism. You cannot know things to be true unless you have the facts and can exercise critical judgement upon them. Excellence in goods and services is predicated upon criticism. We don't get decent theatre unless we have good theatre critics. We get good wine because there are good and independent wine critics, who are not slow to condemn poor stuff if it appears on the market. We now have good beer because of the activities of the Campaign For Real Ale, who were prepared to ctiticise what the big brewers were serving us.

The comparison between wine and whisky is instructive. There does not to my knowledge exist in relation to whisky a constituency of knowledgeable amateurs such as there is for wine. Nor is there any tradition of criticism. Books about whisky (there is very little journalism) are for the most part anodyne. Criticism there is none. There is plenty of bad whisky, but nobody who is willing, or feels qualified, to say so. The big distillers are so big that they can buy off prospective critics, or – what amounts to the same – bring them into the fold by means of consultancies and explain how critical comment will damage the commonweal.

I can think of few knowledgeable persons currently writing about whisky who have not at one time or another taken the distillers' shilling. How else to explain the absence of comment on certain sensitive matters? I should hasten to add that my purpose in saying this is not to blame, merely to understand.

Nor is money the only pressure in favour of dull conformity. The Scotch whisky industry is very important for the Scottish economy: it employs lots of people and consumes lots of locally-sourced materials. So any whiff of criticism causes apprehension on behalf of the whole community. Dissent is censured and thereby censored. A course which is to the long-term detriment of the nation is justified by reference to short-term expediency. The result is that in some of its most important markets – the UK, the USA – Scotch is in long-term decline and nobody knows what to do about it.

I don't suppose for a moment what I say will have much impact on such matters. But the reality of both Scotland and Scotch whisky is much better than the image. My hopes hang on freedom of information: if that reality is better known, people around the world will think better of us than they will if all they know about us is what they get from advertising agencies. The purpose of this book is to make the reality known.

The Book

The book's ten chapters are divided into two sections which I have styled Knowledge and Evaluation. The purpose of the first eight (Knowledge) is to provide you with most of the background information which you will need if you are to make informed judgements on whiskies. The nature of this information is rather varied, for there are various ways of approaching the subject. We begin by looking at taste itself: the least understood because least considered of our senses. Having gained some understanding of what taste is and how it works, we consider the application of taste to whisky: how the notion of taste is used in connection with whisky and how people have in the past described it. (This is not intended to prefigure the more detailed stuff about taste and tasting later in the book, but is meant as a general introduction to taste and whisky.)

We then take a different tack – and for the next five chapters look at why whisky tastes as it does. This is mostly technical stuff and some of it deals with matters which fall within the biological and chemical sciences. I have endeavoured to ensure that this material is self-sufficient and that there is nothing in this which is not accessible to the lay reader who is prepared to work through it. This means inevitably that some of the material will be considered elementary by those who have a scientific background. To them I can only apologise and suggest that they persevere, for I know that I found some surprises when preparing the material, and hopefully, so will they.

The chapters on how whisky is made should be taken as far as possible as a whole. I have always found the traditional way of presenting whisky production pretty indigestible – I mean the approach which is based on drawings of a kit of parts, none of whose functions are immediately obvious and whose interrelation is difficult to understand. If you disagree with me on this and think I am unnecessarily elaborating a well-known and understood process, I would ask you to stop for a moment and look at what you already know, or think you do, and ask yourself what is the function in the distillation process of the low wines and feints receiver and how its management affects the quality of the spirit. I asked a distillery manager (a chemistry PhD who is regarded as a leading expert in the industry) about that very matter. He said he had never been asked about it before, but thinks it possibly the most critical part of the entire distillation as regards flavour.

I have therefore presented whisky production as a more-or-less continuous process, each part of which is closely related to the others and which as a whole is responsible for the development of those flavour compounds which distinguish Scotch whisky from any of its imitators. I have included in this a chapter on grain whisky production and one on blending. Malt is used as the standard for comparison: not because grain is necessarily better or worse, but because malt was the original of Scotch whisky, malt flavour is better-understood, and it is to malt that comparisons may most readily be made.

The chapter on blending is intended to bring a little light into a subject – the relationship between malts and blends – which has been greatly obscured both by the distillers and by malt buffs: the first to the detriment of the malts and the second from prejudice against blends, neither justified.

Since appreciating whisky is about the relationship between people and drink, it is a cultural phenomenon, using culture in the widest sense. It is also to do with culture in a narrower sense, for if we are to understand whisky, we have to understand the culture in which it arose, the culture in which it is produced and the culture in which it is consumed. That, anyway, is my excuse for inserting a chapter on matters social.

The second section (Evaluation) is about using what you know about whisky to appreciate it. You have the information: now is the time to use what you know to acquire or develop your ability to evaluate. The chapter on tasting whisky (see page 140), is a practical guide. With any luck, by using it, you will enhance your ability to discriminate: between different whiskies, and among the flavours you will find within a single malt. The final chapter, Appreciations (see page 153), consists of a few short essays about whiskies and whisky companies. Its aim is to bring together some disparate perceptions and evaluations into what I hope we may call appreciation.

Acknowledgments

My thanks to the following persons, to all of whom I am indebted in one way or another for the contents of this book: David Burton, Derek Cooper, David Daiches, George Dodd, Edwin Dodson at Glen Moray, Tony Edridge, John Grant at Glenfarclas; Bill Lumsden at Glenmorangie; Frank McHardy at Springbank;

Val McDermid; Jim McEwen at Bowmore; John McPherson at Allied Distillers; Dick Pountain; David Rae at North British Distillery; John Ramsay at The Edrington Group; David Robertson at Macallan; Gordon Steele; Tim Steward and Ian Urquhart at Gordon & MacPhail.

I would also like to thank the many individuals and companies who kindly supplied the images for use in the book.

TASTE

INTRODUCTION

Taste is a sensation, a perception, an experience. It is a subjective impression of an objective reality, or so we generally believe. It is purposeful: the means by which we sample our food and drink; how we judge it good or bad. It is a faculty which, like other of our faculties, we can use actively or passively. We can, by and large, choose what we will taste: we taste by the mouth and for the most part, things don't get in your mouth unless you put them there.

The active use of taste goes beyond that: we speak of acquiring and cultivating tastes. That is, adapting our tastes by choosing to accustom ourselves to sensations which in the present we dislike because we believe that by doing so, we shall alter our perception for the future, so that the disagreeable becomes pleasant. This is not the province of the connoisseur alone: most adults have tastes which differ from those which they possessed as children; few kids care for caviare.

What is true of food is true of drink. Teenagers typically drink sweet, fizzy drinks whereas adults mostly prefer drier, less obviously flavoured potations. (It has long been a puzzle to me how cocktails have acquired an image of sophistication, for most of them are pretty vile and suited – in terms of taste if not of potency – more to the kindergarten than the cruise ship.)

The development of taste may be partly down to our biology, but it is certainly within the realm of purposive action. We can and do decide what and how we shall taste. We *cultivate* taste. The term 'taste' is used prescriptively. If we say someone has taste, we mean that he or she possesses an ability to discriminate between good and bad of which we approve. We assume that we can choose to have good taste or not; that couch potatoes who eat hamburgers and drink sweet drinks in front of the television are slobs through moral failure. Indeed, in calling them slobs, we use a term which implies their potential to choose not to be so.

Our choice of whisky lies in this realm. If we have never been exposed to good whisky, we cannot be blamed for drinking bad. But where the possibility exists of choosing between good and bad whisky, and we choose the bad, we are open to censure on moral grounds. And he who censures is exposed to another, quite different temptation: that of self-righteousness. It is a common enough condition which often afflicts born-again malt enthusiasts.

Taste presents us with a predicament: alongside the belief that the cultivation of taste is a duty of maturity, we believe that taste is invincibly personal: *de gustibus non est disputandum*. I don't pretend to be able to resolve this dilemma other than by saying that it doesn't seem to be quite such a problem in practice as it appears in theory. Discrimination in matters of taste, in common with many other human activities, is a skill which is improved by practice, effort and intelligence. Discernment is founded in knowledge. You can't appreciate a masterly golf swing unless you know a lot about the game. You can describe a picture as painterly only if you have an intimate understanding of the artist's technique.

Anyone can watch a football match just as anyone can taste what is in their mouth, but in both cases, the appreciation of what is out there in the world depends on knowledge and understanding. The Inuit have dozens of words for snow, all of them necessitated by the exigencies of the environment. An Inuit child must learn these words and how to recognise each type of snow. It is not a subjective matter at all: survival depends on the ability to discriminate. It is true that I see snow and the Inuits see all sorts of different things; there is no contradiction involved. It is also true that they know a lot more than I do about snow and that their opinions on the subject are worth a lot more than mine.

So with whisky: our tastes are formed by the requirements of our situation. We learn appropriate skills. In an environment of malt and blended whiskies, there are skills of taste which need to be acquired if we are to know what is out there, and a vocabulary to be learned if we are to be able to communicate what we know. The skills of taste are in the realm of tacit knowledge; we acquire them by practice against a background of knowledge. First, that background.

TASTE AND SMELL

We don't generally give much thought to our senses. Everyone knows that we have five of them and we think about them only when something goes wrong – when we try to converse with the hard of hearing, say, or are asked for a donation to a charity for the blind. It is right and natural that this should be the case, and – scientists, psychologists and philosophers apart – nobody takes much interest. Our senses are the channels through which we get information about the world and we are no more concerned with how they work than we are about the insides of a computer. They are, however, deeply mysterious, and the more we investigate the workings of the senses, the more we realise how little we know of them.

This is nowhere more true than as regards the senses of taste and smell. We are generally credited with five senses: sight, sound, touch, taste and smell. In fact, these fall into three main categories. Sight is on its own: the receptor for electromagnetic radiation. Sound and touch resemble each other in that both involve responses to mechanical stimuli. Sound is the more specific of the two: the stimulus consists of variations in the pressure of air and detection is by means of highly-specialised apparatus.

Taste and smell are chemoreceptors, by means of which we detect alterations in the chemical nature of our environment. They are very similar in their oper-ation, though with important differences. It is by taste and smell that we can appreciate our whisky – in as much as appreciation involves enjoyment as well as understanding. We can get information about whisky by the other senses, but we can't really enjoy it except through taste and smell. (You may say that there is pleasure for the eye, at least, since a dram newly-poured is a noble sight. It is, but the pleasure is one of anticipation, and it is the taste that we anticipate. Contemplation of a dram which we were not to be allowed to drink would have exactly the opposite effect.)

In what follows, it should be understood that when we speak of taste, we mean mostly smell. There is a condition known as anosmia, or the inability to smell. People who suffer from this affliction in the extreme form are still able to taste, but are restricted to the four crude tastes of sweet, sour, salt and bitter. This is because those are the tastes which we receive by the tongue alone. All else is got by means of smell.

There are various ways in which this can be demonstrated. Almost everyone will know what food tastes like when under the influence of a heavy cold. When we have a cold, our nasal sinuses – that is, the passages which connect the mouth to the nose – become blocked by the mucus caused by the infection. Vapours from our food cannot travel through those passages to the nose, and expected tastes do not materialise. This is because by far the greatest part of what we mean by taste is the result of stimulation of the smell receptors in the nose. Take those away, and taste becomes a very dull matter indeed.

There is a simple experiment which anyone can do and which is very revealing about the relationship between taste and smell. We all know that apple and onion are very different in taste. Both are sweet because both contain sugar but apart from that, they have very little in common. Cut some small pieces of apple and onion: remove the skin and ensure that the pieces are as similar in size as possible. Close your eyes; hold your nose and, when you open your mouth, ask an assistant to place a piece of either apple or onion on your tongue. Don't chew it (the differences in texture may betray it) but try by taste alone to decide which is which. You will find it surprisingly difficult. This is because almost all of what makes the difference between the two tastes, is detected by your sense of smell – when access from mouth to nose is blocked, your only sensations are those arising in the tongue.

In normal conditions, gases and vapours arising from whatever is in the mouth travel through the nasal passages to the olfactory epithelium, a patch of sensory receptors located high in the nasal septum on either side of the nose. When the receptors of the epithelium are stimulated, we experience smells which, when we are eating or drinking, we generally interpret as tastes.

OUR EQUIPMENT: THE TONGUE

The tongue provides us with four tastes: sweet, sour, salt and bitter. We taste sweet things with the tip of the tongue, salt at the side, sour on either side at the rear and bitter at the back of the mouth. For most adults, there is relatively little

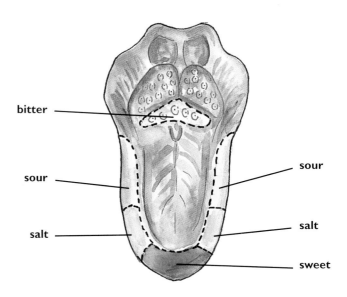

The sensory areas of the tongue.

sensation in the centre of the tongue, which is why in tasting we move the fluids around the mouth. Children are different: they have taste buds all over the surface of the tongue and elsewhere in the mouth, which is probably why things tasted better when we were young.

Taste is detected by the tongue by means of taste buds, of which most people have around nine thousand in all. Each taste bud comprises up to a hundred specialised receptor cells which are served by a rather smaller number of nerve endings. Each group of taste buds is specialised, in that it can detect only the presence of its particular taste: sweetness, sourness, saltiness or bitterness. As we get older, the number of taste buds declines and it seems likely that their balance alters, which may account for the tendency for tastes to change as we grow older.

The mechanism by which foodstuffs coming in contact with the tongue cause nerve impulses to be sent to the brain is not entirely clear, but the leading hypothesis is along the following lines. The surface of the receptor cell contains protein molecules, each of which has a particular spatial configuration which corresponds to the arrangement of atoms at some point on the surface of the molecule which that receptor cell is adapted to detect. It is like a jigsaw puzzle, in which there is one and only one piece which fits any other piece in all respects. When the two are brought together in a perfect fit, a chemical bond is made which causes an electrical signal to be sent to the brain.

All substances which taste sweet are thought to have a molecular structure such that at some point on the surface of the molecule, there is a possibility of its fitting into the protein of the receptor cell. By far the most common naturally-occurring sweet substances are sugars – the simplest of which, glucose, provides energy for both plants and animals. Glucose and fructose (found in many fruits and vegetables) have the same numbers of carbon, hydrogen and oxygen atoms, but a different molecular structure, which gives them significantly different properties – fructose tastes much sweeter than glucose. The sugars which build plants and the sugars which we carry in our blood are all basically the same stuff and all living things – both plants and animals – get their energy by the oxidation of sugars.

Sugar molecules have the ability to join up with each other, a process known as polymerisation. When a glucose and a fructose molecule combine, they produce sucrose, the substance which we know as table sugar. As glucose units are added to the chain, however, the resulting long-chain sugars or polysaccharides soon cease to be sweet. That does not mean that their utility to critters is at an end, though, for starch is a polysaccharide. Starch is the form in which glucose is commonly stored by plants: cereals and root crops of every variety store their sugars as starch. But they don't taste sweet even though they still possess those sections which fit with the sweetness receptors – probably because the larger molecule inhibits the fit of the jigsaw pieces. We shall come back to sugars and starches later, when we come to malting, for the conversion of sugars plays a very important part in the making of whisky.

Various substances other than sugar cause us to register sweet sensations. Presumably all of the molecules are able in some way to fit with the sweetness proteins. This hypothesis is supported by the observations that different forms of the same molecule have differing results as regards their sweetness: certain amino acids are sweet when their atoms are arranged one way, but in the mirror-image arrangement of the same atoms, the substance is not perceived as sweet.

By no means are all sweet-tasting substances either digestible or good for you, though their indigestibility does mean that you can satisfy your sweet tongue without getting fat. Saccharin is around three hundred times sweeter than sucrose, and it is not digested – which made people think it was the answer to a lot of problems when it was introduced, until they discovered that along with the sweetness went a rather unpleasant bitterness. However, people vary in how they perceive such things, and it gained fairly wide acceptance, though mostly among people whose requirements in the matter of taste were pretty crude to begin with.

Some other simple carbohydrates are sweet. Glycerol is found in wines, where it is regarded as desirable, not only for its sweetness, but for the feeling it produces in the mouth – it is mainly when glycerol is present that we describe a wine as smooth. Glycerol is often thought to be responsible for the 'legs' which we see on the side of the glass when we pour some whiskies. The presence of legs is usually associated with a feeling of smoothness, for which glycerol may be responsible. However, the legs are probably the result of more complex causes, to do with the effect of differential evaporation on the surface tension of the liquid.

Diethylene glycol is another simple carbohydrate which tastes sweet. It, too, is sometimes found in wine, but only when the wine has been illegally doctored, as it was in Austria in 1985, by some people who confused it with glycerol. Such doctoring is successful as far as it goes, in that it certainly sweetens the wine, but alas, like some doctoring of another sort, it tends to kill the patient, for diethylene glycol is seriously toxic. It is best left to its more mundane uses as antifreeze and industrial solvent.

Sour tastes are generally associated with acids. Citrus fruits contain citric acid and apples, malic acid. Carbonic acid is the active constituent of soda water, as well as fizzy lemonades. Acetic acid is the cause of the sourness which we detect in vinegar and is the alcohol oxidation product which causes wine to become sour when exposed to the air. (The term vinegar is derived from the French *vin aigre*, or sour wine.) Acetic acid can sometimes be detected in badly-kept whisky, for similar reasons.

Bitterness seems to have more complex causes than sourness. It is a taste of maturity and is almost always an acquired one. Very few children appear to like bitter tastes and many adults never acquire them. The more common bitter tastes, such as caffeine and quinine, arise from nitrogen compounds known as alkaloids. Both of these are enjoyable to sophisticated palates in low concentrations, though in higher doses they become intolerable, as any drinker of tonic water will know if required to take its active constituent, quinine, in medicinal doses. Most alkaloids are poisonous, some of them virulently so.

Discussions of taste and whisky rarely mention any taste sensations in the mouth other than the four primary tastes above. However, the mouth is supplied with many sense receptors other than those of taste, some of which undoubtedly are relevant to tasting whisky. Besides taste buds, the mouth has sensors for hot, cold and pain. The feeling of hotness which we experience when eating spicy food is produced mainly by the stimulation of pain sensors and there is speculation that the feelings of satisfaction which follow a spicy meal may be connected with the presence of endorphins, which are emollient and analgesic compounds produced in the brain in response to pain. Some whiskies produce a feeling in the mouth akin to the pepperiness which we experience when eating food containing peppers. It seems likely that this is down to the stimulation of pain sensors, though its exact cause is not known. However, the feeling of well-being which attends the consumption of whisky is not thought to be a response to pain sensation.

OUR EQUIPMENT: THE NOSE

The nose is a far more sensitive instrument than the tongue. The latter functions by means of around nine thousand taste buds: the nose by contrast has in the region of fifty to one hundred million sense receptors. These are located in the olfactory epithelium, a mucus-covered patch on either side of the nasal septum, high inside the nose. When we sniff, we draw in odour molecules along with the air. Those molecules are caught by the mucus and then brought into contact with the olfactory receptors, which send messages to the brain. When we eat or drink, the air from the mouth passes up the back of the nose to the olfactory epithelium and the odour molecules which it carries create the sensations of smell which are so important a part of taste.

The sensory areas of the nose.

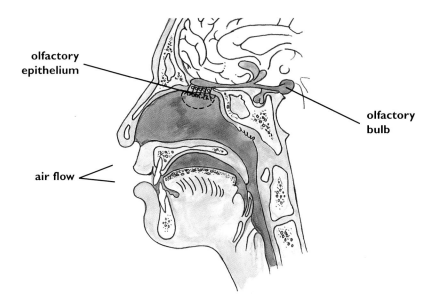

olfactory
epithelium

olfactory
bulb

air flow

Different molecules have different shapes and the leading hypothesis, as in the case of taste, is to do with fit between odour molecules and protein molecules in the sense receptors. When the appropriate pieces of the olfactory jigsaw are brought together, the protein molecule triggers a signal to the brain, announcing the presence of that particular odour. How many different shapes can be accommodated is not known, but the number appears to be very large.

It has been suggested that a clue is to be found in the different types of anosmia or partial odour-blindness. If people can fail to detect a given number of types of odour, it may be that that is the number of particular molecular fits in our jigsaw. This may seem inadequate for the vast variety of smells which we are able to identify. It is not, however, necessary that there should be a fit for each smell. A relatively small number of signals can give rise to a very great number of combinations, each of which is perceived as a distinct odour. In the last twenty years, there has been a lot of interest in devising artificial noses, mainly with a view to process control through detection of odour. Some of these are based on electrically-conducting plastics which swell and alter their conductivity in the presence of a given odour. By using a small number of such materials of slightly differing characters, it is possible to assign to each odour a uniquely identifying electrical fingerprint. Using neural networks, patterns of responses can be learned and the artificial noses trained.

Such things work fine for simple industrial tasks; they are a long way from the sensitivity of the human nose, let alone that of the average labrador retriever. George Dodd, a perfumer who is one of the leading scientists working on olfaction in the UK, describes sniffer dogs as having, in radio terms, the ultimate bandwidth: they can smell everything, but can do so with fantastic sensitivity. For a dog, as for various other animals, smell is not the occasional sensation that it is in humans, but a sense used in a way more akin to the human use of sight, that is, one whose information is continually being processed as an essential component of what we know about our surroundings.

We tend to be very self-centred in matters to do with sensation. The history of philosophy is littered with theories of knowledge which take sight as the paradigmatic form of perception (smell usually comes bottom of any hierarchy of the senses). Yet of the animals alive today, by far the greatest proportion use chemoreception as their principal form of sense perception. Probably only in primates and some birds, is sight the dominant sense. Even for highly evolved mammals, smell is much the more important sense. Dogs quite clearly have an olfactory geography, that is, they operate within a space whose points and boundaries are determined by smell.

It may be that the vast variety of odours is to be explained by a relatively small number of sensations permutated, as suggested above. It may be that we have an enormously large number of different olfactory receptors, or it may be a combination of the two: thousands of different possible olfactory sensations, permutated through the enormous neural networks of the brain, to produce an almost infinite variety of possible sensations. Recent research suggests that this is the most likely scenario.

Besides the endings of olfactory nerves, the mucus of the olfactory epithelium also contains endings of trigeminal nerves, whose stimulation is experienced as pain. It has been suggested that the stimulation of those nerves is partly or wholly responsible for the vigorous reaction to putrid and pungent odours.

We process smells as we process other sensations, by excluding those sensations which we have no particular interest in. This habituation is necessary if we are not to be swamped by information. (If you doubt this, think about the clothes you are wearing. In normal conditions, you do not feel any of your clothes touching your skin unless they are rough or tickly. Yet if, before you dress, you touch any part of your body with the material of any of the clothes which you are to wear, you will feel it quite clearly. It would, however, be intolerable if you were to be made consciously aware of the touch of all of your clothes all of the time.)

Habituation is perfectly compatible with sensitivity. I had this demonstrated most clearly once when visiting George Dodd at his laboratory in Inverness. The lab is located in a nineteenth-century house in the grounds of a mental hospital. The whole building is given over to olfactory research on the therapeutic uses of smell in mental illness. It houses a huge variety of odours for use in that research and when you walk through the door, you are hit by a wall of the most ghastly stink. The people who work in the building are apparently quite unaware of this, and despite it, were able to show me some of the most delicate perfumes – which they are able without difficulty to discern above the background stench.

It is as well to know about this when tasting whiskies: it is preferable to taste whiskies in an environment which is free as far as possible from extraneous odours – but not essential, since one can adjust to most background smells, provided they are constant in nature and intensity.

There is one aspect of the nose which is worth mentioning for its intrinsic interest, though how it may affect our perception of whiskies has never, to my knowledge, been investigated. On either side of the nasal septum, about a centimetre above the nostrils, lies a little dent with a tiny aperture in the centre. This is present in many animals other than humans. It is known as the vomeronasal organ and in some animals contains receptors for pheromones. Pheromones are the compounds which animals use for chemical communication. Recent research in the USA has suggested that pheromonal communication exists between humans and that it has to do with reproduction. Whether this is relevant to whisky is not known. It may be what prompted Ogden Nash's maxim that candy is dandy, but liquor is quicker. However that may be, the utility of whisky for seduction is more likely to be connected with its alcohol content and pleasant taste than the presence of sex hormones.

That said, sexual arousal is known to be enhanced by the presence of certain odours which are definitely present in whisky. Odours akin to human sweat are fairly common in whiskies and it is known that the smell of sweat can lead to sexual arousal among other things. Fresh sweat has little or no odour, but skin bacteria act on it to produce lactic acid, ammonia and various sulphur compounds which soon produce a healthy cocktail of aromas, some of which can be found in your glass of malt. Besides the above, which are known to be arousing, sweat contains a hormone which is closely related to the pheromone which gives truffles their smell – so if you find that a glass of the cratur turns your partner on, it may just be because they are partial to truffles. If, instead of being aroused, your partner merely regards you benevolently over the glass, it may be because he or she sees you as an old lady. Recent research at the Chemical Senses Center in Philadelphia, Pennsylvania, suggests that the underarm odour of old women causes feelings of benevolence. So if you are feeling depressed and can't get any whisky, sniff your granny. If you don't have a granny, sniff someone else's granny – it doesn't seem to matter whether she is related to you for her odour to make you feel good.

SCENT AND MIND

Although both smell and taste involve the detection of chemical changes, the difference between them shows in the arrangement of the nerves which carry messages to the brain. The nerves which end in the olfactory epithelium are not connected to specialised receptor cells such as those which make up the taste buds. Instead, the olfactory nerves merely end in the mucus of the epithelium where they are directly stimulated by odour molecules. This means that the nerve is more or less exposed to the outer world. It has been suggested that this lack of specialised endings indicates a relatively primitive evolutionary status for the olfactory nerves. Whether that is the case or not, it is certainly the case that the neural pathways from the nose lead to a part of the lower brain which is generally regarded as being one of its oldest in evolutionary terms. This, the limbic system, gives rise to the emotions.

The close relationship between smell and emotion may explain why some people feel so strongly about their drink. People tend either to care a lot about what they drink, or not at all. The real ale movement was driven by people with real passion, a depth of feeling which it was hard to explain merely by their being enthusiasts. Ditto malt whisky drinkers, of whom, dear reader, since you are reading this book, you are probably one. In both cases, the passion of the few has done a great good for the many, for excellent beers and whiskies are now widely available, and little thanks to the producers. The latter have only responded to demand, for in neither case did the professionals perceive a potential market until after the amateurs had created one – with a few honourable exceptions such as Glenfiddich.

All humans – all animals for that matter – exude a plume of scent which is detectable for some distance downwind of them. Smells spread even in calm air, due to the action of gaseous diffusion, which does not depend on movement of the air. Over three hundred distinct compounds have been identified in human odour. Each individual has a distinctive smell pattern by which he or she can be identified. It is this olfactory signature which a sniffer dog tracks – and it can track it for a very long way, many hours after it was laid. This gives some measure of how greatly inferior we are to dogs in our ability to smell: most humans detect only the grossest of odours, and those when in fairly close contact.

The perfume industry is possible because we respond to the smells of other people, whether consciously or unconsciously. So is the trade in deodorants and breath fresheners. Sex is involved, both directly and indirectly. Perfumes seek directly to cause sexual arousal through the use of animal pheromones such as musk and civetone. Musk is a substance which is produced by the musk deer, a small deer which is found in central Asia. Known about for a very long time – Marco Polo remarks on it in his thirteenth-century account of that region – the musk collects in a small sac in the abdomen of the deer. Unfortunately for the deer, the removal of the sac involves killing the owner. The musk is used as a perfume both on its own and in combination with other, lighter and more volatile odours. Civet is used in a similar fashion. Civet is produced by the civet cat from a gland which sits between the anus and the genital organs – a fact which is given little prominence in the advertising of the perfumes which contain it. The perfume industry has been remarkably successful in presenting an elegant front which distances it from its grubby origins. I must say I enjoy the perfume departments of big stores (I think it's – literally – the odour of sexuality which they exude). But on occasion, when a painted assistant is just too condescending, it helps to remind oneself – or the assistant, though I find that isn't too well-received – that you get the stuff from a spot between the balls and the bum of a relative of the hyena somewhere in Africa.

The rediscovery of the function in humans of the vomeronasal cavities as specialised pheromone receptors has led in the USA to the marketing of perfumes containing steroid compounds found on male and female skin, designed to be detected by the vomeronasal organs. The perfumes appear to be selling very well, even though there is still a lot of scepticism about whether they really are the ultimate aphrodisiacs.

The removal of offensive odours can be as effective as the presence of attractive ones in encouraging human contact. Anyone who has tried to kiss a partner who has bad breath will know how violent is one's reaction against it and how rapidly and completely sexual desire can be extinguished by mouth or body odour. Bad breath contains small quantities of the charmingly-named nitrogen compounds putrescine and cadaverine, which are more commonly to be found in rotting meat, so that isn't too surprising.

Perfumery and whisky blending work in very similar ways. In each case there is one or more base compounds, which form the substrate upon which other, more accessible flavours or odours are laid – though the base in whisky has rather more savoury origins than perfume's. In a good blend as in a good perfume, the objective is to produce an overall flavour which is not readily separable into its components. This is where blends differ most strikingly from malts in the structure of their flavour: in a good malt, one sees a progressive release of different odours: as the more volatile fractions evaporate, they give access to the underlying flavours in a process which sometimes goes on for a remarkably long time. (I have known malts which were still yielding surprising odours for an hour after first pouring.)

SCENT AND MEMORY

Besides their propensity to excite emotions, smells are very closely associated with memory. There is abundant evidence, both anecdotal and experimental, to support the hypothesis of an association between smell and memory. Most people have experienced the powerful role of scent in memory. Events in childhood are more powerfully evoked by smells than by anything else. People differ greatly in their ability to recollect smells, just as they differ in their ability to smell in the first place, but this seems to be an almost universal experience.

Some people have accurate and detailed recollection of odour. I have known whisky drinkers – usually professionals, but not invariably – who will reminisce about particular casks of whisky and can describe them accurately years after the event. (I can vouch for the authenticity of some such recollections, having on some occasions partaken of the drams described and myself remembering them.) David Daiches and George Saintsbury both evidently have extensive and accurate recall of drams they have taken. Since both were lovers and professors of English literature, one is led naturally to conjecture whether there may be a connection. As far as I am aware, this is a field in which there has been no research as yet.

Some smells stick, in the memory as well as elsewhere. As a young man, I worked for some time as a docker in a Scottish port. One fine morning we were told to unload a row of railway wagons and were offered a bonus for what would be a disagreeable job. The wagons contained glass carboys of formaldehyde. They had been shunted violently and most of the glass had broken. We had to get it out. The smell of formaldehyde stuck to me for days; its smell I can recollect vividly as I write and as long as I live, I expect the recollection of the scene will bring back an olfactory memory of great power.

Fortunately, there seems to be no distinction as regards memory: pleasant smells are as likely to be retained as unpleasant. I find that, merely by thinking about it,

I can bring back a morning when I must have been about six. My father and I were in a wood, and had been picking bluebells. We had so many that I had both arms round the bunch and my nose buried in the flowers. I also remember that some years later, when first reading Wordsworth's 'The Daffodils', I wondered why he had chosen to write about flowers whose scent was so feeble. But then I guess it would have been hard to make the poem work with references to an inward nose, however more distinct the scent when recollected in tranquillity.

SCENT AND PERSUASION

When one thinks of scent and persuasion, the first thing that springs to mind – to my mind, anyway – is seduction. It isn't too surprising, given that that is scent's main function in chemical communication among humans. The connection between scent and sex we have already mentioned. There may be a direct response to the presence of human pheromones. (See 'Our Equipment: The Nose', page 24.) There is certainly an indirect response: some odours cause us to have friendly feelings toward the source of the odours – and people tend to prefer to get into bed with folk they feel friendly toward. So scent may not (*pace* the perfume ads) produce passion, but it's the next best thing.

It is in connection with food and drink that smell is directly persuasive, since odour is usually a reliable indicator of quality. If it smells good, the chances are it is good. The emergence in recent years of in-house bakeries in supermarkets is testimony to the power of smell in the merchandising of comestibles. Fresh bread smells delicious, even if it is of the gutless sort which most supermarkets sell. Fish and meat are pretty reliable: it is difficult to disguise the odours of putrefaction, our old friends putrescine and cadaverine. On the other hand, you should be careful of the smell of almonds: it may come from nuts, but if it is in a chemical laboratory (where you don't normally find a lot of nuts), the chances are it comes from hydrogen cyanide. The latter is to be avoided, for it combines with the haemoglobin in the blood and, rendering the transport of oxygen impossible, produces a speedy demise.

Bakeries are fine, but the best olfactory advertisement I know, is a whisky distillery. There can be few processes which announce the quality of their product in quite so persuasive a way as whisky distilleries. Long before I acquired a taste for whisky, I had a great liking for the smell of whisky distilling. Just about everything connected with distilling smells fine. Still rooms are great; so are warehouses – old-fashioned, stone-walled, earth-floored warehouses by the sea especially. Even maltings smell well, though this for some people is an acquired taste.

Most people like the smell of whisky, even people who profess not to care for the cratur itself. I have long wondered that distillers do not use smells to promote their products. I should have thought that in any whisky promotion, a small quantity of the spirit put through an atomiser would have done more than any amount of advertising – a variation on the principle that one picture is worth a thousand words.

The persuasive power of good whisky is a matter which should be borne in mind in any analytic tasting of the stuff. We shall come to that later, but it's worth a word here. In a tutored tasting, the format is usually for one person to lead the tasting. Whiskies are poured and then inspected. The person leading the tasting noses the whisky, comments on what odours he finds, and invites the others to do likewise. With very obvious scents such as peatiness, there can be little doubt, but as regards the more subtle flavours, one should beware. There is a marked tendency for tasters to perceive those odours suggested by the leader. I have tested this on many occasions: leading whisky tastings, I have announced the presence of flavours which I knew were not present. In almost every case, the other tasters have said they were able to detect the same smells: some more reluctantly and hesitantly than others, but with very few exceptions. Now there may be all sorts of explanations for this, many of which have nothing to do with the odours nosed. It does however seem likely that some odours which actually *are* present incline tasters to think they can smell others which are not.

SCENT AND LANGUAGE

We do things with words: our language adapts to our purposes and our vocabulary mirrors our experience. As observed earlier, the Inuit have dozens of words for snow. Where we see only white stuff, for which we have but a single word, they make distinctions which to us are invisible – but to them are of the utmost importance. In the Arctic, the correct identification of a type of snow can mean the difference between life and death. Mountaineers do the same, though their language is at a lower stage of development as regards snow than the Inuit.

One can give any number of similar examples in which particular interests give rise to specialised vocabularies. The words we use arise from the uses we need to make of them. It is difficult to think of a special-interest group which does not have some private vocabulary. Some private words remain private, while others in time enter the common pool of language. For example, the English language is littered with nautical terms, reflecting the importance of seafaring to Britain over the last thousand or so years, during which the language has developed to its present state. Very few people who ordinarily use words and expressions which derive from the maritime vocabulary have the slightest idea of their original signification. Terms drawn from computing are now become commonplace and it is to be expected that in a hundred years from now, if the technology is not replaced by some other, people who have no knowledge of anything to do with computing will nevertheless use language drawn from that technology.

There is something which is even more fundamental than the way we lead our lives in determining the structure of our language. That is the nature of our perceptual equipment. People who have never been able to see can learn to use the language, but they can never employ terms relating to colour with any assurance – shape, maybe, for you can get the idea of shape by feeling, but not colour or brightness.

The same is true of smell. If you have suffered anosmia from birth, then all smell is a closed book to you. You may learn to use the terminology in such a way that you appear normal enough in conversation, but you can never participate fully in any discourse concerning smell or taste, for you lack the basic referents for the terms which the rest of us employ. Absolute anosmia is relatively rare, but partial odour-blindness is fairly common and most people who suffer from it are able to get by without it being noticed. Some even manage to pass themselves off as experts in matters to do with smells. Two of the most extreme cases of this, which I have met, concern whisky tasting.

To my knowledge there are no connoisseurs of the graphic arts who are blind. You can't judge a painting if you can't see it. Maybe you could do something with sculpture, for you can feel sculptures, if they aren't too big. (I got told off once for caressing a Barbara Hepworth, a lovely thing in rosewood which was surely meant for fondling – but I digress.) One wonders why anyone would want to take an interest in paintings when starting a million miles behind the sighted, and could never, by definition, have more than the faintest inkling of what the sighted get out of them.

Yet I know two people who regard themselves – and are widely regarded by others – as connoisseurs of Scotch whisky, who by their own admission have no sense of smell to speak of. The perfumed garden of fine malts is closed to them forever and all their knowledge is got by peering over the hedge. Nevertheless, both evidently value their status as connoisseurs of fine whiskies and have large collections of bottled malts. Both spend a lot of time in the company of people who share their interest. On the basis of their accepted expertise, they condescend to fellow whisky fanciers, and bask in their admiration. It is astonishing that anyone should want to act such a part; it is more astonishing that he should get away with it, and be able to persuade lots of other people that he knows what he is talking about. We might put it down to some cultural idiosyncrasy – like the Japanese diplomat who wears the kilt – but one of these guys comes from Scotland and the other from the USA.

If this state of affairs is accepted as fact – and I can assure you that it is indeed the case, since in both instances my informant was the individual concerned – then we can infer a few things about the language of smell. First, that it is possible to use odour words in such a way as to disguise a fundamental inability to understand what they mean. Second, that there are few folk out there who take a critical approach to using the terminology of flavour. Third, that you can get away with saying almost anything about whisky. Finally – and this is nothing to do with language, really – that some reputed connoisseurs of whisky are actually less well-endowed in the matter of smell than the rest of us.

The title of the present work being what it is, it is legitimate to ask here whether someone who is odour-blind can be said to *appreciate* whisky. Both of our connoisseurs undoubtedly get satisfaction of some kind from their association with whisky and know a lot about it, but we would not wish to say that they appreciated their whiskies. They have some of the qualifications, namely knowledge about some things pertaining to whisky, but they lack the core experience to which that knowledge is relevant. The blind may enjoy going to exhibitions, but we wouldn't say they could appreciate painting, no matter how knowledgeable they appeared to be about it.

By the same token, we might listen to someone speak about a work of art and – art criticism being what it is – think he made as much sense as most. But if we found out he was blind, I fear we would tend to conclude that he was simply talking nonsense. So what of our anosmic whisky buffs? Both can evidently employ the language of odour in such a way as to convince the great majority of their hearers that they know what they are talking about.

Passing kindly over what this tells us about whisky-tasting notes on bottles, we should think about what inferences we can draw about the language of odours in general and the scents of whisky in particular. It is evident that we do not bring to odour-language the sort of discrimination which we ordinarily employ. If someone describes my cat as a nice dog, I am surprised, and either conclude that he is an idiot or ask him why he uses so perverse a description. I have never known anyone act in such a way as regards smell. So uncertain are we of the objectivity of our olfactory perceptions, that we almost never contradict such an utterance – yet our sense of smell is no less capable of yielding reliable information about our environment than is our sense of sight.

The extent of the language of smell reflects the use we have for it. Perfumers have at their disposal a great range of terms, most of which are unknown to the rest of us. Should we find a need for a smell-language, we would soon develop one. More difficult is to learn to use the language of smell as an amateur, to deploy olfactory terms with an assurance of their being unequivocally attributable in matters pertaining to whisky. That is what the next chapter is about.

If all the above seems a bit theoretical, here is an example which may make things a little clearer. It is a story told by a friend of mine from Prestonpans, a small town near Edinburgh, which served the mines and potteries of Midlothian. Its population is almost entirely proletarian and – most unusually – some of the old miners still take snuff. This habit – which would be misconstrued elsewhere – involves sniffing a pinch of tobacco dust from the hollow of the thumb. It is a relic of the eighteenth century, having survived in the mines, where no flame of any kind was permitted.

Life in the 1950s was very different from what it is today. Tobacco was scarce. Horses were common on the streets. So was horse dung. A resident of the Pans, finding his snuff running low, thought to eke it out with a little dried and ground horse dung, which looked and smelt not unlike tobacco. That night at the Labour Club he offered his tin of snuff round, as was the custom. One of the lads, who had a cold, accepted. He took a pinch, sniffed, sneezed and declared it to be fine snuff, for his head had cleared most wonderfully. It was a mixed blessing though: as he said, he now realised that there was 'An awfy smell o' shite aroun' here.' 'Can ye no smell shite?' he asked. The others all took a pinch. One said, 'Man, that's guid snuff. I can smell shite noo.'

The use of the odour term is confident. The user – paradoxically, in the circumstances – has no doubt that there is something in the world to which his term refers. There is none of the doubt or assumption of subjectivity with which most people approach whisky. Taking snuff is the olfactory equivalent of drawing a curtain – to reveal what is there. All the guys know what the term refers to, and each has confidence in his nose as a way of finding out about the world, just as a perfumer will identify an odour, however faint. The rest of this book is about the acquisition of this ability in relation to whisky.

HOW WHISKY TASTES

DESCRIBING TASTE IN WHISKY: TASTING NOTES

We ended the last chapter by speaking of taste and language. We begin this one in the same way. There is no point in talking about how whisky tastes unless we have a grasp of the language we shall use, and a reasonable assurance that we are able to communicate meaning when we talk about our drams.

It is rarely these days that one comes across a malt whisky – or even a good blend, for that matter – which does not have, either on the label or attached to it by a little booklet on a string, a description of the whisky. The description is usually in the form of tasting notes which suggest that the taster will experience some rather remarkable flavours, few of which bear much resemblance to what he or she knows as whisky. Tasting notes are one of the current fashions in whisky marketing – and since they are fashionable, everyone provides them. As far as I have been able to discover, the effect is further to confuse a public which is already pretty hazy about what it should be looking for in a whisky.

There are a lot of people out there who genuinely want to learn about Scotch whisky, but putting daft tasting notes on (often indifferent) whiskies is not the way to enlighten them. Tasting notes can be of use in indicating the qualities of a drink, but only if the reader is able to interpret them with understanding – which means a degree of cynicism, and an ability to separate truth from advertising. People's response to advertising depends largely on the degree of their knowledge of the advertiser and the product. The less you know of the truth about the product, the more likely you are to be influenced by advert-communicated values which are extraneous to what you know. Most people who use detergents know very little about their chemistry. If you understand something about how a detergent works, how it is made and what it is made from, you are liable to be a bit cynical about the claims of rival manufacturers. The same is true of whisky. If you know nothing about

TASTING NOTES

Age: 10 years old

Colour: Rich mahogany gold

Nose: Soft luscious tones linger in the background, with a hint of wood. Elegant and refined.

Palate: Soft, rounded tones reward the palate. Almost a wood spicy feel to it.

it, chances are you will be dead impressed by tasting notes, regarding them as authoritative and yourself as a worm when you can't find the whiff of lily-of-the-valley beneath the orange-peel surface. It won't occur to you that your expensive purchase in the duty-free is in fact a pretty dubious bottling out of a job lot of poor-quality casks which have been left too long in the warehouse.

So you need to know about tasting notes. What do they mean and how much reliance can you place on them? Before we turn to describing taste in whisky, we should look at how it is described and why. That means a bit of history because the thing has roots, and to know where you are, you need to know where you came from.

Scotch whisky hasn't had a lot of big ideas. It first crossed the Scottish border on a raft of notions it got from the Romantic Revival: Victorian gentlemen drank it because in their minds it was associated with kilts and tartans and misty highlands. Later it crossed the oceans on the back of the British Empire, together with the conceptual baggage of imperialism. Later still, it sold in the USA because it was prohibited and thought desirably wicked. In none of these guises, did the people who sold it feel the need to mention its taste. Curiously enough, they would sometimes mention the mouth-feel (as in *smooth*), but never taste. You bought whisky because it brought some form of gratification other than its taste.

Only in the last ten years or so has anyone thought it desirable to mention how the stuff tasted – and then, having discovered (only 150 years late) that maybe it would be a good idea to tell people that whisky tastes nice, they go and spoil their act with all these daft tasting notes. Some whiskies are undoubtedly worth writing notes about: they have a range and depth of flavour which do not strain credulity. But if all whiskies are described in similarly extravagant terms, the consumer is left once more in the dark.

The idea that whiskies ought to taste delicious came out of the malt revolution which began in the 1960s and really gathered pace in the 1980s. Until the 1960s, nobody drank anything but blended whiskies except a few folk in Scotland who knew where to get a malt. The emergence of malts was driven mainly by customer demand: people who liked malt whisky told their friends about it, and gave them drams. People bought the stuff because they liked the taste of it.

When the distillers came to market malts, for the first twenty years or so they failed to realise the difference and used the same brand-marketing techniques that they had employed with blends. Gradually, in the 1980s, marketing departments awoke to the novel idea that maybe folk drank the whisky because they liked it and maybe it might be possible to use this strange notion to sell it. But, as we have seen in the previous chapter, describing taste is no simple matter. Even less simple if you have to try and sell your malts because they taste great, but you must at all costs avoid implying that by the same token your blends taste less than great. It isn't an easy circle to square, and one which the whisky industry is still wrestling with – somewhat unnecessarily, as I hope shall become clear.

The vogue for using tasting notes arose from the need to describe flavour. It was not until the late 1970s that anyone in the Scotch whisky industry thought an investigation of flavour in whisky desirable. With the establishment in 1979 of the Pentlands Scotch Whisky Research Centre, the effort began to find a way of classifying whisky flavours with a degree of objectivity. This was done, not as a way of selling whisky, but with a view to systematising the assessment of spirit – a function which until then had been purely traditional.

The methods used to assess and describe flavour were similar to those which were already in use to describe wines. Wine had the advantage of a longer lineage – one of the first attempts in English was by a Scottish doctor, Alexander Henderson – in 1824, in *The History of Ancient and Modern Wines*, he listed terms which might be used to characterise a wine. By the 1970s, tasting notes had long been used to describe wines, though most folk who did not regard themselves as connoisseurs of wines – which means a lot fewer than today – tended to be pretty sceptical about such things. Until recently, nobody thought of using tasting notes as a way of selling whisky. The origins of this may be of interest.

In 1983, a few friends and I set up an organisation called the Scotch Malt Whisky Society. We bought casks of whisky, bottled the contents and sold them by mail order to others of our friends who had become members of our Society. It was something unheard of in relation to whisky and prophets of doom were not lacking in the whisky industry. We needed a way of telling people at a distance what the contents of our casks tasted like, so hit on the idea of applying wine-tasters' terminology to whisky, in the form of tasting notes.

We were all amateurs, save one who was a chemist and had been professionally involved in the research at Pentland. We set up a tasting committee which met in my kitchen and whose business it was to inspect the whiskies and write the tasting notes. Membership of the committee was by invitation and qualifications were knowledge, wit, scholarship, or being around if we needed someone to make up our numbers. Our little committee had some very distinguished members, but distinction was no guide to ability when it came to describing whiskies. David Daiches was probably the best of us, for he brought vast scholarship to a subject – whisky – which he both knew and loved, and employed poetry in its description. Hamish Henderson, on the other hand, was useless. Hamish, the only one of us who could compare with David in knowledge of Scotland and experience of drinking drams, had two problems. First – and we are talking of one of Scotland's best-loved poets here – he could think of nothing to say of the malt, but that 'It's a lovely whisky.' He would savour the whisky, an expression of bliss cross his features, and then he would give a considered judgement: 'Chust a *lovely* whisky.' Hamish reacted with great indignation to the idea that he should spit the stuff out. 'Spit it out? Spit out such a lovely whisky? Indeed I will not.' After drinking a large number of large drams at 60 per cent, he subsided altogether.

There were a few such difficulties, but in the end we generated a dialectic which produced such descriptions of whisky as the world had not seen before. Some of them were none too serious, for nobody spat out all the whiskies, and people seemed to like the descriptions. We were admittedly fortunate, not only in the quality of our people, but in the excellence of the spirit which we inspected. In those days, the distillers literally did not know what they had in their warehouses and would sell to us spirit the like of which we shall not see again, certainly not at the prices at which we bought, and sold, it.

No one in the whisky industry paid any attention to this. We were so small as not to be worth bothering about, and anyway, we would soon disappear. Well, we didn't, although at one point it was a close thing. Very gradually – it took about ten years – our big idea caught on: that whisky which had been matured in a really fine cask and was bottled straight from that cask without diluting or chill-filtering was about as good as distilled liquor can get. The news spread, purely by word of mouth. Not surprisingly, we soon found we had thousands of members, all delighted by such amazing whisky.

It took about ten years for the big distillers to realise that we were creaming off their finest products and selling them. When they did, they figured that we were making profits which they should be making, so started selling them themselves. They copied various aspects of what we had done, though never all of them. The most obvious of our devices which they adopted was the use of tasting notes. A few years ago, malt whiskies started appearing with tasting notes appended. As far as the public were concerned, these were authoritative descriptions of the contents of the bottle, written by people of impeccable qualification. You had to know the liquor business pretty well to understand that anything which appears on a bottle is driven by marketing alone, and marketing pays no service to any value other than propelling sales. The result is tasting notes whose relation to the contents of the bottle is, to put it politely, driven by considerations other than accuracy or illumination.

There is also the matter of how the descriptions are made up. Simile and metaphor have a place in this as in most other uses of language. But when such figures of speech are employed without real flair or panache, the result is whimsy. Trouble was, our tasting committee had some people of real ability doing it for love. That's not the same as hiring someone to do it for money: the difference shows in the quality of the language. Moreover we were writing to amuse – ourselves as much as others – as well as to advise, and we never intended the notes to be taken seriously. To be honest, it never occurred to us that anyone would be daft enough to do so. I'm sorry to say that the day came when even the Society would do so, but that's another story.

So when you find a bottle of whisky with some pompous tasting notes purporting to describe its contents, don't be impressed, because the descriptions are probably nonsense. Don't be put off the whisky, though: it may be perfectly good. Try it and decide. Your judgement is the only judgement that matters, and you don't need to be able to put words to your tastes to know that the tastes are good.

DESCRIBING TASTE IN WHISKY:
SCIENTIFIC DESCRIPTIONS

Morphology is an important and respectable stage in the history of science. When people first try to understand the world, they begin by looking around them, making collections of the objects or phenomena which interest them, classifying their collections and giving things names. They move from naming individual objects to naming classes of object. You feel you have got some kind of a handle on things when you have names for them and you know how they resemble other things, for which also you have names. Names make things more familiar and less scary. We can begin to build explanations only once the foundation of classification has been laid.

The use of tasting notes which became widespread in the early 1990s was facilitated by the work at Pentland, which had laid down a classification of the tastes of whiskies. The drive to develop comprehensive and objective descriptions of flavour in whisky was undertaken originally in the interest of process control in the production and maturation of whisky. The maintenance of quality standards depends on the knowledge and judgement of the distillers and blenders. The maintenance of consistency in a whisky brand from one generation to the next depends on the people who put it together – be it malt or blend – being able to transmit their judgements from one generation to another. This has always been done by word of mouth and by traditional apprenticeship methods; it still is. But in the last few years, the training of new blenders has been facilitated by the use of the systems of classification begun at Pentland.

Sensory analysis is now well-developed as a way of classifying the odours to be found in a whisky. The main centre for this in the UK is at the Scotch Whisky Research Institute at Riccarton, near Edinburgh. The Institute has a purpose-built laboratory in which its sensory panel assess the effect of the various flavour compounds which have been found in whisky. Since to date over seven hundred of these have been identified, it will be apparent that sensory analysis of whisky requires to be both organised and precise. By using a large pool of trained assessors working in a controlled environment, the Institute is able to provide information on the effects of variations in materials and processes in the production and maturation of whisky. New-make spirit is assessed as to the effects of alteration in the raw materials, fermentation and distillation. Mature spirit is assessed in terms of the contribution made to flavour by different cask types and conditions.

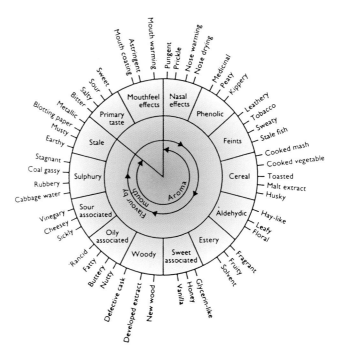

The flavour wheel, as devised by the Scotch Whisky Research Institute.

Flavours are identified and classified. In the tradition of biological - morphology, classification is logically in tree-form, with categories of high generality at the top dividing to give more particular descriptors as you descend. Graphic presentation of the results of the Pentland research followed the wine tradition of using flavour wheels, which Aberlour famously used in its advertising posters as 'The Aberlour Flavour Wheel'. I must say that while the device of a wheel is convenient – it fits into a small space – I find it less than transparent in practice.

The classification enterprise has prospered in recent years and we have seen the emergence of flavour wheels whose purpose it is to encompass and classify every odour detectable in whisky. (See, for example, in Charlie Maclean's excellent book, listed on page 191). Such is the complexity of odour recognition, however, that even the most comprehensive flavour wheels cannot do justice to the range of flavours detectable by a moderately sensitive nose. Nor can they cover the metaphorical use of many flavour terms – and it is the use of simile and metaphor which gives rise to some of the most striking descriptions.

As is the case with any system of biological taxonomy, views as to how things should be arranged change from time to time. There has been a lot of discussion in the scientific press recently regarding species boundaries in the natural world. You might think, if you were not a biologist, that the attribution of species in animals and plants was pretty well fixed. It isn't, and a lot of critters which were thought to be so different that they were obviously different species, are now being found to hybridise, which suggests that the accepted taxonomy is incorrect. So if you think that the scent of tar should be classified as falling under smoky rather than medicinal flavours, well, you're entitled to say so, and no one can gainsay you.

In any science, explanation follows taxonomy. That is, once we have got a grip on things by sorting them into categories, we can make a start on looking for explanations as to why things are arranged as they appear to be. In the case of taste, that means looking for reasons why particular flavours occur and why very different substances have similar flavours. As we have seen in the section on taste above, the aim of the search must be to establish a correspondence between the presence of certain molecules and the perception of a given taste. This is a big job, given that over seven hundred different flavour-inducing molecules have been identified in whisky, and that a particular taste may result from the interaction of several molecules. The number of possible permutations of seven hundred is very large.

However, our concern here is with the use of flavour classification as an element in the appreciation of whisky. Most proprietary bottlings of whisky exhibit only a relatively small number of the possible flavours and most tasters are able to discern only those flavours which are present in fairly high concentrations. So there isn't too much point in our going into enormous detail. Our object is to give you the basic olfactory tools; the more refined ones you can develop for yourself.

BASIC WHISKY TASTES

The simplest way of showing a person how to use a vocabulary is by showing him or her examples of objects which have in common one and only one striking characteristic. Thus, if we show a child a collection of differently-shaped bricks, and we pick out all the red ones, he pretty soon gets the idea that 'red' refers to the colour of the bricks and not to any other attribute. However deeply mysterious this ability may turn out to be when you investigate it, it is simple in practice, given a smart kid. But imagine a situation in which we had to put across the idea of red, where we could only point to the red things from a distance. And we had to do it in a poor light. Then even a really clever child would have difficulty.

Now, think about teaching someone what to look for in a glass of whisky. For that matter, think about your own experience of tasting whisky and trying to identify the aromas. If you are an amateur – or even, in many cases, a professional – you are in a position analogous to the one described: you don't quite know what you should be looking for, and the light is very dim indeed, and there are lots of things which you can't identify which seem to be getting in the way. No wonder folk have problems identifying simple tastes, let alone the higher flights of olfactory fancy.

Whisky tastings are usually little help. Most whisky tastings are either recreational or promotional. If the former, people mostly go around drinking drams and having a good time. If the latter, any structure provided by the organisers is intended to get you to buy the whiskies, rather than to enlighten you as to their true qualities. Even if you are fortunate enough to come across a well-organised tutored tasting, you have to contend with difficulties which are intrinsic to tutored tastings.

We have discussed the close relationship between smell and emotion. It is a two-way process, for not only can our emotions be aroused by odours, but our perception of smells can be influenced by our beliefs and desires. If, after a tutored tasting, you ask the tasters to describe what they have tasted, you will find that they rarely disagree with the tutors. This may be because the tutors know what they are doing, but it may also be down to the tendency for objectivity to fly out of the window when we are in a tasting situation. We tend to taste what we are told to taste. Thus, if we are to discover whisky tastes for ourselves, we require a method which is free from extraneous influences. This means a systematic method which we may employ in solitude, as follows.

The perceptibility of a particular aroma depends on several things. Firstly, on whether it is present at all, for no whisky is likely to exhibit all of the odours listed and some will show only a few. Secondly, on the concentration at which it is present. There is a threshold, which varies with the individual, below which scents are not discernible at all. Technique helps with this, as described in the chapter on tasting (see page 140), for you can enhance the perceptibility of smells by doing it in the right way, under optimum conditions. Thirdly, on the presence of other aromas: some smells mask while others enhance. Peatreek, for example tends to mask other, more delicate odours; vanilla typically enhances sweet scents. Technique and experience are again valuable for they allow us to see what is behind the mask.

The aromas listed below are those most likely to be met with in any Scotch whisky. I have put them in two ranks: the first being scents easy to detect, the second less so. The examples given in each category are intended only to give

EASY	NOT SO EASY
Smoky peaty, phenolic, medicinal	**Soapy** candles, wax
Fruity apples, pears, bananas	**Sulphury** rubber, drains
Floral heather, rose, geraniums	**Caramel** toffee, burnt sugar, treacle
Vanilla toffee, vanilla pods	**Nutty** coconut, almond
Pungent hot, peppery	**Woody** newly sawn timber, resin, pine
Cereal hay, grass, porridge	**Sour** vinegar, cheese
Musty cellars, cork, mothballs	**Sweet** cloying, sickly
Harsh bitter, astringent	

Six of the basic whisky tastes: smoky, fruity and floral (above); vanilla, cereal and sulphur (opposite).

you an idea of the sort of flavour. In practice, most flavours are encountered in combination with others, as compound tastes or smells. Thus caramel and vanilla are commonly experienced together as the odour of toffee or honey. (There is a difference, which is contributed by other flavours which are present in lower concentrations.) Or fruit cake, which may be both of the above together with fruity odours. Or a specific scent such as gardenias, which has a flowery fragrance with slight sourness.

Smoky tastes are by far the easiest to detect. They form the great divide in malts and most people either like them or loathe them. (I think it is a taste which can be acquired, though to do so demands perseverance.) The smoky taste derives from the phenols and related compounds got from burning peat, which are to be found in whisky made from heavily-peated malt. It has nothing – contrary to common belief – to do with peat in the water. The presence of peat in the water used to make the whisky may well have some influence on the taste of the mature spirit, but its influence is of a different order of magnitude compared with the use of a heavily-peated malt.

There are probably more myths associated with smoky flavour than with any other matter in whisky. I have heard it said that it is a taste peculiar to all Islay malts. It isn't – Bunnahabhain and Bruichladdich are both extremely fine Islay whiskies, neither of which uses heavily-peated malt and neither tastes smoky. Highland Park uses a peated malt (though not so heavily-peated as, say, Laphroaig) and it doesn't come from Islay. I remember some Glen Garioch which was pretty smoky; it was many years ago and the whisky was old: presumably at some point someone at Glen Garioch distillery had made whisky using malt more heavily-peated than usual. By the same token, I was once given a glass of Laphroaig which was very old and which bore no trace of peating. I assumed that it must have been made with unpeated malt.

Smoky flavours are the worst offenders when it comes to masking other tastes. In a young whisky which has been peated to a level of 50 parts per million, it can be hard to discern anything at all except smoke. The trick is to make use of our friend and nuisance, habituation: in tasting the whisky, you must give the nose time to accustom itself to the peat. As it does so, it progressively ceases to register smoky odours, and other smells, which hitherto have been completely masked, are able to present themselves.

After peatiness, fruity odours are those most commonly encountered in whisky. Fruit odours are typically produced by esters (see Why Whisky Tastes As It Does: Chemistry, page 63) and develop during fermentation. In an unpeated or lightly-peated whisky which has been well-matured in a good cask,one would expect to find fruity aromas coming off as soon as the spirit is poured. Esters are generally volatile, so that the fruity aromas will quite quickly disappear. In whisky which has lain for a long time in a nearly-empty bottle, it is common to find that the fruity character has gone.

Floral scents also arise from the fermentation process and are in some cases closely related to fruitiness. The compounds which give rise to floral scents are, however, more varied and more complex than those which produce fruity flavours. Floral scents tend also to be volatile and evanescent.

The scent of vanilla is commonly found in well-matured whisky. Both fermentation and maturation give rise to vanilla flavour. Diacetyl, which occurs at the fermentation stage, can give a vanilla flavour. However, it is more usually the product of the extraction of vanillin from the oakwood during maturation.

Pungency is the result of stimulation by ethyl alcohol of pain receptors in the mouth and nose. A little can be desirable, but in excess the sensation is disagreeable. It is easily diminished by diluting the spirit.

Cereal notes arise from a variety of causes, not all of which are presently understood. They tend to be associated with immature spirit and are character-istic of feints. (When we describe a whisky as 'feinty', it is to cereal odours that we mainly refer.) Too late a cut in the spirit run tends to yield feints. Under 'cereal', I include the grassy aromas of aldehydes. This is disputable, and some people would say that the latter require a category of their own. They are, however, reasonably close enough to be brought under the single heading.

Musty flavours too can come from a variety of sources, most of which are undesirable. Bad wood, poor bottling practice, bung cloth disintegration all produce complex compounds such as chloroanisoles and naphtha compounds which give the whisky an off-taste. Almost all of these flavours make for bad whisky but surprisingly, some are not only tolerable but almost pleasant if in sufficiently low concentrations.

Harsh flavours are difficult to describe but instantly recognisable. They are caused mainly by tannins which leach out of the oak of the cask and into the spirit. Whiskies which have been too long in an active cask tend to be high in tannins. While a certain level is tolerable for the sake of the flavours which sometimes accompany it, once a whisky has begun to pick up tannins, it can only go downhill. This is the taste which is described as 'woody' in relation to an old whisky. It should not be confused with the same word used of resinous, aromatic flavours in younger whiskies. Very old whiskies commonly exhibit high levels of tannins: they are tolerated, mainly by people who have paid a lot of money for a bottle of too-old whisky and who, being convinced that the stuff must therefore be wonderful, are able to persuade themselves that bad whisky is good.

All of the above are fairly easy to detect if present in sufficient proportion. The first four are easy to recognise; pungency is a feeling rather than a taste; the final three are usually associated with off-notes and if present, readily identifiable. The second-order flavours are much harder to detect and to identify once detected.

Soapy odours come from long-chain esters formed during fermentation. They are not on the whole desirable, particularly as long-chain esters tend to mask the short-chain, which produce the agreeable fruity aromas.

Sulphurous smells are the product of various compounds, formed mainly in fermentation. Organic molecules such as thiols are formed when a sulphur atom replaces an oxygen in an alcohol molecule. Other sulphur compounds arise in malting and in maturation. It is the practice to sterilise sherry casks prior to transportation by burning sulphur candles inside the cask. It certainly kills off any bacteria; it also introduces sulphur which, in the course of ten or twenty years, markedly affects the taste of the whisky matured in the cask. As with other flavonoids, small concentrations are acceptable to some people and may contribute to an overall flavour which is greatly to be desired. Some people think sulphurous tastes indicate good sherry-cask maturation and therefore convince themselves that they are likeable, even in quite high concentrations.

You might think that the flavour of caramel would be easy enough to pin down to burnt sugar or something of the sort. However, the source of the taste in whisky is anything but easy to attribute. It mostly comes from wood sugars, created by the breakdown of long-chain lignin molecules into their constituent sugar units. There is a popular belief that the caramel used in colouring blended whiskies is a powerful source of caramel flavour. That in fact is not the case, though one could occasionally be forgiven for thinking so. The caramel which is used for colouring is made from sugars, but their oxidation is so complete that little trace of the original sugar is left. If too much caramel is used, its presence is detectable not as sweetness, but as a bitter flavour.

I recall once, many years ago, paying a visit to some old friends who were showing their Highland ponies at the Royal Highland Show, Scotland's premier agricultural show. My friends were as usual installed in a cabin in the show-ground, and acting as hosts to everyone who had any interest in Scotland's indigenous horse. The hospitality meant pouring drams for grizzled farmers and classy ladies in dungarees and rubber boots. I had brought along a bottle of a particularly fine Glenfarclas. The company drank the Glenfarclas until it was gone, whereupon an old farmer produced a bottle of The Famous Grouse. We all duly had a dram, and then another. What struck me most forcibly, was the taste of caramel. Now I was familiar with The Famous Grouse, but I had never before noticed that it had a powerful flavour of caramel. It became perceptible by contrast with the Glenfarclas. (See the next section about the use of contrasts.)

There is a sequel to that story, which I may as well tell you while I'm about it. That year, my friends' stallion was judged the overall champion of the show. Duncan had to take him on a strutting victory parade round the ring – a fact of which he was evidently well aware. As the stallion came up to the judges' stand, he paused, and produced an astonishing erection. The judges said nothing, but I noticed that various old ladies thought it perfectly commendable.

Back to the whisky. Nutty flavours are happily quite common. Coconut and almond flavonoids are both to be found in whisky and when they are – never in high proportion – they make a delightful addition. They arise from oak lactones in the maturation and benzaldehyde produced as part of the fermentation.

Woody flavours of the non-tannic sort are occasionally to be found. These probably come from the cask wood, but the mechanism is not known.

Sourness arises from the presence of organic acids. These arise mainly during fermentation, though they can be produced by distillate reactions in distilling, and at the maturation stage, both by distillate reactions and by extraction of wood components. Acids react with alcohols to produce esters, which are among the most important flavour components, so they are essential to the production process. The presence of free acids in mature whisky is not desirable, save in two respects. First, some very old whiskies develop sour notes, which may be acceptable because of what goes with them. Second – and more - importantly – acidity together with other flavour components, especially sweet and nutty ones, may give rise to compound flavours which are pleasing. Tartness (which is caused by acid) combined with caramel, vanilla and some nuttiness, gives the rich, fruit-cake aroma of many well-matured whiskies.

There is a sweetness – quite different from the fresh sweetness of fruity and floral tastes – which can arise from various causes: malt, fermentation, maturation. Reactions to this vary a lot: some people like it, some don't. Aberlour springs to mind: a very sweet malt, of which many people have a very high opinion.

All Scotch whiskies will contain one or more of these odours. Some will contain lots of them. Before you set out to look for them by sticking your nose into glasses of Scotch, there are a few things you should bear in mind.

You are more likely to find these aromas in a malt than in a blend. This is not because they are present in malts and not in blends. It is caused by the different ways in which malts and blends exhibit their character. Blends are assembled so that the malts and the grain whiskies will *blend* together: that's what blending is all about. On the whole, the odour elements of a blend tend to present jointly, not separately. Malts, on the other hand, tend to reveal themselves progressively, layer after layer peeling away to show what is underneath.

The way in which flavours combine is hugely variable: some malts show lots of quite distinct and identifiable aromas; others have as many or more, but hold them, as it were, bound together, so that what you get is not a series of distinguishable flavours but one overall impression of goodness. And what is worse, great malts seem to be able to integrate flavours in different ways. (This is not only my idea: I am reporting an impression shared by many expert tasters.) Take for example the Macallan and Highland Park: in both the flavours are well-integrated, but in the Macallan they present (as it were) vertically, and in the Highland Park, laterally. So in the latter, it is easier to separate and identify them. (I hope this makes sense in the reading. It seems to as I write and it certainly did so at the tasting last night, but that may have been the whisky talking. But this is a book about whisky, so the cratur should be allowed a voice occasionally.)

In tasting notes, especially the more fanciful ones, you will find many flavours or scents described other than those referred to above. There are two reasons for this, apart from bullshit. One is that primary flavours can combine to yield a vast variety of complex flavours. Most floral scents, for example, are made up of dozens of different esters – and a good nose can distinguish hundreds of flowers. Some have compounds other than esters: gardenias, for example, which have an acidic component.

The second reason is that there are enormous numbers of compounds which have distinct aromas and which may be present in whisky in concentrations high enough to be perceptible. Tasters commonly say a whisky smells of new-mown hay; less commonly, of raspberries. Both hay and raspberries contain a molecule known as ionone, which may be present in whisky. Eugenol is a related compound which gives their aromas to bay leaves and to cloves, both of which may occasionally be detected in a whisky. It is a very large field and one which is well outside the scope of this book, whose purpose is to act as an introduction, not a manual for advanced students

The presence and balance of flavour elements in a whisky are what makes it a good or a bad whisky. Whisky can be bad just because it is lacking in character. That is, there are few flavours discernible and those at low levels. Or it can be bad because flavours which at low concentrations are pleasurable, are present in excessive quantities. Or because there are flavour compounds which are disagreeable if perceptible at all.

TASTE RECOGNITION: DIFFERENCE ANALYSIS

The purpose of this section is to show you how to discover for yourself some of the flavours mentioned in the last. First, you must equip yourself with a knowledge of the basic odours. It is desirable that as far as possible you should do so by direct experience. For example, in the case of vanilla, you should procure a vanilla pod or two, for nothing smells quite like the real thing – and having sniffed them, you should store them in a jar of sugar: they last forever and you have a constant supply of vanilla-flavoured sugar if you keep topping up the jar. Some scents are easier than others: 'musty' covers a wide range of scents – but if you sit on cork in a damp cellar with a few mothballs about, you will get the idea. Or sulphury: I recommend cleaning drains downwind of an oil refinery dressed in rubber boots and wearing rubber gloves. If that seems fanciful, I can tell you, I've done it. I must say, it didn't occur to me at the time that the experience would be useful later on.

At the start of the preceding section I mentioned the difficulty of identifying an odour which is surrounded by others. In the section which follows this one, there are tasting notes, mainly in terms of the flavours described before, of a number of commonly-available malt whiskies. You could of course simply drink your way through a bottle of each, and try to see if you can distinguish some of the aromas we discovered. That would be expensive, bad for the liver and methodologically suspect.

The best course is to use a technique which has been used in this and other fields, known as difference analysis. It consists of inspecting two or more objects, only one of which has the characteristic we wish to identify. By comparing that which has it with that which does not, it becomes easier mentally to isolate the impression. In whisky tasting, this can best be done by taking a standard whisky and spiking it with some of the compound we wish to discern. Because we have a standard base, we can readily discern any strange flavour. However, many of the flavour components would be classed as poisons, so that isn't an option, save in certain circumstances for industrial training by certified expert institutions.

The next best thing is to look at two whiskies, one of which has the flavour and one which has not – or one which has it in much greater concentration than the other. Compare and contrast them, and see whether we can discern the difference. Now if we have a very large number of whiskies to choose from, that shouldn't be too difficult, for we can choose those which have singular characteristics. The problem is that there are very few whiskies commonly available which exhibit isolated or striking flavours. Most whiskies have lots of flavours – that is why they are good whiskies and why they are marketed. If you could choose from single-cask bottlings from all the distilleries, you could just about do it, but not otherwise. So we are left in the position described at the start of the previous section: seeking to identify one flavour among many others.

Together with some of my colleagues in the Malt Masterclass, I have put together a group of proprietary bottlings of malt whisky from which, with some care, it is possible to discern most of the flavours mentioned by means of a difference analysis. The whiskies we propose you use are as follows:

  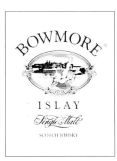  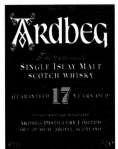

| Glenmorangie 10-year-old | Macallan 10-year-old | Bowmore 12-year-old | Glendronach 12-year-old | Ardbeg 17-year-old |

You will require two nosing glasses and a couple of watch glasses or similar to cover them. The technique is fairly simple: select two whiskies to be compared; put a little of each whisky in a glass, cover the glass and then proceed to nose the contents in quick succession, looking for a specific aroma which is present in the one but not in the other. (It is possible to use more than two at a time and to isolate an aroma from one out of three, say. That, however, can become confusing and there is a problem with the effects of habituation, so we have decided to stick to a two-glass system.)

Applying this technique to the five whiskies chosen, we can analyse their flavours as follows.

	Glenmorangie	Macallan	Bowmore	Glendronach	Ardbeg
Smoky			✗	✗	✗
Fruity	✗	✗	✗		
Floral	✗	✗			✗
Vanilla	✗	✗	✗	✗	
Pungent			✗		
Cereal	✗				
Musty					✗
Harsh					
Soapy	✗				
Sulphury		✗		✗	
Caramel	✗		✗	✗	
Nutty		✗		✗	
Woody			✗		
Sour		✗	✗	✗	
Sweet	✗			✗	✗

You will note that there are no entries under Harsh and only one each under Woody and Musty. None of the whiskies we chose could be described as harsh and those which show woody and musty flavours do so in very low concentrations indeed.

The smoky aroma is by far the easiest, and few tasters will be in need of instruction. Compare the Bowmore or the Ardbeg with any of the others, and the smoky flavours will immediately become apparent. Less obvious is a comparison between the Glendronach and the Macallan: the latter shows fewer phenolic flavours than the former, though they are present at low levels in both.

For fruity scents, the Glenmorangie is the obvious choice, since it is high in esters. So is the Macallan, but in combinations which produce different results. Compare the Macallan with the Glendronach: the first has dried-fruit odours (esters in combination with some acidity) which the second lacks. Comparison of Bowmore with Ardbeg will show a similar disparity.

The Glenmorangie is strong on floral notes, also mainly down to esters. So strong, indeed, that you should be able to detect them without using a comparison. Once you have got an idea from the Glenmorangie of what you are seeking in the matter of floral odours, try comparing the Macallan with the Glendronach: the former has them and the latter does not.

Vanilla is easy: all of the whiskies have it except the Ardbeg. Compare that with the Bowmore: give yourself time for the nose to accommodate to the phenolics, and then look for the vanilla in the Bowmore. It's there, though it is not too easy to discern. It isn't present in the Ardbeg – or if it is, it is too weak for any of us to detect, which amounts to the same thing.

Pungency is more of a prickle than a taste. It is caused by stimulation of pain sensors in the mouth and nose, not by the olfactory receptors. You get it with almost any strong alcohol, though it is also caused by capsaicin and piperine, which are the active compounds in peppers. In this case, the Bowmore exhibits it most clearly – though only if taken without water. The water kills it dead. No need for a comparison with this: you either get it or you don't. If you don't, try using cayenne for snuff. Then you'll get it – though you'll wish you hadn't.

Cereal aromas are not so simple. In our sampling selection, only Glenmorangie has them in any marked degree. They tend to be obscured by the esters and sweet flavours. Fortunately, these are more volatile than the cereal odours, so the trick is to look for the latter later in the tasting. Put some water in the glass and let it stand for a little, uncovered. Then you should be able to discern a scent as of newly-cut grass, or hay. None of the other whiskies will give anything remotely similar.

Musty mostly means nasty. I remember a cask whose contents we nosed for the Scotch Malt Whisky Society, of which the bung cloth had disintegrated. (The bung cloth is a piece of hessian sacking they wrap round the bung before driving it into the hole in the cask.) The whisky was a pale green colour and decidedly off. It tasted as it would if you had drunk it sitting in the garden shed with an old sack over your head. Now that scent is not necessarily unpleasant: everyone likes the smell of a garden shed, of which a musty base is part. Well, the Ardbeg is very similar in olfactory terms: there are lots and lots of fine aromas, all blending together to give a charming sensation of organic smokiness and freshness, with beneath them, a base note of something musty. The best comparison here is the Bowmore, which hasn't got it at all. Many people, of whom I'm one, think that that base flavour actually improves the Ardbeg.

Harsh we have not got. Try any really bad, cheap liquor taken without mixers and you will get the idea. You will probably get a bad head as well, but then you have probably had a bad head in a less worthy cause, so no whining.

Soapy is difficult, though once you have the idea, it sticks. Glenmorangie has it, but in very low degree: certainly not enough to diminish the flavour – and possibly just enough to enhance it. Look for it after you have let the whisky stand in an open glass, after you have looked for the cereal. I think it smells more like candle wax – and perhaps that is the thing to look for, since nowadays so few people have any experience of unscented soap. I have been unable to detect the aroma in any of the other whiskies we are considering – which is not to say it isn't there, so it's worth looking.

With sulphury odours we are on surer ground. Macallan and Glendronach both have them, the latter in much greater degree. Think bad eggs, rubber, old farts. (My father was a notable farter, so I am on safe ground here.) There is enough sulphur in the Glendronach for some people to dislike it on that ground. It occurs at the end of the Macallan, but in such low concentration that it merely adds a topping to the richness, as asafoetida does to a curry.

Caramel is one of the components of rich, sweet tastes and is commonly found in association with vanilla and sweetness in foodstuffs. As a result, it is not as simple as you might think to detect the flavour of caramel, as opposed to its associates. The best course, as in so much to do with flavour, is to do a lot of cooking. If you have made a lot of toffee, or understand the function of burnt onions in savoury dishes (which is surprisingly uncommon) then you will recognise caramel. If you don't have this sort of experience, then I suggest you get it – take up cooking in the interest of enjoying whisky. If you think that's beneath you, remember Brillat-Savarin. Interestingly, none of our tasters mentioned caramel as a component of the richness of the Macallan, though it has all of the other sweet-associated tastes. Glenmorangie certainly has it: you will find it up-front, as a different sort of sweetness alongside the esters. Try comparing the Glendronach and the Macallan: the former has it and the latter does not, or not so markedly.

Nutty flavours come from wood extractives, so they depend more on the cask type and quality than on the distillate. That means that if you are bottling individual casks of a whisky, some will yield spirit with nutty notes and some will not. Happily most of the distillers nowadays are fairly consistent in the sorts of casks they use, so we can generalise with some confidence. The Macallan is certainly nutty and so is the Glendronach, about equally so. Try comparing either with the Glenmorangie, as regards nutty aromas – the peating in the other two will make comparison difficult. Both the Macallan and the Glendronach are matured in sherry casks, which are mostly made of European oak, which is where the nuttiness comes from. The Glenmorangie on the other hand, is matured in *Quercus alba*, the American white oak, which is not so high in the relevant compounds.

Woody is difficult. By 'woody' here, we don't mean the tannic woodiness of very old whiskies. We are speaking of the aromatic, resinous sort of woody flavour which you get from freshly sawn pinewood. Bowmore has it and – the obvious comparison – Ardbeg does not. That said, it is not present in any very high concentration in the Bowmore, so is none too easy to spot. In making the comparison, you will have to nose both whiskies for some time in order to allow your nose to accommodate to the phenols. Once you have done that, with any luck you will be able to discern the scent of pines beneath.

Sourness is present in three of the whiskies as a component of more complex flavours. In the Macallan and the Glendronach, you will find it in the dried-fruit tastes: more sweet than sour, but sour none the less. In the Bowmore, it lies alongside a fresher fruitiness, though you have to delve for it and pay close attention.

The Glenmorangie, the Glendronach and the Ardbeg all have a sweet note upfront, which is lacking in the other two. The best comparison is between the Glendronach and the Macallan. When you make it, remember you are looking for a first, immediate impression: not the deep-down fruitiness associated with vanilla or caramel, but something more immediate and sugary.

WHY WHISKY TASTES AS IT DOES: CHEMISTRY

ow that we know how whisky tastes, we can sensibly ask why it tastes as it does. As you might expect from what has gone before, the answers to this question are not simple, nor are they all to do with what we might call objective factors. Whisky tastes as it does because of what it is made from and how it is made. Then there is the matter of what is done to it after it has been made and before it gets in the bottle. And once it has been let out of the bottle, genie-like, the taste can take myriad forms: the cultural context in which the tasting is done is as important as the physical environment.

In the following chapters, we look at all of these in turn. First, however, we will make a short excursion into the chemistry of whisky production and maturation. It is surprising how few people who consider themselves connoisseurs of whisky know even the rudiments of its chemistry. Indeed, there is a point of view to the effect that chemistry is a lower-class, mechanical sort of business and that the cultivation of taste does not require any knowledge of how those tastes arise. That's like saying you can appreciate Mozart without being able to read music. You can, but you will do it better if you know the language.

The stuff on chemistry is pretty elementary, so my apologies to any readers who find it tedious. I think it more important that people who do not know much about the chemical basis of whisky tastes should learn something, than that I should entertain those who already know lots. Anyway, in my experience, the latter are few and the former many.

ORGANIC CHEMISTRY

The science of chemistry, like all other sciences, is made up of observations, concepts, theories and techniques. What follows is a summary only of results: that is, theories which are generally accepted and conclusions which may be regarded as established. As with most other sciences, it is possible to have some understanding based on an acquaintance merely with the results of several hundred years' work by a great many people, without knowing how those results were arrived at. This is a long way from a systematic grasp of the science, but better than nothing.

The central concepts of chemistry – which, for our purposes, may be taken as facts – are to do with what matter is made of and how the basic parts combine to make different sorts of matter. Everyone knows about atoms: how they were thought to be the fundamental particles until it was found that they could be broken up to release huge amounts of energy. For our purposes, we can take atoms as fundamental, with the reservation that each atom is made up of a central nucleus round which whizz one or more electrons. The nucleus has a positive electrical charge and the electrons a negative charge. Atoms are very small: the dot at the end of this sentence is made up of several hundred million atoms.

Atoms vary in how they are made up: hydrogen has only one electron, carbon has six, nitrogen seven and oxygen eight. Depending on how they are constituted, atoms have different characteristics. There are just over a hundred types of atom, each type being known as an element. All matter is made up of atoms of those hundred elements, usually in combination with other atoms of the same or other elements. Combinations of atoms are called molecules, and it is as molecules that we mostly experience atoms. Just about everything is made up of molecules. The writing on this page is made up of molecules; so is the page; so are you.

Atoms differ in their propensity to combine with each other. This difference is expressed numerically as the *valency* of the atom. Hydrogen has a valency of one; oxygen of two; carbon of four, which means that one carbon atom can combine with four hydrogen atoms and two oxygen, yielding methane, CH_4, and carbon dioxide, CO_2, respectively. One oxygen can combine with two hydrogen, to produce a compound commonly known as water, or H_2O.

In conventional depictions, each atom is represented by a letter. Thus carbon is C, oxygen O, hydrogen H and nitrogen N. Some elements have two letters such as lead, Pb (from the Latin *plumbum*, meaning lead.) The number of atoms of a given element in any molecule is shown by a numeral at the bottom right of the relevant letter, as methane CH_4, in which one carbon atom has combined with four hydrogen atoms. Similarly, water is H_2O, meaning two hydrogen atoms attached to one oxygen. This notation is known as the molecular formula.

The properties of any compound depend not only on how many of each element are combined in the molecule, but on how the atoms are arranged. Different arrangements of the same atoms can lead to wildly different properties.

It is therefore desirable to indicate in any molecular formula the way in which the different elements are combined. The use of letters and numerals as above is suitable up to a point, but its inadequacies soon become apparent, especially as regards compounds which have the same numbers of elements in varying arrangements. By arranging the element-symbols (the letters) spatially, it is possible to show how the atoms are arranged in the molecule. Bonds between atoms are depicted by lines, hence water is shown as an oxygen atom with a hydrogen attached to either side of it:

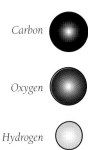

Carbon

Oxygen

Hydrogen

and methane as a carbon with a hydrogen on each of its four prongs:

Ethane, the next-largest molecule in the series, is, like methane, an odourless gas. Its molecular formula is C_2H_6 and its arrangement is:

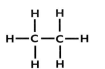

With larger organic molecules, it becomes impracticable to show all of the carbon and hydrogen atoms, so a convention is adopted in which lines are used and every line is assumed to have one carbon atom attached to each end of it. Each carbon atom is assumed to have a hydrogen atom attached to any of its four prongs which are not otherwise occupied.

Thus ethane is shown as a line representing the two carbons. One at either end, and the six hydrogens, three attached to each carbon. Thus:

———————

Carbon atoms have very peculiar properties and are quite unlike any other kinds of atom. Organic chemistry is the chemistry of the carbon atom in all its compound forms, of which there are millions. There are so many of these and they play such an important part in our lives, that they warrant special attention. The chemistry of living things is organic chemistry, for all living things are made up of organic molecules. We are made of organic compounds and so are most of the things we taste and smell, so the chemistry of taste is organic chemistry. That is, it is about one lot of organic compounds reacting with another lot. The difference is that the first lot – us – is alive and the other, by and large, isn't. (There are exceptions: we eat oysters which are alive as we eat them, which some vegetarians find disgusting. So are most fruits, though nobody seems to be disgusted by the idea of eating apples.)

The main difference between carbon atoms and other atoms is that carbon atoms show a strong propensity to join up with others of their sort. Thus molecules arise in the form of long chains and with the addition of each link to the chain, a new compound is born which has properties entirely different from those which precede it in the chain, or those which follow it. The simplest compounds of carbon and hydrogen – the hydrocarbons – are the long chains which occur when carbon atoms are added to the methane – ethane series. Thus propane and butane – which we are familiar with in the form of bottled gas – are the next two in the series, having three and four carbon atoms respectively (see left) or in line formula:

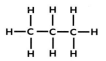

Propane

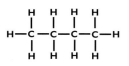

Butane

Methane, propane and butane are gases. Pentane, hexane and octane, which come next in the series, are liquids. We mostly experience these in the form of petrol and diesel. As the chain gets longer, the substances get more dense and the heaviest hydrocarbons are solids such as paraffin wax, which you use to light barbecues.

ALCOHOLS

After carbon, by far the most common elements found in organic compounds are hydrogen, oxygen and nitrogen. Every variation in form or content of an organic molecule results in a compound with highly individual characteristics. For example, if we add one oxygen atom to methane (illustrated on page 55), we get not a gas but a liquid, methyl alcohol.

Methyl alcohol is the simplest in a series which contains a truly enormous number of compounds. Like the hydrocarbons, the longer the carbon chain, the heavier the molecule gets, and the more viscous the substance. Ethyl alcohol –

the next one up the chain – is not so volatile as methyl; by the time we get to amyl and hexyl alcohols, the fluids are beginning to look like oils. Indeed, in the whisky industry, they, along with other even higher alcohols, are known as fusel oils. Being heavier and less volatile, they evaporate later in the distillation process and are sent to the feints receiver. The middle cut, which is what becomes whisky, contains only traces of the higher alcohols. Though present in infinitesimally small quantities, they nevertheless make a significant contribution to the flavour of the finished whisky.

Methyl alcohol is also present in most wines, but in concentrations so low that it does no harm. (You can't drink enough of it in wine to hurt you: you would die of ethyl alcohol long before the methanol got you.) In whisky, it is present in the wash, but being very volatile, is normally lost in the foreshots. That is not to say it isn't dangerous, though, and it should on no account be consumed in any appreciable concentration. A single measure of the pure stuff will kill you and much smaller doses will attack your optic nerve and blind you. It is commonly used as a domestic solvent, in which form it is sold coloured purple and spiked with the odour of rats' piss. Some desperate characters have been known to drink it none the less. Not for long, though.

All of the alcohols are characterized by the possession of the -OH group. Also known as ethanol, this is the substance which we usually refer to as alcohol, since it is the alcohol which we normally encounter in our drinks. The term comes from the Arabic *al kuhl*. This phrase originally meant the fine powder, antimony sulphide, which is used to darken the eyelids to make the wearer more alluring to the members of the opposite (or in some cases, the same) sex. (I bet you thought there would be no sex in a chapter on chemistry. You were wrong.) Anyway, these Arabs – chaps, mostly – thought pretty highly of the stuff they put on their eyes. It seems they thought it the very essence of sexuality: so much so that the phrase came to be used to refer to the essence of just about anything. It is a short step to the application of the term to distillate, given that the Arabs invented perfume as we know it and they used distillation to extract essential oils from flowers.

The Arabs are commonly credited with having invented distillation. This is probably not true. There is evidence that Gnostic Christians used distilled wine in their religious ceremonies, long before anyone had heard of the Arabs. The Gnostics were an early Christian sect, deeply influenced by Neoplatonism, who were heavily into spirituality. This got them into trouble with the Church, which even then was over-bureaucratic and kept its spirituality at a comfortable distance. The Gnostics thought that the soul was akin to the volatile component

Methyl alcohol or methanol

Ethyl alcohol or ethanol

of distilled wine and that when people died they more or less evaporated. Heaven was a kind of celestial condenser in which the purer part of us would be reconstituted. It has been argued recently that the origin of the phrase 'baptism of fire' was the Gnostic practice of baptising their converts with a mixture of distilled alcohol and water, in which the alcohol was sufficiently concentrated to light with a flame but not enough to burn the person baptised. I'm sceptical about this, having tried it and got burnt.

Anyway, it's pretty clear that the Chinese knew about alcohol long before the Gnostics. Being Chinese, they did things differently from the rest of the world, and though they knew how to make hard liquor, they didn't drink it – much as they knew how to make gunpowder and used it in warfare to make firecrackers to frighten their enemies, rather than bombs to kill them.

MAKING WHISKY

The -OH group, known as a hydroxyl group, is significant in matters of taste, for compounds in which it is present are commonly perceived as sweet. True, ethanol itself doesn't taste sweet, but if another hydroxyl is added to the molecule it becomes ethanediol, which does. This compound is also known as ethylene glycol (see page 20) or antifreeze. Its molecular formula is $C_2H_6O_2$. and in line formula

Ethylene Glycol

As hydroxyl groups are added, the sweetness increases. If you have a molecule consisting of six carbons and five hydroxyl groups, you get sugar. Glucose is $C_6H_{12}O_6$. and in line formula

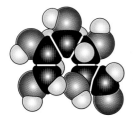

Glucose

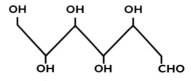

It also exists in the form of a closed ring of five carbon atoms with one oxygen (see opposite).

The same lot of atoms – $C_6H_{12}O_6$ – in a different arrangement is fructose. Both combine readily with oxygen (that is, burn) to form carbon dioxide and water and give off energy. Both are also highly soluble in water and it is the combination of those two attributes that enables them to constitute the energy source of all living things. Being soluble, they can be transported between cells and within them; being capable of oxidisation, they act as fuel. Glucose is the form in which energy is stored by plants: the energy of sunlight is used to synthesise sugars from water and carbon dioxide.

Glucose and fructose molecules have the ability to join together – a process known as polymerisation – to form sucrose and maltose, types of molecules which are known as disaccharides. As with hydrocarbon chains, the process can go on, building polymers which consist of ever-longer chains of glucose and fructose molecules, known generically as polysaccharides. Starch is a polysaccharide. Some plants such as beets, fruits and sugar canes store their energy directly as sugars, but most do so as starches: cereals and root crops such as potatoes contain their energy in the form of starch. When we eat starchy foods, our digestion breaks down the starch molecules into their constituent sugars.

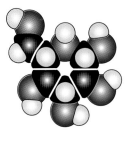

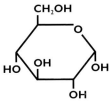

Glucose ring

The business of whisky making begins with starches and ends with alcohols. We take a grain of barley, which consists of two things: a barley-plant embryo and a store of energy in the form of starch. We convert the starch into sugar. We then ferment the sugar to produce weak alcohol; we distil to concentrate the alcohol.

The barley plant needs to be able to access its energy store to provide for the growing plant. This it does by using enzymes which split the long-chain starch molecules into shorter sugar molecules. (Enzymes are organic catalysts which, though they enable a process to take place, are not themselves used up in the process. Your car probably has a catalytic converter in its silencer: it works by

The two varieties of glucose polymer that starch consists of: amylose (top) and amylopectin (bottom)

converting poisonous compounds in the exhaust gases into harmless ones.) The whisky maker exploits both parts of the barley grain – the enzymes and the starch. The process of malting barley consists of dampening the grains, so that they begin to grow. In growing, the barley grain produces the enzyme, maltase. The maltase acts on the stored starch, and converts it into maltose, a disaccharide sugar. You can taste the difference between malted and unmalted barley: the latter tastes dry and mealy; the former tastes distinctly sweet. As soon as the malting is complete, the process is halted, otherwise the plant would grow and use up the sugar. At this stage, the barley is still alive. The kiln which dries the malt, kills it. This is what prompted Burns to say:

And they hae sworn a solemn oath
John Barleycorn should die.

Starch is not soluble in water, but sugar is. The next stage in whisky making is the grinding of the dried, malted barley in a mill until it is a flour. That flour is dissolved in water in the process known as mashing. Once the solid, insoluble part of the malt is removed (the *draff*), we are left with a sweet liquid: water containing dissolved sugars, which is known as *worts*.

Fermentation is the process which converts sugars into alcohols, mainly ethyl alcohol. It is called brewing. It has been known about for a very long time: almost every culture has its own way of brewing alcoholic liquor. The Scots, in common with most other people who live in cold temperate climates, have traditionally used grains as the source of sugars. Barley is easy to use for this purpose, since it produces relatively large amounts of the desired enzyme. Other grains can for the most part be malted, but not as easily. Rice and millet are both used: the one to make rice wine, the other for mealie beer.

In warmer climates, fruits are used: grapes for wine, apples for cider, cherries, pears, plums, any fruit with sugar in it. There are other sources: the heart of the agave cactus contains high concentrations of sugars which, when fermented yield pulque, which is distilled into tequila. The sap of some palm trees gives us palm wine; distilled it becomes arrack.

In most cases, the fermenting agent is a yeast. (Rice wine is different: the agent is an organism called *Aspergillus oryzae* which grows on the rice.) Yeasts, of which there are a great many different varieties, are relatives of fungi. They thrive on sugars and, as a by-product of their metabolic activity, produce alcohol. The kinds of alcohol – and the amounts of compounds other than alcohol – which result from fermentation, depend on the species of yeast employed. For control of flavour, brewers generally prefer to use only pure strains of certain yeasts. Unless they do so, they are unable to predict the outcome of individual brewing processes. Wild yeasts abound in the air, and tend to contaminate batches of malt. When they do, the fermentation which takes place is significantly different from that which is desired.

Historically, all wines, beers, etc., were fermented by wild yeasts, so the quality of a brew depended on which wild yeasts happened to float by at the time. The resulting potations were mostly pretty vile, but they did have two important attributes: they got you drunk and they were sterile. Even at the low concentrations produced by fermentation (up to about five per cent by volume), alcohol is toxic to most organisms. In the absence of a pure water supply, beer or wine was the only stuff safe to drink. Excessive alcohol in society had become recognised as a social evil in most Western societies by the nineteenth century, round about the first time since the Romans that most cities had achieved a decent municipal water supply. Because everyone then took the water supply for granted, the public health virtues of alcohol disappeared from view.

The emergence of whisky as a potation for polite persons happened toward the end of the eighteenth century. Its quality had improved, partly through better distilling and maturation processes, partly because of developments in the understanding of the place of yeasts in brewing and control of flavour resulting therefrom. Today, the brewer is one of the most important people in a distillery and the contribution of fermentation to the flavour of the mature whisky is not in doubt.

AFTER ALCOHOL

The chemistry of maturation is a pretty tough subject which, if you don't already know a lot of chemistry, will require a good many years' study. However, there are certain basic things which happen to alcohol which you ought to know about and whose chemistry can be outlined fairly briefly.

Aldehydes

When an alcohol is exposed to air, the oxygen in the air combines with the hydrogen of the alcohol, leaving it short on a couple of hydrogen atoms per alcohol molecule. In that state it may be described as having been dehydrogenated. Hence the name given to the resulting class of compounds, of aldehydes. The compound produced by the dehydrogenation of ethanol is called acetaldehyde, and its molecular formula is C_2H_4O. Acetaldehyde occurs naturally

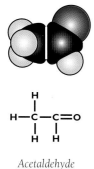

Acetaldehyde

in beers and wines, through exposure to oxygen and by the action of yeasts. In small quantities it makes a contribution to the flavour, though in excess it is not agreeable. In some fortified wines, though, it is encouraged, since an aldehydic taste is desired: flor yeast is allowed to develop on fino and manzanilla sherries, in which the acetaldehyde produced gives them a nutty flavour.

Acetaldehyde is one of the main causes of hangovers. An enzyme called – rather obviously – alcohol dehydrogenase which is found in the liver, converts ethanol in the blood to acetaldehyde and makes us feel bad the morning after. (This is a subject on which I can claim some expertise, having suffered all my drinking life from really desperate hangovers.)

It is difficult to describe the smell of acetaldehyde, though it is easy enough to recognise once you know it. Characteristic of old whisky, cognacs and armagnacs, as well as fortified wines such as sherry and madeira, it is also to be found in bottles of whisky which have lain too long on the shelf in a near-empty state.

There is a common belief to the effect that whisky does not go off in bottle and that consequently nothing need be done to keep bottled stocks in good condition. This is not the case: whisky left in the presence of a relatively large volume of air for a long time will form acetaldehyde. People sometimes ask me what whisky I drink in a bar. I usually tell them I have a very simple principle: I order a dram from whichever bottle is fullest, as it is likely to be in the best condition.

I do not know of any sommelier or bar manager who does anything to ensure that his whisky is kept in perfect condition. Indeed, I do not know of any who are aware of the problem, since I know of no book which has mentioned it and certainly none of the distillers seem interested. I know also a number of self-proclaimed connoisseurs of whisky who have large collections of malts, all of which are in a more or less advanced stage of dehydrogenation. This situation provides an interesting insight into the level of expertise – or rather the lack of it – which is current in respect of whisky.

There are two ways round the problem: either you drink the whisky before it has a chance to go off, or you get rid of the air in the bottle. The former is much the simpler and more agreeable. Dehydrogenation is a slow process, so you have weeks, maybe months, to get through the contents of the bottle. But if you must keep the stuff, you can preserve the contents of the bottle either by pumping out the air – there are various wine bottle pumps on the market – or by using a gas blanket to cover them. The latter is preferable, since it seals the whisky off completely. In the UK, a firm called Winesaver markets an aerosol-type bottle which is simple to use and appears to be very effective.

Ethanol is not the only alcohol to undergo dehydrogenation. Formaldehyde, which comes from the oxidation of methanol, is perfectly ghastly. It was responsible for one of the worst olfactory experiences of my life (see page 27) It is used to preserve dead flesh and is what gives a dissecting room its stench. There are only two things you can say for it: it probably doesn't smell as bad as dead bodies did in the days before it was discovered – and it provides the best evidence one could desire for the effect of habituation: when you first enter a dissecting room, you think you have never smelled anything so vile, but after an hour or two, you don't notice the smell and must make a conscious effort to register it at all.

Fortunately, the aldehydes of the longer-chain alcohols are far more agreeable to the nose and palate than those which contain only a few carbon atoms. Aldehydes formed by some of the higher alcohols are vital flavour congeners in whisky. Vanillin, $C_8H_8O_3$, is an aldehyde and also a flavour component of good malt whisky. While its main source is the oak wood used in maturation, it also results from the dehydrogenation of a higher alcohol, eugenol, $C_{10}H_{12}O_2$, which is the active component in oil of cloves and closely related to nutmeg. Cinnamaldyde, C_9H_8O, is what we taste as cinnamon.

The higher aldehydes tend to appear during distillation – in the pot-still only: in patent-still distilling, the higher aldehydes are discarded along with the fusel oils, which is one reason why patent-still whisky is less flavoursome than pot-still.

Acids and Esters

There is a further stage in the interaction of alcohols with oxygen, of which you should be aware. This is oxidation proper – the gaining of an oxygen atom rather than the losing of hydrogen. When the aldehyde molecule gains one oxygen atom, it becomes acetic acid, $C_2H_4O_2$. This is the acid which is formed when wine and beer go sour. It is also the acid in vinegar – indeed, the term vinegar derives from the French *vin aigre*, meaning sour wine, and is also present in sourdough bread.

Acetic acid is not normally a problem as regards the taste of whisky: oxidation does not usually proceed much beyond the aldehyde stage in distilled liquors. It, and the acids (such as butanoic acid and propanoic acid) formed by oxygenation of the higher alcohols, are, however, important in the development of whisky flavours. This is because those acids react with the alcohols to form a new group of compounds called esters. The best-known is the reaction of ethanol with acetic acid to form ethyl acetate, which gives many fruits and

Acetic acid

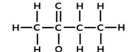

Ethyl acetate

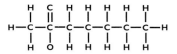

Amyl acetate

berries their characteristic scent. Since ethanol is the main alcohol present in whisky and acetic acid the principal organic acid, ethyl acetate is the ester most likely to be found. It and amyl acetate are common organic solvents: they are likely to be encountered as the solvent in such things as glue and nail polish. Amyl acetate, which is the product of amyl alcohol and acetic acid, has the smell of peardrops. Its presence is one of the indicators of a well-made whisky, well-matured. I suppose it would be possible to have too much of this, as of any other scent, but I cannot recall ever having found it present in excessive quantity.

Esters are the stars in the worlds of whisky and perfume: they are responsible for most of the lovely scents. There are lots and lots of esters: if you permutate the number of possible alcohols with the number of possible acids – and an acid can react with any alcohol, not just the one whose oxidation produced it – you get a huge number of possible compounds. So when someone says he can smell pineapple in his whisky, he may be kidding himself and you, but he may be detecting a trace of ester, namely amyl butyrate. Over a hundred esters have been identified in malt whiskies. Some of the more common ester odours are shown below.

Ester	Odour
n-pentyl acetate	bananas
octyl acetate	oranges
ethyl butyrate	pineapples
amyl butyrate	pineapples
pentyl butyrate	apricots
ethyl formate	rum

The odours of fruits are usually made up of large numbers of different esters and the characteristic odour may result either from one dominant odour or from the mixture. For example, the smell of Bartlett pears is known to contain at least 53 different esters.

Esters are formed during fermentation and maturation. The fruity aromas of young wines are mainly down to esters, as are some of the odours of good ale. During maturation, acids from the cask – which are a different lot from the acids formed in the production process – react with alcohols in the whisky to produce even more and different esters.

Ketones

Molecules which contain the carbonyl group C=O are called ketones. They are the source of many natural odours. Diacetyl, one of the simplest, $C_4H_6O_2$, is the ketone based on butane. Its line formula is:

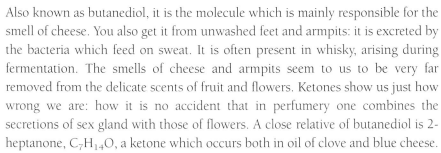

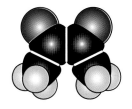

Diacetyl

Also known as butanediol, it is the molecule which is mainly responsible for the smell of cheese. You also get it from unwashed feet and armpits: it is excreted by the bacteria which feed on sweat. It is often present in whisky, arising during fermentation. The smells of cheese and armpits seem to us to be very far removed from the delicate scents of fruit and flowers. Ketones show us just how wrong we are: how it is no accident that in perfumery one combines the secretions of sex gland with those of flowers. A close relative of butanediol is 2-heptanone, $C_7H_{14}O$, a ketone which occurs both in oil of clove and blue cheese.

A rather complicated molecule called 3-(para-hydroxyphenyl)-2-butanone – though it is in reality one of the smaller, simpler ketones – has the molecular formula $C_{10}H_{12}O_2$. It is the molecule responsible for the scent of ripe - raspberries. Raspberries when newly picked have a wonderfully fresh smell, which is due to a compound of the same three atoms in a slightly different combination. This is ionone, $C_{13}H_{20}O$, and is the essential oil extracted from violets; it also causes newly dried hay to smell so pleasant – which of course is one of the aromas to be found in good whisky.

It will, I hope, have become apparent that a tasting note which describes a whisky as being floral, smelling of pears and violets and new-mown hay, while it may be down to the fancy of the taster, may also be the result of an accurate sensory assessment. All of the scents mentioned do in fact occur in whisky and they come from compounds of the same three atoms: carbon, hydrogen and oxygen.

Terpenes

Rubber isn't exactly what one thinks of in connection with refinement, whether of the social or the chemical variety. But then we should by now be accustomed to the conjunction of the base with the exalted in matters olfactory. Natural rubber is a polymer made up of lots of molecules of a hydrocarbon known as isoprene, C_5H_8. Carvone, $C_{10}H_{14}O$ is a terpene. It is the compound which gives its flavour to oil of spearmint. Spearmint is related to menthol, $C_{10}H_{20}O$, which in turn is related to camphor, $C_{10}H_{16}O$. All of these rather exotic molecules can from time to time be detected in a glass of whisky.

THE CHEMISTRY OF FLAVOUR

Now that we have some understanding of the basic chemistry of whisky production, we may address the chemistry of flavour production. Ethanol itself is flavourless and odourless; it is detected only as pungent, hot or peppery feelings in the mouth or nose. All of the flavour in whisky comes from the congeners, compounds which arise as by-products of alcohol production or maturation and which are present in very low concentrations.

All stages of whisky production and maturation make some contribution to its flavour. It isn't always easy to say at what stage a particular flavour has been produced, for several reasons. The chemistry of some flavours is reasonably well understood; others, scarcely at all. A given flavour may develop at more than one stage in the process; it can be difficult to tell at which. Research into whisky flavour has revealed more than seven hundred compounds, each of which may contribute to the flavour of the mature spirit. Most of these compounds are very complex and well outwith the scope of a book such as this. We mentioned on page 41, fifteen basic flavours detectable by the amateur sensory analyst. We shall confine ourselves to those – and that's quite enough, for tracing their origins is far from easy, and if you can identify all of them in a whisky, you will be one in a million.

Smokiness

Just as the most immediately recognisable flavour is peatiness, so its origin is the most easily attributable. Before we begin, perhaps it would be as well to dispel a widely-held belief: that the presence of peat in the water which is used to make a whisky, causes the whisky to taste peaty. It doesn't. You can make whisky with water which has so much dissolved peat that it is almost black, and you will get no flavour of peat in the finished spirit if you use unpeated malt. The source of the smoky taste in Laphroaig, Lagavulin, Talisker and all the other peaty whiskies is the peat smoke which has been used to dry the malted barley. The more peat is used, the smokier the whisky. The degree of peating is measured in parts per million (ppm) of phenols (the main smokiness-producing family of compounds) and the higher that rating, the wilder the smell of smoke.

When you burn wood or peat, if you burn it slowly – as is the case with a peat fire – the combustion is incomplete, and lots of compounds go up – literally – in smoke which in a more efficient furnace would have been burnt and converted to carbon dioxide and water. The most important of these for our purposes are the phenols. Phenols are aromatic compounds whose odour most people will recognise as tar. The basis of all aromatic compounds is benzene. It is a hydrocarbon, but with the difference that the carbons are arranged in a hexagon. Its line formula is

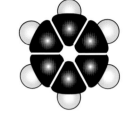

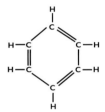

Benzene

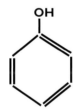

If instead of one of the hydrogens, an OH molecule is added, you get phenol:

When we think of alcohol, smoke is not a natural association. However, it will be apparent that there is a similarity in the molecular structure and component elements. Both alcohols and phenols are hydrocarbons with an added hydroxyl group. The difference lies in the fact that in alcohols, the carbons run in a chain, while in the phenols they are arranged in a ring (for which read hexagon). So there appears to be a natural communion between whisky and peat reek.

Phenols are very persistent. They stick to the barley grain, dissolve in the water in mashing, survive brewing and distilling, and then after ten or twenty years in cask, they still haven't gone away. The intensity of their taste does, however, diminish with time. Those heavily-peated whiskies which are bottled at different ages show a decline in smokiness with time. At the time of writing, it is possible to buy Laphroaig at ten and sixteen years old; the sixteen is noticeably less phenolic than the ten. Ardbeg is now available in a number of bottlings, in which the decline of peatiness with age is evident. Having said that, I should enter a caveat: you can't always assume that the level of peating is a constant. Practice varies from time to time and distilleries will for various reasons – mostly to do with their perception of future demand – vary the level of peating of the malt they use. Ardbeg now uses malt peated to 30 parts per million, where before it was 50 ppm. Ditto Laphroaig.

A good many years ago, I wandered into Berry Brothers and Rudd, in St James's in London. Berry Brothers – who own Cutty Sark – are the oldest and poshest wine merchants in London. The shop has been there for three hundred years and looks it. I found myself, somewhat to my surprise, being treated as a celebrity by some of the staff, who were members of the Scotch Malt Whisky Society. They asked me if I would like to taste some of their malt whisky. A bottle was produced which bore a handwritten label saying Laphroaig and a date some forty years back. A dram was offered, which I didn't refuse. The whisky was good, but bore no trace of peat. I was assured that it was indeed Laphroaig, but no further information was to be had. Two possibilities suggest themselves: that Laphroaig had at some point made a wash from unpeated malt; or that so great was the age of the whisky that its smokiness had declined to invisibility. I rather suspect the former, for the whisky wasn't woody, which it would have been had its age been that great.

A final word on smoky whiskies, to clear up a few misconceptions. Some folk think all Islay whiskies are smoky and that it is to do with their being from an island. Neither is the case. Of the eight Islay whiskies, Bruichladdich and Bunnahabhain both use lightly-peated malt and neither tastes particularly peaty. A mainland whisky which uses heavily-peated malt will taste just as peaty as an Islay. I came across a Glen Garioch some years ago which was moderately heavily-peated. Springbank now makes a malt – Longrow – in Springbank distillery from malt peated at 45–50 ppm. It could easily pass for an Islay.

Fruitiness

Fruity aromas are among the easiest to detect when they are present. That means that if they are not present, one can be fairly categorical about it. They are, as we have seen in the last section, mainly caused by esters which are formed from reactions between alcohols and acids. It is well-established that esters are formed during fermentation; whether they are also formed during maturation is less clear. Experiments with bourbon casks have shown that the rate of ester formation is constant throughout the maturation period. This suggests that the distillate is the source of the esters; the rate of formation of flavour congeners derived mainly from the wood tends to decline over time. However, it has been shown that storage of spirit in a sealed container with no access to air, does not produce esters in appreciable quantity. (I recall John Grant at Glenfarclas telling me he once had whisky which had been put in a tar barrel. To everyone's surprise, when the barrel was opened, it appeared to be almost new spirit.)

The acetic acid required for ester formation is, as we have seen in the last chapter, formed by an oxidation reaction. The requirement for oxygen appears to be the reason why whisky stored in a sealed container will not mature: the oxygen which permeates through the walls of the cask is part of the maturation process. Certainly, observation of variation among casks tends to support this hypothesis: if the distillate is the source of esters, then one would expect all of a given batch of distillate to have much the same concentration of esters. That is not the case: the same whisky will mature differently as regards floral flavours, depending on the quality of the cask. Research into the effects of different casks on the flavour of brandy has shown that American oak contributes much higher levels of esters than does the oak from Limousin – a difference which would be hard to account for on the hypothesis that esters are formed only by the acids in the distillate.

Floweriness

Flowery smells are not so easily assignable to a particular class of compounds as are the scents of fruit. Some of them indeed come from esters, but others from a variety of sources, almost all of them complex.

Floral scents are most often used in perfume, and it is to perfumery that we must look for analysis of the components of floral odours. As mentioned earlier, the Arabs used distillation to extract the essences of flowers for use in perfumes. Those essences, together with musk and civet, are the basis of the modern perfume industry. Over three thousand different natural essential oils have been identified. Some of them contain hundreds of different organic compounds.

Esters are most commonly represented among floral odours by benzyl acetate, $C_9H_{10}O_2$, which is a large part of the odour of jasmine. It is formed by the replacement of one of the atoms in the methanol molecule with a benzene ring. Another ester, geraniol, $C_{10}H_{18}O$, is found in the leaves of geraniums and the flowers of the rose.

Floral scents arise during the fermentation process and are easy to detect if present. They are usually less easy to identify.

Vanilla

Vanilla is one of the most common flavourings in sweet foods. It is one of the two main components of the scent of chocolate, of toffee (in which it is allied to caramel), and in ice cream. The vanilla-like aromas in whisky are caused by two main compounds: vanillin and diacetyl. Diacetyl we dealt with in the last chapter: it gives the buttery flavour to toffee and some whisky. In whisky, it is formed during fermentation.

The vanilla flavour we get from another single-compound organic odour molecule, $C_8H_8O_3$, vanillin. The line formula looks like this:

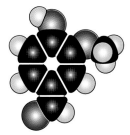

Vanillin

As you can see, the molecule has both hydroxyl and carbonyl side chains. The flavouring can be extracted from the fermented seed pods of the vanilla orchid, which was originally to be found in Madagascar. Or it can be synthesised (as it commonly is nowadays) by the oxidation of eugenol. It is an important element in the character of matured wines as well as whiskies. It is perceptible in extremely low concentrations and it is curious in that once it is present, the flavour of vanilla does not increase appreciably, irrespective of how much of the compound is present.

Vanilla is extracted from the barrel wood during maturation. Lignin in the oak undergoes oxidation when in contact with spirit and oxygen to form aromatic aldehydes, of which vanillin is one. The amounts of vanillin present vary with the type of oak wood used, American white oak generally yielding lower concentrations of vanillin than do European types. How then do we explain the very strong scents of vanilla to be found in bourbons, which are all matured in American oak? The answer is to be found in the practice of charring.

The oak staves which are used to form a cask are not cut on the curve – which would be very wasteful of timber – but are bent into the required shape by steaming or toasting. These are techniques as old as the use of formed oak itself: when you heat oak wood, what had previously been perfectly rigid becomes pliable – as long as it is hot. When it cools, it adopts the shape to which it was bent during the cooling. Boats used to be built by this method. In some cases, they still are. (As I write, it's a lovely day and I ought to be doing that very thing, namely shaping oak for boatbuilding, so I hope you appreciate my sacrifice in writing this instead.) The heating process degrades the lignin in the oak and produces aromatic aldehydes, of which vanillin is the most important.

In addition to heat-treating the oak wood for construction purposes, the bourbon distillers subject the finished cask to a further charring, which is purely for flavour. This produces the sweet flavour which is characteristic of bourbon. It is not judged suitable for whisky, distillers preferring to use casks which once held bourbon, from which the greater part of the vanilla flavour has been extracted.

The Scotch whisky industry has experimented with recharring as a way of rejuvenating casks. Casks which, though virtually inactive through long use, are still watertight are heavily charred and then refilled with whisky. It is successful up to a point – but, as with other such expedients, the spirit matured in a treated cask cannot compare with that which has lain in a new sherry or bourbon wood.

Pungency

This we have already mentioned. It arises from the stimulation by concentrated ethyl alcohol of the pain centres in mouth and nose.

Cereals

This is a rather vague category of flavours. Like the scent of acetaldehyde, it is easy enough to demonstrate and once known, it is not readily forgotten – but it is difficult to describe. Not least because it seems to partake of several sorts of aroma – all of which, however, are so commonly spoken of together that they are classed as one. Feints are the single most evident component. These are always present in immature whisky, but tend to decrease with maturation. In small proportions, they make up an essential element in the flavour of whisky, but beyond a low thresh-hold, they become unacceptable to most tastes. (Though it should be said, not all. People who work in distilleries commonly acquire a taste for new spirit, they being the only folk who can generally lay hands on such a thing, if illegally.)

Descriptors of this flavour usually associate feints with grass, hay, barley, oats and other such grassy and cereal vegetables. Some of them are ketones, such as ionone, mentioned earlier. One of ionone's relatives is methyl 2-pyridyl ketone, C_7H_7ON, the molecule responsible for the odour of popcorn. A cousin of that, 2-methoxy-5-methylpyrazine, $C_6H_8ON_2$, gives us the smell of peanuts. This molecule is a pyrazine. Pyrazines are organo-nitrogen compounds, typically formed by the action of heat. They consist of benzene-type rings known as pyrenes, in which one or more of the carbon atoms has been replaced by nitrogen.

Soapy flavours

Typically described as being waxy, candle-like, soapy, these flavours derive from long-chain esters formed during fermentation. They tend to be present when other, more desirable esters are formed in fermentation. Soapy flavours, as you might have guessed, are not generally reckoned a good thing. (Few folk like eating soap.) See below.

Sulphury flavours

This flavour is usually lumped together with soapy flavours, probably because neither is desired and because the two tend to be found in association. Organo-sulphur compounds on the whole don't taste pleasant and some of them are really vile. Sulphur compounds form during fermentation and, to a lesser extent, in distillation, where they tend to result from a late spirit cut.

Sherry casks are commonly sterilised after use by burning a sulphur candle in the cask. This certainly kills off any bacteria – it would kill anything at all – but it leaves a residue which is taken up by the whisky during maturation. It is common to find that whisky which is strongly-sherried also has a trace of sulphur.

This again is a field in which exact specification of the compounds and mechanisms giving rise to the flavour are as yet not well understood.

Caramel

The flavour of caramel is well known and its presence is easy to recognise, especially when a whisky with a lot of caramel is contrasted with one which does not have it. Identifying it isn't as easy as you might think, however. Caramel is added at the bottling stage to give colour to most blends (and some malts, though no malt distiller will admit to the practice). It is the only additive permitted by law – though some companies today are steering pretty close to that law by using treated casks in which substantial residues of the treating compounds remain.

Some people like the taste of caramel in their whisky. They tend to be folk who prefer blends and are therefore accustomed to it. Very few malt buffs can be found who will approve of the addition of caramel, though in recent years a certain malt from heavily-treated casks which contain a lot of caramel has been marketed in the USA with great success. However no names, no pack drill.

Nuttiness

Nutty flavours are almost universally associated with good whisky. (I can't remember a nutty whisky which wasn't good.) They derive from benzaldehyde produced during fermentation and from compounds extracted from the oak wood during maturation. Benzaldehyde, C_6H_5CHO, is the compound which gives us the flavour of almonds. It is related to cinnemaldehyde and vanillin.

Coconut is a common flavour in well-matured whiskies, and is due to the presence of lactones, which are extracted from the oak wood. Lactones, which occur also in red wine, are beneficial to flavour in small quantities, but in excess are detrimental. They are cyclic esters, having five- or six-member rings in place of the hydrocarbon chains of the esters discussed earlier.

Coumarin, which is a lactone, gives us the smell of new-mown hay which is found in whisky. Nepatalactone is a related compound. It is the active ingredient in catnip, though whether it is found in whisky, I do not know – though I have to say that my cat shows an unhealthy interest in certain malts. (He is also partial to newly-removed boots, so there may be a connection.)

New-wood flavours

There are certain new-wood flavours which are occasionally to be found in whisky. These are the odours of pine resin and new wood, and are not to be confused with the tannic flavours referred to when whisky is usually described as 'woody'. They almost certainly are extracts from the cask wood, but their chemistry is not understood. Over two hundred volatile components of cask wood have been identified, and there are probably a lot more, so it isn't as surprising as it may seem.

Sour flavours

Some whiskies have a sour, vinegary, cheesy odour. While this odour may be tolerable at very low concentrations, it is not desirable. Such flavours arise from the formation during fermentation of excessive quantities of acids such as acetic acid and butyric acid.

Mustiness

Occasionally one comes across a disagreeable, musty odour in whisky. It is as though the spirit had been kept in a cupboard with mothballs rather than in a decent damp cellar. This can have a number of causes, most of which occur during maturation or bottling. Compounds of naphtha, a polycyclic hydrocarbon, have been implicated in this. Since, however, the presence of such compounds is never wanted, attention has been given to the elimination of causes through good techniques and materials.

In this context, I recall a cask of Ben Nevis which had bungcloth contamination, which would have fallen within the present category. The cloth which surrounds the cask bung had disintegrated and affected the whisky, which smelled very strange and had a curious greenish colour. Strangely, it didn't taste too badly.

Sweetness

A variety of sweetness is found in the taste of whisky which is very different from the fruity or floral sweetnesses which are so desirable. It is sweetness simple, as in sugar. Obviously, tastes differ in this as in all other matters, but there is general agreement that, though minimal levels of sweetness of this sort are tolerable, any more makes for a bad whisky.

Sweetness may be attributed simply to the presence of sugars in the spirit. As we have seen, the formation of sugars in the malting barley is an essential part of the production process, and it has been suggested that some sugar finds its way through the distillation process. Exactly how this could happen is not clear and the source of sugars in mature whisky can more profitably be sought in the cask. Glucose and fructose are both found in oak wood, and levels of sugars have been shown to show a hyperbolic increase during the maturation period. Such sugars probably derive from the breakdown of hemicellulose and hydrolysable tannins.

Tannins

Wine drinkers will be familiar with the bitter, astringent taste of wine tannins; cheap Australian chardonnay in particular. Tea drinkers, too: when tea is stewed, tannins are extracted from the tea. Tannins are detected by the tongue alone: their taste is a physical rather than an olfactory sensation.

Tannins in whisky are oak-wood extracts (unlike in wine, where they come from the grape as well as from the wood – and in some cases, from additives). Low concentrations of tannins are acceptable in whisky. Generally, the longer the whisky lies in cask, the more tannins it will acquire. This leads some misguided souls to think that the presence of tannins in whisky is an indicator of quality. It isn't. It usually only indicates age and, as we discuss elsewhere, old whisky isn't necessarily good whisky.

Tannins are a group of phenolic compounds which are synthesised in the growing oak. They are phenol polymers and have as their basic structural unit, a glucose molecule. There are large numbers of different tannins and their chemistry is complex. Opinions vary as to the mechanisms by which tannins contribute to maturation.

WHY WHISKY TASTES AS IT DOES: THE FIVE MATERIALS

I t will be apparent from what you have read so far that some of the origins of flavour are to be found in infinitesimals, and that very small changes in material or process can bring about quite major changes in flavour. We now look at what whisky is made from and how it is made – and how every stage affects the flavour of the finished product. That said, we should recognise from the outset that some influences are more important than others. Two stand out: the peating of the malt and the cask used for maturation. Those two have more influence on how malt whisky tastes than all of the other factors put together. Note: on how *malt* whisky tastes.

BARLEY

For the first reason why malt whisky tastes so much better than any other kind of whisky – or indeed, than any other kind of distilled liquor – is that it is made from malted barley and from no other grain. Barley contributes more in the way of flavour than any of the other cereals. You may have wondered why real ale tastes so much better than factory-made beer: it's because real ale is usually made only from barley, whereas the keg beers of the big brewers are made mainly from maize. Grain whisky is much less flavoursome than malt, not only because of the patent still, but because it is made mostly from maize or some other grain. The best-flavoured grain spirits are those whose makers use the highest proportion of barley in their mash.

Barley, *Hordeum polystichium*, has been used as a food grain for a very long time. It has been found among Mesopotamian and ancient Egyptian grave goods. The Egyptians discovered that sprouted barley was more palatable than unsprouted and made cakes of it which were used both directly as a food and indirectly as the base for beer – the sugars in the malted barley were fermented by wild yeasts.

Barley, like many other grasses, has a propensity to mutation, which means that it is not difficult to produce strains which differ widely in both the nature of the grain produced and in the conditions in which it will flourish. Thus some barley strains will grow in warm, dry climates; others in cold, wet conditions. Scotland's climate falls, of course, into the latter category. Happily for the Scots, barley varieties which thrive in the cold and wet were discovered and cultivated very early in our history – or, strictly, our prehistory, for the use of barley long pre-dates written sources in Scotland.

Barley was widely used as a food in Scotland until fairly recently: oats and barley were the two main food grains until the development of wheat in the later eighteenth century. Barley bannocks (flat cakes) were eaten as a staple, as in the old song:

> Bannocks o' bere meal, bannocks o' barley,
> Here's to the Hielandman's bannocks o' barley!

The grain was also taken boiled, usually with meat or greens, but its principal use as a food was in beer making. Ale was the drink of the poor; wine that of the gentleman – though many who considered themselves gentle saw wine but rarely. Brewing was mainly a domestic employment until increasing urbanisation in the later eighteenth century saw the rise of large brewing concerns. Many of the most important of the early distillers in fact began as brewers: distilling was a way of adding value to their product. The conversion of breweries to distilleries was common in the later eighteenth and early nineteenth centuries.

The 'bere' referred to in the rhyme above was the original of Scottish barley. It gave a low yield but would tolerate very wet and cold climatic conditions and would thrive on the acid, undrained soils which at one time covered most Scottish arable land. The eighteenth century was a period of unprecedented innovation in agriculture and it is to that period that we owe the ancestors of modern barleys. The use of both terms in the rhyme indicates that the improved version was known and used alongside the unimproved.

The barley grain comprises, within its husk and a covering skin, both a barley-plant embryo and an energy store with which to sustain the growing embryo until such time as it can draw nourishment from the soil and the sun. The energy is stored as starch, which will be hydrolised into sugars as required by enzymes also contained in the grain.

As far as mere alcohol goes, the starch is the main thing, for it is the starch which becomes first sugar and then alcohol. However, the enzymes which convert starch to sugar are just as important. So are the other yeast metabolytes, the other nutrients which the yeast requires to fuel its activity in converting the sugars to alcohol. Besides carbohydrates, the main nutrients are fatty substances known collectively as lipids, and nitrogenous materials. Traces of sulphur compounds are also present. Both the nitrogenous and sulphurous materials are potential sources of undesirable flavonoids.

Barley starting to germinate. The grain stores its energy as starch, which it converts to sugar as it begins to grow.

All barley carries a microflora of bacteria and fungoid organisms. (So do we.) Wild yeasts and bacilli such as, lactobacilli, pediococci, micrococci, enterobacteriacae and acetobacter, are all potential sources of disagreeable flavour compounds. It is here that such apparently unrelated functions such as harvesting and storage, steeping and germination become important, for undesirable bacteria grow if poor practices prevail.

The brewer requires three main things of a barley: that it have a supply of the minor yeast metabolytes, that it have optimum fermentable sugars, and that it produce a free-running wort. The last is in order that a clear wash may be produced which does not stick to the bottom of the pot still and burn. The need for yeast metabolytes is obvious, or shall be shortly.

It is widely maintained in the whisky industry that the only thing which matters in a barley is the amount of fermentable sugar obtainable from the malt, and that provided the grain is not mouldy, variation in type will have little or no effect in the flavour of the whisky. But then, for years, distillers have been saying – and believing – things about whisky which are manifestly untrue. I suspect this may be one of these. Nobody disputes the importance of the brewer in a distillery: as far as flavour is concerned, he is crucial. For unless we can make good ale, we can't distil good whisky. Now I have met a lot of brewers, both those who brew for whisky and those who brew beer, and I have yet to meet one who doesn't think that the type of barley matters. Indeed, a lot of the new generation of real ale makers specify the type and quality of barley very closely, and will brew with nothing else. One suspects some whisky distillers haven't moved much beyond the days of keg beers – when we were told that the type of barley didn't matter much as regards the flavour of our beer. That was true, but only because the stuff was all pasteurised and kept pressurised in fizzy casks. The parallels with the blended whiskies of former times need not be laboured.

There plainly isn't agreement within the whisky industry, either. Macallan, who make what is indisputably one of the finest malts, will use nothing but Golden Promise barley, as do some of the best beer makers.

WATER

Making whisky uses a lot of water. It is involved at every stage in the process, from malting the barley to tasting the final product. Brewing beer has traditionally required ten litres of water for every litre of ale. Whisky uses even more: water is used for steeping, germinating, brewing, mashing, sparging, propagating yeast, fermenting and condensing the distillate. Fortunately, Scotland has rarely been short of water. Our usual trouble is rather that we have too much of it when we don't want it, especially in August and September, when the barley crop is harvested.

I recall an occasion about thirty years ago, in late August, when two old friends of mine had bought a small, very run-down farm in the Howe of Alford in Aberdeenshire. The farm included a field of standing barley, and also a combine harvester of great antiquity which had not run (we later discovered) in twenty years. Neither Duncan nor I had the least idea of how such machines worked but, by the application of first principles and a lot of oil, we got it to go. As we weaved our way up and down the field, missing bits and losing bags, all the surrounding country turned out to watch and laugh at the townies trying to be farmers. Well, we got the harvest in – too early, they all said – before anyone

else had even begun. As we put the last bag in the barn, the heavens opened and the rain came down. There was not a dry day from then until the beginning of November. We had the only barley crop in the entire howe. Two hundred years before, that would have meant at best no whisky, at worst, starvation.

My justification for telling this story, is that the farm was the same one at which I first tasted the Glenfarclas straight from the cask. That tasting led to the Scotch Malt Whisky Society, which began the bottling of single-cask malts at cask strength. Without the exploit with the harvester, this book would probably not have been written.

I have heard it said that what distinguishes Scotch whisky from any of its many imitators, is the quality of the water. I'm not sure I agree with that, for I have been unable to discover any convincing evidence that beyond certain basic requirements – which are to be got from any clean water source – there is anything in the water which makes much difference. Water for whisky making must meet certain physiochemical and bacteriological standards: yeast metabolism requires trace compounds, and levels of undesirable bacteria must not be excessively high. But these are standards which all potable waters must meet – and bacterial infections would usually be insignificant compared with the microflora populations of the barley, as regards flavour components. It must have acceptably low levels of metallic salts which would inhibit malting and fermentation. The presence of high concentrations of dissolved substances such as peat is said to have an effect, though, as mentioned elsewhere, it is difficult to detect the influence of these in the finished product.

Levels of calcium and magnesium carbonates seem, rather surprisingly, to have little effect. Most Scottish water is soft, but some of the great distilleries such as Glenmorangie use hard water. I have sometimes wondered whether, following Chernobyl, the presence of radioactive isotopes in the water supply might have an effect. I am pleased to say that enough time has passed for us to say that none are detectable.

YEAST

Yeast is a single-celled micro-organism. It is a very simple creature, usually regarded as a plant, though at unicellular levels the distinction between plant and animal tends to become irrelevant. Yeast is a member of the class of thallophytes, which also includes algae and fungi. Yeast cells are present in the environment in enormous numbers and are frequently airborne, so that any vessel exposed to the atmosphere is liable to find itself home to a colony of yeast

The combination of four different strains of yeasts used to create The Macallan.

cells. If the vessel contains dissolved sugars of any sort, then that colony will grow, for yeasts live mainly on sugar. You may have noticed that if you leave a container of fruit juice exposed to the air for any length of time, it will go off and start frothing. That is because it has been colonised by yeast cells and they are feeding on the sugars in the juice. The frothing is caused by the carbon dioxide which the yeast gives off as a result of metabolising the sugars. This process is called fermentation.

The yeast cells floating around in the air are usually referred to as wild yeasts, which distinguishes them from the cultivated yeast used to make some wines, beers and bread. There are lots of varieties of yeast and different types of yeast produce fermentations which have very different end-products. This means, in the production of beverages, different tastes, for the fermentation brought about by the yeast is a principal source of flavour. The yeasts which float in the air are known to brewers as ambient yeasts. Some wines and beers use ambient yeasts for fermentation, since the local population of yeasts is fairly stable and produces flavoursome and distinctive potations. Such uses tend to be on a small scale, for the use of ambient yeasts is a chancy business with an ever-present risk that a wild stranger may float in and spoil the brew. Some wine makers return the lees from the winemaking to the soil of the vineyard to maintain the local yeast population.

Many wine makers and all whisky makers use cultured yeasts. These are grown from pure strains in sterile conditions and their use enables the brewer to predict with some assurance the outcome of his fermentation, both as regards alcohol yield and as regards flavour. The price to be paid for the use of cultured yeasts is in a diminution of desirable flavour elements. Different yeast strains yield different levels of higher alcohols, fatty acids and thus esters. Cultured yeast is grown in large vessels and can be dried and stored. In that form, it is possible to calculate the quantity of yeast injected into the wort and therefore to control the fermentation.

The classification of yeasts is not simple and has changed radically over the last couple of centuries. The genus is *saccharomyces* and the species most usually employed in wine, beer and whisky making is *Saccharomyces cerevisiae*. There are thousands of varieties: for purposes of whisky making, three main types are used: distillers' yeasts, brewers' and bakers' yeasts. Brewers' yeasts are less able to metabolise dextrins such as maltotetraose and maltopentaose than distillers' yeasts. They are, however, cheaper, and this is a consideration which the distiller must set against the lower alcohol yield. Brewers' yeasts tend also to produce more flavour elements. Some bakers' yeast is occasionally used, mainly with a view to economy.

Most distillers use several varieties of yeast, balancing flavour against yield. The distiller's requirements of a yeast are first, that it provide a good alcohol yield per unit of malt, for on that depends the economics of the production; second, that it give a good flavour; third, that it convert the sugars in the malt efficiently; fourth, that it give a rapid fermentation, and last, that it be resistant to infection.

In whisky making, the wort is not boiled as it is in brewing for beer. As a result, wild yeasts which are present in malted barley, if they survive malting, are able to infect the fermentation. If they do, they may cause the formation of compounds such as ethyl acetate at levels which are higher than is desirable. Bacterial infection may also occur, which shows up in high levels of acids and low alcohol yield.

Yeast uses carbohydrates as its primary food source: the sugars which have been produced by malting the barley grain. It also requires small quantities of various other nutrients such as nitrogen, minerals, vitamins and sulphur and potassium salts, all of which it finds either in the barley grain or in the water. The main source of nitrogen is the amino acids in the proteins of the barley.

We mentioned earlier that the metabolisation of sugars is the main energy source in all organisms. The metabolisation takes place in a complex series of reactions known as glycolysis. Yeast behaves no differently: it produces enzymes whose action breaks down the sugar molecules. If oxygen is present in large enough quantities, the sugars are broken down completely, to carbon dioxide and water. If, however, the oxygen supply is limited, as it is in all brewing, the yeast produces an intermediate stage in the process, resulting in alcohol and carbon dioxide.

PEAT

The first people who arrived in Scotland found a country which was covered in forest, save for the upland areas and the great tracts of the north and west, which

Cutting peat by hand in the traditional manner.

81

consisted of rock and bog. The forests provided a convenient source of fuel, but they were not renewed as rapidly as they were used – when Dr Johnson came to Scotland in 1773, he remarked that between Berwick-on-Tweed and Edinburgh, he had not passed a single tree. He was probably exaggerating – Johnson had no high opinion of Scotland and agreed to visit only because Boswell pestered him – but the point is made: by the late eighteenth century, Scotland was seriously short of trees. Firing and boatbuilding had largely destroyed the forests of oak, birch and pine. For the Lowlands, this was no great problem: coal seams lay close to the surface and could be mined. But in the Highlands, people had no coal of their own and were unable to buy any from the Lowlands – most of them had, literally, no money – and even if they could have got coals, there were no roads on which to transport them. Highland people turned to peat as their only source of fuel.

They fell back on that least efficient of fuels, bog peat. Peat is what you get when moss and heather grow on acid, ill-drained rocks for a few thousand years. Because of the acidity of the environment, the dead plants do not decay as they would elsewhere, but form a subsoil of partly-decomposed organic remains. Over millennia, this is compacted to a black, fibrous material which if dried, will burn. In the north and west of Scotland, vast tracts of peat bog have accumulated since the last Ice Age. The peat is dug – or, rather, cut – from the surrounding material, stacked and dried. The cutting is usually done in the early summer, in order to give it as much exposure as possible to drying wind and sun. Rural populations in Scotland – which until a century or so ago meant almost everyone – had traditional rights to cut peats from specified sections of bog. Even today, if you buy a house on one of the islands, chances are the house title will include a legal right to take peats from a designated piece of moor.

Peats had always been the fuel of the very poor. They did not burn as well as wood, producing lots of smoke and little heat. Fires work as an energy source in much the same way as the biological systems which we have already discussed: the oxidation of hydrocarbons to carbon dioxide and water. Coal, wood and peat all contain mostly carbon and hydrogen, but they vary in the manner in which those elements are held. Most of the hydrocarbon compounds will oxidise and release energy, but unless the combustion takes place in a very efficient furnace, it will be incomplete and instead of a lot of heat, you get a lot of smoke. That is what happens with peat, as anyone knows who has had to depend on the stuff for heating. In much of Highland Scotland, the method of burning was about as inefficient as could have been devised: people lived in low

Adding peat to the malting kiln at Glenmorangie Distillery

houses with turf roofs; the fire was in the middle of the room and the smoke found its way out through a hole in the roof. Life can't have been much fun in the Northern winters, but one did acquire a taste (literally) for peat smoke.

When, some time in the last millennium, people began to make whisky, they would naturally use peat to dry the malt and heat the still. It is therefore to be expected that the original Scotch whiskies would have been heavily-peated. (It is possible that malt may have been dried without peat smoke, but this is very unlikely, given the lack of alternative heat sources and the dampness of the Scottish climate.) I have found no reference to smoky taste in any contemporary sources, but this could be accounted for by the fact of its being universal and therefore unworthy of mention. Also, until the end of the eighteenth century, most whisky was highly flavoured by botanical additives, which would have disguised a peaty taste.

Coke is what is left of coal after the volatile carbon compounds have been evaporated off. The process was invented in the eighteenth century for the purpose of iron smelting. Around the same time, whisky had begun to be made on an industrial scale in the Lowlands, and later in the Highlands. By the mid-nineteenth century, courtesy of the rapidly-expanding rail network, coal was used to fire Highland stills and coke to dry the malt. Because coke burnt in a furnace produces hardly any smoke, it became possible to make malt which had little or no aroma of peat – more or less, peat was added to the coke fire to produce the desired level of phenols in the malt. This method is used today by those distilleries which still have floor maltings, such as Laphroaig, Bowmore, Springbank and Highland Park.

Most distillers buy their malt from commercial maltsters. They specify the level of peating which they require, expressed as parts per million of phenols. A typical Speyside whisky will use malt peated to one or two ppm; Bowmore's malt has 20, Lagavulin and Laphroaig around 30, Ardbeg a thumping great 50. Some distilleries use a mixture of peated and unpeated: Highland Park peats about 20 per cent of its malt to around 30 ppm; the balance is unpeated. The part which is peated is all floor-malted and dried in a natural-draught kiln, using only Orkney shallow-bed peat burnt on a cool fire. Jim Robertson, who is in charge of all Highland Park's materials, explains that this gives the malt a spectrum of phenols which is quite different from that which is obtained from a commercial maltings.

This rings true: it is typical of much of the Scotch whisky industry. People will go to great lengths to secure those materials and processes which they believe contribute to the flavour of their product. The fact that they differ greatly as to which is the right stuff to use and the right way to use it, doesn't mean that some of them are wrong.

WOOD

Of all the materials of which whisky is made, wood is easily the most important. Whisky derives more than half its flavour from the cask in which it is matured, and estimates of the extent of the influence of the wood range up to over 80 per cent. Casks are made from oak. The flavour which the oak contributes to the whisky is determined by the type of oak, its previous use, where it was grown, when felled, how dried, how coopered and how treated. Some of the flavour contributions are substantial, some minimal – but as we have already seen, flavour is a field in which infinitesimals matter.

There are hundreds of different varieties of oak and it is often difficult to tell which is which. The genus is *Quercus*. The species commonly used to mature whisky are American white oak, *Quercus alba*, and the European oaks, *Quercus robur* and *Quercus petraea*. In the past, things were a lot simpler. (They always were.) *Q. alba* was used for bourbon and *Qs robur* and *petraea* for sherry, and everybody knew where they stood. Nowadays American oak casks are widely used for maturing sherry and the Americans buy something like a quarter of all European oak casks. What is more, we know that American oaks, classed as *Q. alba*, are a very varied lot, and an American bourbon barrel may be made up of timber from a dozen different varieties of oak. Even worse: oaks hybridise readily, so *Q. robur* may fertilise *Q. petraea* and your whisky gets matured in wood which has a bit of both. It's like hiring a hippogriff to look after your kids.

The American white oak is a lovely tree: it grows tall and straight in the forests of eastern North America. (It was involved in the American War of Independence: there were influential people in Britain who would have been happy to write off America as a loss-making enterprise, had it not been that the Royal Navy needed American oaks as timber for shipbuilding.) The timber is straight and close-grained and a joy to work. It bends easily when heated, is good for cooperage and is stable and long-lasting. The closeness of grain makes it an excellent material for containing spirits: the timber is resistant to penetration by the contents of the cask and losses by leakage or evaporation are minimised. Low in tannins, the wood does not impart unpleasant tastes to the cask contents; it has high levels of volatile compounds which, when released into spirit, contribute agreeable flavours. Altogether great stuff.

The great forests which cover much of Spain and southern France are made up mostly of two varieties of oak: *Q. robur* and *Q. petraea*. There are lots of other species, but none of them are important for the cooperage industry. It is only fairly recently that the Scotch whisky industry began to take an interest in the type of cask used to hold its spirit. In the past, distillers used to specify the source of their casks, but identification was by the port of origin, rather than the species of oak or the previous use. European oak wood is more easily penetrated by spirit than American oak; by the same token it more easily yields the flavour congeners which it contains and admits atmospheric oxygen. It is high in tannins, lignin degradation products such as vanillin, lactones and aromatic compounds.

The previous use of the oak wood is of great importance. Scotch whisky matured in new oak casks acquires disagreeably high levels of various flavour components and there is general agreement that new wood does not produce mature whisky of an acceptable quality. As mentioned above, the two main prior fillings are bourbon and sherry, and for simplicity we should think of the latter as being put in European oak and the former in American.

Until recently, it was thought (and still is, in most quarters) that as regards sherry casks, the remnants of the previous filling have a direct and substantial influence on the flavour of the mature whisky. Research recently carried out by Messrs Tatlock and Thomson for the Macallan distillery has provided evidence that this is not the case. They have demonstrated that there is little difference between a cask which has held a fino sherry and one which has held an oloroso, despite the great disparity in flavour between the two types of sherry, provided they have been put in the same sort of wood. The importance of the previous filling is indirect, its role being as modifier of the influence of the wood itself. The same series of research papers shows that the main difference is to be found between the types of wood, *Q. alba* consistently yielding a flavour different from that produced by a European oak, irrespective of what the cask contained in its previous incarnation. A whisky matured in a fino cask tastes different from the same whisky matured for the same time in an oloroso cask, because the fino sherry has been matured in an American oak cask and the oloroso in a European. Which goes to show that we should be wary of folk who confidently pronounce a particular flavour to have derived from a fino sherry: they may be right, but not for the reason they give.

The oak tree should ideally be cut down in autumn or winter, when sap levels are low. The trunk having been felled, it is sawn to length and then the billets

Different styles of cooperage.

Traditional European cooperage

The log is split into
quarters lengthwise
so that the axe blade
can follow the grain

Each quarter is then
further split into
sections from which
the staves are then cut.
This procedure is
extremely wasteful as
more than half of the
timber is lost

American barrel-sawn cooperage

The log is sawn into
quarters lengthwise

Using a curved-band
barrel saw, staves
are cut from each
quarter so as to
maximise the yield
of each log

taken from it which will form the staves of the cask. American and European practices differ greatly in this. In the latter, traditional, low-tech methods are used. The log is split or quarter-sawn and the quarters are split vertically, as shown above.

As can be seen, this is a practice which is very wasteful of wood, for much of the log is lost. And once the stave has been cut, more wood is lost in shaping it to the curve of the barrel. American practice is to saw the stave, using a band-saw with a curved blade, as shown in the drawing.

The advantage of splitting, apart from requiring much simpler tools, is that the stave presents no end-grain to liquid contents which might then diffuse length-wise and evaporate. This, it is argued, is necessary, given the more open texture of the wood of the European oak. The tighter-grained American can be sawn with confidence that even if some end-grain is exposed, the cask will not leak. That, anyway, is the general belief. Various studies have cast doubt on it, and have suggested that the advantages claimed are not found in practice. The fact that Portuguese coopers make casks which do not leak from sawn staves of Limousin oak, is reason for scepticism. The difference may be down to culture and technology. On the other hand, that there may none the less be flavour considerations for whisky is suggested by French studies in which, in blind tastings, experienced tasters consistently prefer wine matured in casks made of traditionally-split staves. It has been suggested that this is because more tannins are extracted through the exposed grain of the sawn timber. The lower tannin levels of American oak may account for the greater acceptability of staves sawn from that timber.

The stave is cut only from the heartwood. Sapwood is much more open-grained than heartwood and not as stable, so that casks made from it are more likely to leak. Once cut, the stave billet must be dried. This is traditionally done by stacking the billets in the open and allowing them to dry in the air. It takes anything up to three years for the moisture content of the timber to diminish to an acceptable level of 15 per cent, depending on the drying environment. The wood shrinks as it dries and if staves were made from wet wood, the cask would leak as the staves dried. The alternative to air drying is kiln drying. This takes much less time and gives the cooper more flexibility in meeting demand. Beginning in the 1970s, most US coopers changed to kiln drying.

Those whisky producers who take an active interest in the quality of their cask wood tend to prefer air drying, since it produces a better flavour in the mature whisky. Wine makers, too, prefer air-dried timber, for the same reason. Wood which has been air-dried has lower levels of tannins and phenolic acids than kiln-dried timber, and higher levels of vanillin and lactones. Studies by French wine makers suggest that moulds forming on the wood release enzymes which neutralise bitter components. American and European oak differ in the degree to which they are affected by the air/kiln-drying issue. Since American oak is lower in tannins and higher in some other components to begin with, it is less affected by the results of kiln drying. Also, some flavours which are desirable in a bourbon are not wanted in a wine or a whisky. Nevertheless, some bourbon producers have been so concerned for the quality of their product as to specify air-dried wood – and Glenmorangie went to the length of having its own casks coopered

Spanish oak from the northern forests of Galicia in Spain is brought down to Jerez and dried in the baking Andalucian sun before being transformed into the casks to hold first sherry and then whisky.

from air-dried wood and hiring them out to bourbon producers. That said, most Scotch whisky is now matured in casks, whose wood has been kiln-dried.

The making of wooden casks is a very ancient technology, which requires only the simplest of tools and materials. The materials are timber for staves and ends, and iron for the hoops. (Even the iron isn't essential: before iron hoops became widely available, the staves were held together by wooden bands, usually of hazel or chestnut. Stewart's Bar in Edinburgh has a row of particularly fine whisky casks bound with hazel.) The tools required were saw, axe and adze: the saw for cutting to length, the axe for splitting and the adze for shaping. Most manufacturing cooperage today is mechanised, but much of the cooper's work is in repair, and a great deal of that is still done by hand.

The staves, which start life straight, must be bent to take the familiar bellied form of the cask. (They are not cut on the curve, which would be difficult and very wasteful.) This is possible because of the propensity of oak wood to bend when hot. When the cask staves have been shaped, they are heated and bent into the required shape. Once bent, they are held together by the hoops and when cooled, they retain the shape to which they were bent.

Without the ability of oak to bend, it is I think no exaggeration to say that there would have been no oak casks. And no oak casks, no whisky, or at least no decent whisky. It is one of the happier accidents of the cosmos. For the business of bending contributes greatly to the taste of the whisky. The heating of the staves can be done by steam but is more usually by direct exposure to flame, either from a fire or a jet of burning gas. The greater the degree of heat-

Finishing the cask by smoothing it down and ensuring it is tightly sealed. Cask assembly is a work of pure craftsmanship.

treatment, the greater the effect, from the mild toasting of sherry casks all the way to the deep charring which is required by bourbon producers.

Toasting and charring affect the ability of cask wood to mature whisky in two ways: they alter the chemistry of the wood, and, in the case of charring, the physical structure, which allows deeper penetration by the distillate. Charring also produces a layer of active carbon, which may remove undesirable flavour compounds. The heating of the timber has a radical effect on its chemical composition, decreasing levels of flavour compounds such as phenolics and soluble tannins, while increasing the quantities of lignin degradation products, aldehydes, acids, furans and many volatiles.

After a cask has been used two or three times for the maturation of malt whisky, it will have little to contribute to the spirit. The rate at which the cask matures the distillate declines sharply after the second fill and only by leaving the whisky in wood for a very long time, will a flavoursome whisky be got from a third-fill cask. (When very old whiskies are still drinkable, it is usually because the cask they were put in was worn-out to begin with, so that it took ages for the whisky to extract enough flavour components to make the stuff palatable. This consideration does not appear to inhibit people who wish to spend large sums of money on very old whiskies.)

After they have been exhausted in the service of malts, serviceable casks are generally used to mature grain spirit. It is not therefore surprising that the grain whisky acquires few desirable characteristics by maturation. North British distillery uses some first-fill bourbon casks for its grain, with admirable results.

The whisky industry is a victim of its own success as regards the supply of casks. It is estimated that there are some 17 million casks currently in use in Scotland – so great is the production of whisky. The output of used bourbon casks is around 750,000 per annum; the number of sherry casks very much smaller. There is demand for casks from the producers of wine, brandy and rum, so by no means all of the casks come to Scotland. You need only simple arithmetic to figure that by no means all of the casks used in the whisky industry can be first- or second-fill. Since the quality of the whisky depends on the quality of the cask, it follows that the industry is locked into the production of a lot of fairly low-quality whisky.

The demand for good-quality casks far outstrips their availability.

Faking It (1)

The enormous demand for casks has led to research into ways of rejuvenating old ones. This involves taking casks which, though worn out, are nevertheless physically intact, and treating their wood in such a way that once again it is able to contribute to the development of flavour. It is largely a matter of opinion as

Casks are charred to open up the wood in order to release its natural seasoning.

to how far you can go down this road without being open to accusations of faking. The whisky industry has found that the best thing to do about this is to keep it as quiet as possible. It is, however, a subject which is directly relevant to the appreciation of whisky and one which we must address.

Re-charring casks can improve them substantially. The cask has its end removed and is subjected to a fierce flame until the old surface is burnt away and a new one charred. This process increases the levels of tannins and aromatic aldehydes which can be extracted from the cask, as well as enabling it to impart colour to the spirit. While the process is effective, recharring cannot replicate the influence of a new cask and the effects quickly diminish with use.

Some coopers scrape the inside of the stave to expose new wood to the distillate. Research has shown that whisky penetrates the wood to a depth of a little less than a centimetre, so that the removal of that amount of wood will yield the possibility of a new source of extractives. That theory is borne out in practice, and scraping is usually combined with recharring. Since the average barrel stave is less than three centimetres thick in the first place, though, it will be evident that there is limited scope for scraping. If, however, the previous use of the cask was important, and if the contents do not penetrate far into the cask walls, it follows that a thoroughgoing rejuvenation would require refilling with sherry or bourbon for an appropriate period. As far as I am aware, this is never done.

Faking It (2)

Wine-treatment of worn-out casks has been widely used to simulate the effects of new sherry wood. This is one of the best-kept secrets of the Scotch whisky industry. Indeed, a perusal of all of the books on whisky on the shelves of a leading Edinburgh bookstore failed to discover any mention of it, despite the declared intention of many of the authors of revealing the secrets of how whisky is made.

In wine-treatment, a sweet, dark sherry, such as pedro ximenes, is introduced and the cask is pressurised in order to force the potion into the wood. For many years, a potion called paxarette was used, which combined sweet dark sherry with other flavourings and colourants. The use of paxarette has now ceased, but of course we shall continue to see casks which had been treated with the stuff for many years. The effect in both cases is to inject colour, sugars and some esters. After a time – hours rather than months – the cask is depressurised and the remaining wine removed. The cask is then refilled with whisky and left to mature.

The results are not impressive: whisky from a treated cask of this sort smells slightly sulphurous and sweet, but that is all. Of the lovely aromatic flavours of a true sherry-cask maturation, there is no trace. It tastes sweet and flat and is a very dull potation. That has not prevented one of the largest distillers from marketing, mainly in the USA, a single malt matured in treated, recharred casks. For the sake of decency, it shall remain nameless, but it is recognisable by its colour, which is almost black, and by the absence of any of the flavours which arise from long maturation in good sherry wood. It must be said in the distiller's favour, that that has not prevented its being well-received by a great many people who consider themselves connoisseurs of malt whiskies. At the time of writing, however, I am informed that it is to be withdrawn – which reminds me of a saying by a great American, to the effect that you can fool some of the people some of the time ...

The main advantage of treated casks to the distiller is that, while their absence of flavour is lost in a bottling of many casks, they contribute large amounts of colour, which allows the distiller, when asked whether any colouring is added to his whisky, to lay hand on heart and to say with conviction that 'Our whisky gets all of its colour from the cask. No artificial colouring is added in the bottling.' When a practice such as this has been sanctioned by an interest as powerful as the Scotch whisky industry, it becomes part of the belief system of the culture.

I once paid a visit to a famous Speyside distillery in the company of Paul Levy. Paul is a very sharp American intellectual, who has the enviable job of covering, for the *Wall Street Journal*, all matters in Europe to do with the arts and food and drink. We were shown around the distillery and the manager offered us drams of its single malt, which we happily accepted. He explained that it is company policy to mature all the whisky in refill casks. I asked why, since so many fine whiskies produced in the same valley use first-fill, was this malt not so treated? He replied, that first-fill sherry wood was ill-suited to its particular character. By way of proof, he pointed to a decanter full of very dark-coloured liquor, which he said had come from a first-fill cask. He invited us to try. We did. It was foul: sweet, heavily sulphurous, and dead flat. We said we saw what he meant, and left soon after. Paul asked me what on earth that had been about. I explained that what we had seen was whisky from a paxaretted cask. I should say in mitigation, that the manager gave every appearance of believing what he had told us. Paul, reflecting, mused on the fact that as an American journalist, he once thought that there could not be a better source of information about a Scotch whisky than the manager of the whisky distillery which made it. Such is the influence on belief of large organisations: propaganda as an instrument of policy is not confined to politics.

WHY WHISKY TASTES AS IT DOES: THE FIVE PROCESSES

MALTING

Every stage in the whisky process has an influence on flavour. The first stage is malting: this produces the sugars whose fermentation will result in alcohol and the trace compounds which will turn into flavour congeners. Physically, malting consists of three processes: steeping, germinating and kilning. Before the malting begins, the maltster must ascertain that the barley is of a quality and in a condition such that it will produce malt of the quality required. The barley is brought to the maltings mainly by truck. When it arrives, it is inspected for the presence of alien seeds and rodent droppings. The former are undesirable because they may introduce alien flavour elements. The flavour considerations of rat shit will need no elaboration for those who have any acquaintance with it. Microbial contamination may also influence flavour; fortunately infestation by micro-organisms is easily detectable by smell. Analysis in the laboratory establishes that the barley has appropriate levels of moisture, nitrogen and sulphur compounds.

Steeping

When barley is harvested, it is or ought to be dry. In the dry state – that is, when it has a moisture content of less than 12 per cent – the barley grain becomes dormant and can be stored for long periods. The purpose of steeping is to raise the moisture content of the barley grain to a point at which the grain will germinate. Given the right conditions, when the moisture content of the barley grain exceeds about 40 per cent, it will begin to germinate. The readiness with which it will do so depends on the type of grain and on how it has been treated. Barleys vary in their ability to germinate: in their experiments with bere, Highland Park found great difficulty in getting the grains to germinate. If the barley plant has come to fruition in cold, damp conditions (not uncommon in Scotland), it can become stubbornly dormant and requires warm storage and

The steep tank, where the dry barley is soaked to raise the moisture content of the grain to a point at which it will begin to germinate.

abrasion before it will consent to germinate. Some barleys are sensitive to immersion in water and require dampness rather than soaking, together with a plentiful supply of oxygen before they will germinate.

Steeping methods are adjusted to the requirements of the barley. Steep tanks vary greatly in their form, but have in common the provision of varying amounts of water and plenty of air. In large maltings, steeping is done in hoppers with provision for aeration and drainage. Movement of the barley is automated and can be carefully controlled. This is not universal, though. At Springbank, steeping takes place in a long, narrow steep tank in which aeration and movement are provided by a man with a shovel. When first introduced to the water, the barley grain takes up moisture rapidly. Steeping is interrupted after twelve or twenty-four hours and the water drained. After a resting period, more water is then introduced and this alternation continues until the first rootlets begin to appear, usually after around two days' steeping. Burns tells us, in the eponymous poem, what happened to John Barleycorn:

> *They filled up a darksome pit*
> *With water to the brim*
> *They heaved in John Barleycorn*
> *There let him sink or swim.*

Germinating

Steeping ends with the appearance of the rootlets or chits 9seen in the illustra-

*Turning the malt at
Benriach Distillery*

tion on page 77). The malting barley is transferred from the steep tank to the malting floor or drum. The traditional form is floor malting. Malt floors are usually light and airy, the floor being of concrete or other impermeable material. The steeped grain is spread out on the floor to a depth of about a foot and germination takes place. The barley embryo begins to grow and in doing so, converts the starch of its foodstore into sugars whose oxidation fuels its growth, yielding energy, carbon dioxide and water. The germinating grain is turned periodically, either by a turning machine or, if by hand, using a malt shovel. The turning allows the grain to access oxygen in the air and dissipates heat and carbon dioxide. It also stops the rootlets from becoming matted. Germination continues for four to six days, depending on conditions:

> *They laid him out upon the floor*
> *To work him further woe;*
> *And still, as signs of life appear'd*
> *They toss'd him to and fro.*

You can see floor malting at Laphroaig and Springbank distilleries, Glendronach, Glengarioch and a few others. But most malting today is done in large, automated maltings, in which conditions can be controlled much more closely than is possible in a floor malting. In such places, the grain is introduced into a drum or tank fitted with a perforated floor through which water may be drained and air introduced. Drum malting is quicker than floor malting, taking normally three or four days. The result is much the same – or so say the big distillers. Other folk say differently: Springbank has gone back to floor malting after years of buying malt in, on the ground that if the distillery could produce perfectly wonderful whisky using purely traditional methods, that surely is the best thing to do, and beggar the expense. Given the result, it is hard to argue with them.

During the period of growth of the barley embryo, hydrolytic enzymes are produced which break the starch molecules down into sugars. The sugars produced are mainly maltose 35–50%, maltotriose 10–25%, glucose 7–11%, fructose 5–7%, sucrose 2–3% and the remainder as dextrins.

Enzymes also break down the lipid and nitrogenous materials into fatty acids and amino acids. The distiller seeks as high as possible a conversion of starch, but is less keen to have the other sorts of compound. Fortunately, the lipase and protease enzymes (which convert the lipid and nitrogenous materials) are more sensitive to heat than the carbohydrases and tend to be deactivated during kilning. Even so apparently simple a matter as the timing of the kilning may have an influence on flavour. And economic policy may impact on flavour: there has been a movement toward lower-temperature kilning over the last decade or so, resulting in the presence of higher levels of free fatty acids and amino acids in the worts.

Sulphur compounds are produced during malting, which can sometimes persist all the way through to the final whisky. Normally, however, these are removed during kilning, as are many of the disagreeable aromas which arise from the action of microflora present on the barley. During malting, many carbonyl compounds are formed, which give the cereal its malty flavour. Most of these are lost during kilning and mashing and what carries over into the worts is mostly lost in fermentation – which is why for the most part, malt whisky doesn't taste of malt.

Kilning

When the barley has germinated, it must be stopped. Otherwise, it would continue to grow until the sugars were consumed in the interest of the new barley plant. The developing embryo is killed by roasting in a kiln. Besides arresting germination, the purpose of kilning is to dry the grain so that it may be milled, and to add flavour from the kiln gases. The traditional malt kiln is the pagoda-roofed building which is so characteristic of malt whisky distilleries. (I have heard various fanciful explanations of the form of roof and of its origins. In fact, it was invented by an Elgin architect by the name of Charles Chree Doig in 1889. It was claimed that it made the malt kiln draw better, but since malt kilns draw if anything too well, its popularity can be put down to fashion and its use by the Doig family firm as its trademark.)

The traditional pagoda-roofed kilns of Strathisla Distillery

Modern kilns run mainly on coke, whose burning produces carbon dioxide and water and not much else. Peat was originally used as the sole source of heat for drying the malt, in which case, some very tarry whiskies must have resulted. Now peat is burnt on top of the coke to give whatever degree of peating is required. Glengoyne, for example, uses none at all, while Ardbeg peats to a mighty 50 parts per million. Combustion products such as phenols and cresols, which adhere to the malted barley during kilning, persist all the way to mature whisky in cask ten or fifteen years later and we taste them as smoky, fishy flavours. The strength of such flavours depends on the amount of peat used and on the temperature at which it is burnt. When a malt is heavily peated, the flavour dominates all other flavours. That is not to say that peatiness can conceal off odours – it can't, for the other flavours are discernible through the peat reek by a practised nose.

The finished produce: malted barley.

MASHING

The malt which comes out of the kiln is sweet, dry and friable. In that state – when it is known as 'grist' – it can be put through a mill – as in 'It's all grist to the mill' – which grinds it to a rough powder:

> *But a miller us'd him worst of all,*
> ~~*For he crush'd him 'tween two stones*~~

Once ground, the powder is mixed with water. Even in such a mechanical-seeming an affair as milling, there are still flavour considerations. The more finely the distiller mills the malt, the more the starch is converted to sugars and the more sugars are extracted Fine grinding also releases higher levels of husk components such as tannins and phenols, and these are less desirable. Malt mills are often of considerable antiquity and rather stylish design. Stones are their bane, and some form of screening for stones in the malt is normally employed.

At one time, it was thought that the sole purpose of mashing was to extract as much as possible of the fermentable sugars produced during the malting stage. It is now known, that the process of converting starch into sugars continues during mashing, since the carbohydrase enzymes are not destroyed by kilning and continue to work during mashing.

It is at this stage that water quality becomes important: the water used in mashing may contain trace nutrients, but also contain minerals such as copper and iron which can inhibit fermentation. Water may also be a source of bacterial infections, though these are normally killed during fermentation. The acid/alkaline level of the water matters at this stage, since it affects the activity of the malt enzymes.

During mashing, protease enzymes release nitrogen-containing compounds from the malt, which are important in the flavour of the final whisky. The amounts of available nitrogen affect the fermentation by determining the amount of yeast growth in the wort. But more importantly, nitrogens tend to be present in the form of amino acids, and amino acids can be precursors of fusel alcohols and their esters.

The mashtun is a large tank, usually constructed out of cast iron or stainless steel, with a perforated floor through which the tank is drained. It is equipped with mechanical stirrers and normally has a cover, which is sometimes made of copper. Grist and hot water are pumped into the tank, and after a little while, stirred. The water is given about half an hour to dissolve sugars and other compounds, and then drained off. A second, hotter, water is then pumped in and the process repeated. At that stage there is very little left to extract from the malt. A third, almost boiling, water or 'sparge', is introduced which takes away what little remains. This third water is used as the first of the subsequent mashing.

The filtration of the mash can have an effect on the flavour of the whisky. The filtration must be fine enough to prevent relatively large particles passing over into the wort. However, it has been found that the removal of all of the solid material will depress the level of the higher alcohols which are such important flavour congeners.

Inside the mashtun, the ground malted barley is muxed with heated water and carefully stirred or 'mashed' to convert the starch in the grain into sugar.

BREWING

The worts from the mashtun are taken via a receiver known as an underback, through a cooler to the fermenting vessel or washback. (The cooler is required to reduce the temperature of the worts to a level – about 23 °C – at which the yeast can survive.) In the washback, yeast is added and fermentation begins. The process of fermentation in whisky-making is much the same as that in any other alcohol production, though with certain differences of detail, namely in the raw materials, the yeast strains used, the fermentation conditions and the local bacterial populations. The wort is not boiled, as in beer brewing, so malt enzymes are not destroyed and a secondary conversion occurs during fermentation.

Fermentation is an important source of flavours: higher alcohols, fatty acids and esters are all formed at this stage. Indeed, most of the important flavour congeners or their precursors are formed during fermentation by yeast or other micro-organisms. The principal purpose of fermentation, however, is to convert the sugars in the worts into potable alcohols.

The product of mashing, the hot, malty, sugary liquid known as the worts, is drawn off ready for fermentation.

The worts are inoculated with yeast: either a single distiller's yeast or a mixture of that with brewers' yeast. Following that inoculation, there is a quiet initial period which is followed by a short and furious phase of yeast growth lasting for 12–16 hours. In this stage, huge amounts of carbon dioxide are produced and the wash becomes wildly turbulent, even to the extent of shaking the washback and its surrounds. Many distillers employ a beater device to break up the froth which, driven by the carbon dioxide, threatens to boil out of the vessel. If you are fortunate enough to visit a distillery while this is going on, by all means look into the washback, but don't breathe while you do it, else you may get a lungful of carbon dioxide, which is a startling experience, to put it mildly.

During this phase, the most readily-accessible sugars are used up. The order is roughly sucrose, fructose, glucose, maltose and then the higher sugars. Alcohol fermentation is generally complete in about 36 hours, at which point some yeast strains lyse (break down) and release their contents into the wash. Contemporary with the yeast fermentation, there is a competing lactic acid bacterial fermentation. Following the lysis of the yeast, the activity of the lactic acid bacterial fermentation increases, as the bacteria grow on the released nutrients. Besides lactic acid, the bacteria at this stage produce important congeners, some good, some not. The timing of the point at which the wash is distilled is important for flavour, since bacterial fermentation produces certain acids which, if they carry over into the distillate in appreciable concentration, can produce undesirable aromas. By the time the fermentation ceases – or rather, is stopped – ethyl alcohol makes up about 8 per cent of the total volume.

The chemistry of flavour congener production during fermentation is hugely complicated and well beyond the scope of a book such as this. We must content ourselves with noting that besides alcohols, esters, fatty acids, and aldehydes are produced, together with carbonyls, such as diacetyl and butanediol. Higher alcohols arise, both from amino acids – in the earlier stage of fermentation – and from carbohydrates in the later.

There are many different factors determining the congeners which are produced and, if that were not complicated enough, most of those factors interact with each other. Besides the yeast strain, the temperature and pH value of the wash have an effect on congener production, as do oxygen and carbon dioxide levels, and bacterial population growth. Many of these are determined not only by outside influences, but by the shape and size of the fermenting vessel.

Washbacks vary hugely throughout the whisky industry. Some distilleries

Traditional and modern washbacks

swear by their original wooden washbacks, others by modern vessels of stainless steel. Some are open to the atmosphere, others have copper or steel lids. Some distilleries, which converted to stainless steel washbacks in the 1970s and 1980s in the course of what was then described as modernisation, have gone back to using wood. Some, such as Springbank, never modernised in the first place. The claims for wooden and stainless steel washbacks are diametrically opposed. Those opting for the latter cite the absence of bacterial contamination and consequent controllability of conditions as factors in the production of high-quality wash. The people who favour wooden vessels say that the excellence of their product is down to the presence of flavour-contributing bacteria and the natural variations in process which result from a lack of control. The funny thing is that both may be right. Certainly, both produce good whisky.

DISTILLING

Distilling is the spectacular part of whisky production: great, shiny copper stills steaming gently away in the gloom; clear spirit running in a gleaming brass safe; the stillman quietly going about his work. This is where mere beer turns, miraculously, into fiery spirit. In the stillhouse of an evening, it is not too hard to imagine why people once thought that alchemy was related to magic. It still is: we just know a bit more about it – though little by comparison with what we do not know. What has changed is our attitude. We no longer regard anything as unknowable: we think distilling whisky is magic because it is enormously complex and wondrously subtle.

Yet distilling seems very simple. It was when you tried it at school: you boiled up alcohol and water in a flask; the alcohol boiled at a lower temperature than the water, so it came off first and the vapour turned to liquid in the condenser. The latter, being glass, allowed you to see both the condensing alcohol and the cold water which cooled it. It is not too difficult to visualise the whisky distillery in terms of this image: the still is the flask, the lyne arm the tube which connected it to the condenser, the worm tub and tube condenser are not intuitively different from the laboratory version. They even use hydrometers to measure the density of the liquid and therefore the proportion of alcohol to water.

So the principle is simple enough, as regards the separation of water from alcohol: low-strength ale turns into high-strength spirit. The devil is, as they say, in the detail. For the ale is much more than just water and alcohol, as we have seen. And what happens in the whisky still is not just about concentrating the spirit. In a vodka still, yes, for what you want there is pure ethyl alcohol, which has no taste. In a whisky still, the object is the conservation of the flavours present in the wash and the production of yet other flavours in the still.

Most books about whisky have a schematic representation of the whisky process which consists of containers and their connections. That is fine and, one would think, unexceptionable. It is, with the reservation that it implies that the functions are perfectly separate and distinct. This is not the case, as we have seen in the transition from malting through mashing to brewing. The same is true of distillation: some of the processes which take place during the preceding fermentation continue in the still. Some indeed become more active. Acids and alcohols react to make esters; reduction and oxidation reactions occur, with aldehydes becoming acids and alcohols.

We spoke earlier about enzymes, which are organic catalysts. Copper is an inorganic catalyst; the copper of the still catalyses many of those reactions, which take place in the body of the still, in its neck and arm, and in the condenser. The size and shape of the still, the rate and temperature at which it is worked, all influence those reactions. The smaller the still, the greater the area of copper exposed to the contents and the stronger the catalysis of the contents. A tall, narrow still will cause more components to condense and fall back to be evaporated again, than is the case with a short, fat still. On the other hand, a short still which is fitted with a purifier and a reflux condenser will do the same trick, but not in the same way. A still with a plain, straight neck will catalyse a different lot of reactions from a still which has a lamp-glass neck, or one with a boil collar.

A still which is worked off quickly at a high temperature will produce a whisky quite different from that which runs from a slow, cool still. In the early

Boil-ball and lantern stills at Cragganmore Distillery. The 'boil ball' chamber at the base of the still-head (seen on the first still) causes heavier vapours to collect and fall back into the still to be redistilled.

nineteenth century, before the invention of the patent still, the distiller paid a licence fee based not on the amount of spirit produced, but on the size of the still. Consequently, the faster the still was worked the greater the profit. Some stills could perform a complete distillation in about five minutes. The whisky they made was quite vile. That said, there is scope for plenty of variation, for within certain limits good whisky can be produced, and variations in still size, shape and working merely make for variety in the distillate.

Most malt whisky is twice-distilled. A few distilleries distil more than twice: Auchentoshan and Bushmills spring to mind, and Springbank distils two-and-a-half times in a process which is hard to understand, but which evidently works. It is said that triple distillation yields a lighter, purer spirit, but I can't say I have ever seen any evidence of that in the mature malts. Anyway, it's far from clear that anyone wants a purer spirit, if purer means having fewer flavour congeners.

The first distillation is of the wash which, carrying a considerable quantity of solid materials over into the still, continues many of the reactions which were set in train earlier. The presence of solids causes problems for the distiller, since, as in any cooking pot, things tend to stick to the bottom and burn. Burnt bits do not improve the flavour of the whisky, any more than they improve that of other sorts of cooking. Various devices are employed to combat this, of which my favourite is the rummager, a heavy copper chain which is swirled round the bottom of the still and dislodges any material inclined to stick. It works fine and incidentally introduces another copper surface to the wash, available for use as catalyst. Springbank have a delightfully low-tech device to let the stillman know when the rummager is working: the shaft which drives it has a little chain attached and at each revolution, the chain strikes a bell.

The wash still is worked until 99 per cent of the alcohol passes over into the low wines receiver, at which point it is around 21 per cent alcohol by volume. From there it is pumped into the spirit still. Since the volume of liquid has by now considerably diminished, spirit stills are smaller than wash stills. The process is repeated, with the difference that the stillman takes a greater interest in the spirit running off. His business now is to take from the effluent of the still only that part which will taste well in ten years' time. Happily, he has various ways of discerning this. He knows that the first fluids emanating from the still, the foreshots, are pretty unpleasant. By manipulating the levers of the spirit safe, he directs those back into the feints/low wines receiver, to be distilled again. When next that particular lot of compounds comes back to the still, they will have altered greatly.

The spirit in its first flush is around 80 per cent ethyl alcohol. It is, however, mixed with various other alcohols and esters and is not considered fit for consumption. After about half an hour, things get better; the alcohol level has declined to 75 per cent and the spirit does not cloud when mixed with water in a glass. Then begins the middle cut, which the stillman directs, by manipulating the spout of the spirit safe, into the spirits receiver.

This is what is destined to become whisky. It is high in esters, with their fruity, flowery aromas. As the run of the still continues, the nature of the distillate changes and feints begin to appear. These are the higher, long-chain alcohols or fusel oils and their esters; the nitrogenous compounds derived from amino acids and, eventually, the sulphur compounds. In low concentrations, feints are not only tolerable but desirable, since they give whisky its characteristic taste. Sweet flavours appear fairly late in the run, and in some whiskies are considered very desirable. However, the stillman's problem is that the sulphurous congeners follow hot on their heels and if there is to be honey, there's a risk of getting rubber and drains as well.

When the spirit is between 60 and 70 per cent alcohol, the stillman redirects the spout in the spirit safe and the rest of the distillate is run off into the low wines receiver to be distilled again. The distillate, which at this point is still of high alcohol content, raises substantially the input concentration to the spirit still, as it is mixed with the next distillate of the wash still.

So far, so good. No doubt it is a story you have heard often enough, if you have

The 'middle cut', the most desirable part of the distillation, is drawn off in preparation for the final stage of the process, maturation.

any interest in whisky. I confess I had heard this process explained many times before I came to feel that there was something I wasn't quite getting. A nagging doubt which, being inarticulate, doesn't quite surface, but creates a feeling of unease. Recently I managed to drag my gremlin into the light and asked a distillery manager the obvious question: if the foreshots and feints are returned to the low wines/feints receiver and redistilled, and the same thing happens again and again, is there not a build-up of some pretty hefty organic compounds? And if so, what does it do to the whisky? My distiller – who runs one of the most prominent of the malt whisky distilleries – was a little taken aback. He told me that he had been talking to people about distilling and taking them round distilleries for many years, and nobody had ever asked the question, so he had no ready answer. He did volunteer, however, his opinion: that as distiller, the management of the feints receiver is probably the most important single matter he has to deal with.

He says that when the distillery is closed in the summer for its annual maintenance, the receiver is opened and cleaned. Its walls are thickly coated with a dark, waxy, oily substance which has accumulated over the preceding year's distillations. Its chemical nature he can only speculate about, but suggests it consists of a great variety of very large, very exotic molecules. What he can tell me is that he is sure that deposit makes a contribution to flavour, for when he restarts the distillery, the quality of the spirit is poor for the first few runs of the still. This may be explained by the need for the foreshots and feints to mix, but my informant is certain that the build-up of goo in the feints receiver is what really matters.

The stillman checks the distillate as it flows through the spirit safe, deciding at which point to begin collecting that part which will taste agreeable after maturation. The padlock is present courtesy of the exciseman.

Later I asked some of the scientists, who confirmed what the distillery manager had said. I then went to the whisky books on my shelves, but nowhere could I find any mention. Now I don't claim any great originality in this enquiry, but the

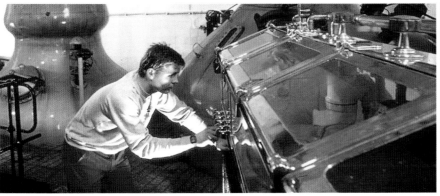

fact that there seems to be no other public mention of the matter, confirms some long-held opinions about whisky experts and the whisky industry.

The condenser is the Cinderella of the distillation kit. The stills are in the forefront and get all the attention; the condenser sits behind, or even outside the stillhouse. Condensers come in two main forms: tube condensers and worms. The tube variety is like a locomotive boiler in reverse: a cylinder with cold water pipes running through it. The distillate condenses on the outside of the pipes and runs off. The worm is the traditional form, in which the arm of the still continues as a coiled copper tube which sits in cold water. The heat of the spirit vapour passes to the water and the condensed distillate runs out the bottom of the tube.

Even in the condenser, the reactions continue and different condensers will yield different levels of flavour congeners. Again, we have seen a reversal of the changes brought about in the last few decades in the name of modernity, with a return to traditional types of condensers. When Dalwhinnie distillery was renovated in the early 1990s, worm condensers were installed. Now on a winter's day, as you drive up the A9 road to Inverness, you can see on your left the steam rising from the worm tubs of the distillery – a pretty sight in that desolate valley.

Private distilling was common in Scotland until the end of the eighteenth century. Every house of any size had a whisky still in which it produced spirit for use by the people of the house. The spirit produced was of variable quality, depending as it did on so many factors beyond the control of the distiller. However, it was held in many quarters that small stills made for better whisky – an opinion which can now have some scientific support, on the ground that in a small still, there is more copper available to catalyse the reactions which take place than in a large one. Much the same goes for maturation: a small cask will mature whisky more rapidly than a large one, simply because the spirit has a greater area of cask surface per unit of volume available for extraction of flavour.

Some years ago, I obtained permission from HM Customs & Excise to distil whisky in a small still which had been given to the Scotch Malt Whisky Society by Sir Kenneth Alexander. (Ken had been given it when he was chairman of the Highland Board by a man who had once been an illicit distiller.) The permission was given for one run of the still to mark, of all things, the opening of the Cheltenham Arts Festival – a typically zany idea from my friend Ralph Steadman, the cartoonist and artist, whose job it was to declare the festival officially open. Well, after a lot of coming and going and talking to the Excise, we got our permission and at the grand opening, we distilled whisky. Ralph said

The Malt Masterclass still.

afterwards that he had been completely upstaged, despite doing his well-known W.C. Fields impersonation, for everyone wanted to see whisky being made.

A few years after that, when some pals and I had started the Malt Masterclass, we had thought it would be a good wheeze to do some distilling. The business of the Masterclass was to inform people about every aspect of whisky making and it seemed only logical for us to be able to distil whisky, preferably as part of the class. (I can confirm that there is no difficulty in keeping the students' attention.) I therefore approached HM Customs with a proposal that they give me a licence. They refused, saying it was against the law. I asked why, as I had been given permission before? They replied, ah, that was given by the Bristol office, seeing the distillation was to happen in Cheltenham, and the folk in Bristol, being English, naturally knew nothing about whisky. I said, but surely if I could have permission once, I could get it again? They said no. Things went on in this way for a year or so, until either there was a change of policy or they just got tired and wanted me to go away. Whatever the reason, they said we could have a licence, but that it was a special case and nobody else should try the same. And we had to provide a floor plan of any premises in which we wanted to distil and give a guarantee that no spirit would be consumed without payment of duty.

The result is the still pictured on the previous page. It was made for us by Norman MacLeod, who was Glenmorangie's coppersmith and the maker of their new pagoda roof. It holds about seven litres and will work by an electric heater, bottled gas or peat fire. The latter is the best, but the copper is a swine to clean afterwards.

The spirit was pretty foul to begin with, we think because it was picking up brazing flux remaining in the still. After half a dozen runs, however, it began to improve and now I am pleased to say, it produces very respectable spirit. We haven't as yet laid any down in cask, but who knows, that may come.

MATURING

Maturation is easily the most important part of the whisky production process as regards flavour. A malt whisky acquires more than half of its flavour during maturation; some would say as much as 80 per cent of the final flavour of the spirit comes from the cask.

People had come to realise the importance of maturing in wood by the beginning of the nineteenth century. In *The Diary of a Highland Lady*, Elizabeth Grant describes the Glenlivet which she sent to King George as 'whisky long in the wood, long in uncorked bottles, mild as milk, and the true contraband *gout* in it.' There is reason to believe that the Grants were not alone in appreciating cask-matured malt. George Saintsbury in the *Notes on a Cellar Book* tells us that whisky in cask was kept 'by all persons of some sense and some means north of the Tweed'. He is writing in 1920 and referring to the mid-nineteenth century. Saintsbury is a delight, but you must interpret him: when he says 'of some means' he means seriously rich.

The rest of the drinking public got whisky which, far from being long in wood, was hot off the still. Until Lloyd George's legislation of 1915, most whisky was sold new or at least very young. The great majority of the whisky-drinking public was taking its drams complete with all the undesirable flavour compounds which are converted during maturation. This, I believe, explains the rise of blended whiskies from the 1860s onward. (see Why Whisky Tastes As It Does: Blending, page 116). Prior to 1915 there had been a trend toward better (that is, more mature) whisky, but in terms of two-year-old, not twenty. In the advertisements of the later nineteenth century, words such as 'smoothness' are commonly used to describe whiskies. The terms are undefined, but it is reasonable to assume that some of them at least must have referred to qualities incompatible with really raw hooch. The Royal Commission of 1908 (the same which declared blended whisky to be the genuine article) says, 'compulsory

Contrary to appearances, the maturation process is a very active affair …

bonding is … a means of securing the maturity and flavour … of spirits … A very much longer period is required for the maturation of a heavy pot-still malt whiskey. [*sic*] Even in the case of spirits of the same character, differences in the condition of storage, such as the nature and size of the vessel in which the spirit is kept … have a considerable effect in determining the rapidity of maturation.' The Royal Commission took evidence from all the leading scientists in the field, so we can assume that this represented informed opinion at the time. None the less, it took legislation and a war to make a significant change.

The Royal Commission denied the malt whisky distillers the sole right to describe their product as Scotch whisky. This judgement merely accelerated a trend which was already well-established, for blended whisky was to eclipse malt as a popular drink. Single malts went into a decline which continued for another sixty years. 'Whisky' came to mean blended whisky for all but a tiny band of aficionados in Scotland. Blended whisky was taken with mixers by a docile public whose criteria were ideological rather than gastronomic. Consistency of flavour was preferred to quality by both producers and consumers. In such circumstances, and in the absence of any critical milieu, it is not surprising that product quality declined and little attention was paid to the role of the cask in maturation.

With the beginning of the malt revival in the 1960s, the mature spirit began to be more closely examined – exposed as it was by the malt drinker's preference for taking it straight or with a little water. There was no ice or soda or other mixers to disguise off-notes. As the demand for high-quality bottled single malts developed, people started looking at the influence of the cask in the production of mature spirit. Traditional practices began to acquire a much-needed basis in scientific understanding. Those distillers such as Glenfarclas and Springbank

... although some distilleries would have you believe otherwise.

who had always spent money on good casks found themselves in an advantageous position and enterprising companies such as Macallan which were prepared to examine and adapt traditional practices, began to reap rewards. Even the big corporations such as Allied and United Distillers eventually awoke, and were able from their vast stocks to find enough good casks to supply a growing demand. The common factor in the development of single malts as a genre was the importance of the cask in production of mature spirit of high quality.

To describe whisky as ageing in the cask, is to imply something passive. It is not: ageing is a very active business indeed, if slow. Congeners in the distillate react with each other, to make acetaldehyde, acetic acid and ethyl acetate, to name but a very few of the aldehydes, acids and esters which continually form to yield important flavour compounds. The wood provides – by solution or reaction or both – sugars, tannins, lignin, ethanol, lactones, glycerol, fatty acids, furfural and aromatic aldehydes. The wood also gives the colour which distinguishes mature from immature whisky – so long as no caramel obscures it. Depending on the environment – the type of cask, size of cask, warehouse temperature and humidity – reactions proceed to differing degrees. It is no wonder, therefore, that the resultant spirit is highly varied. The chemistry of maturation is a large subject and it is not possible in a work such as this to do more than inspect a few of the more prominent aspects.

Reactions among distillate flavour congeners yield acids, esters, tannins and furfural. Acids and tannins increase in concentration over the first year or two but thereafter level out. Aldehydes and esters, on the other hand, increase in concentration gradually over the whole maturation period, which explains why fruity, floral aromas are to be found in mature whiskies to a greater extent than in younger spirit. Ethanol oxidises to form acetaldehyde and acetaldehyde to form acetic acid. The higher alcohols do likewise, creating a vast number of compounds, all of which may figure in the final flavour spectrum. This part of the maturation process requires the presence of oxygen, which is got from the air by diffusion through the wood of the cask. If the cask is painted or otherwise treated so as to destroy its porosity, the whisky will not mature to any appreciable degree.

Various solids are present in mature whisky, dissolved in the alcohol. These contain sugars and glycerol, which contribute to the sweetness of the mature spirit. Both derive from the wood itself: hemicelluloses are polysaccharides which, being broken into some of their smaller components during maturation, yield sugars which sweeten the mature whisky.

Aromatic aldehydes, which are such important flavour congeners, are probably formed by breakdown of the lignin in the barrel wood by a process of hydrolysis similar to that which releases sugars, but more complex. It is to this that we owe the flavour of vanilla, which is produced by vanillin, an aromatic aldehyde. Lactones also derive from wood reactions during maturation: they give the flavour of coconut, which is often found in well-matured whisky. The presence of furfurals, besides having a direct effect in the flavour of the whisky, affects our perception of the flavour of lactones. Low concentrations of furfurals accentuate the pleasant flavour effects of lactones, though beyond a certain level, this is balanced by the disagreeable flavours of the furfurals themselves.

The practice of charring casks enhances flavour by providing quantities of flavour congeners available for solution and reaction. Amino acids, pyridines and pyrazines are extracted from the charred oak. The latter two are known to have very low flavour thresholds and almost certainly have an effect on flavour. Various compounds of the terpene family are also found in oakwood and it seems likely that they contribute to whisky flavour. Terpenes are aromatic compounds which are found in many spices and perfumes.

Various phenols besides those mentioned above are present in oakwood and may be extracted during maturation. Phenols too have low flavour thresholds and may be detectable in the mature spirit, hence the possibility of smoky flavour from sources other than peated malt, though in very low concentrations.

It will be apparent from even so brief a survey that small variations in maturation factors may produce large alterations in the mature whisky. As more is discovered about the mechanisms of maturation, the temptation is to use that knowledge to intervene in the process. Mention has already been made of cask finishes and wine treatment, both of which in unscrupulous hands can be used to simulate maturation. Happily the trend in the industry is away from the latter, and cask finishes, properly used, are legitimate extensions of traditional practice.

There can be little doubt that the best results are got from scrupulously applied traditional methods. Good casks must be sourced, from Spain and from America; whisky must be laid down, preferably in cool, damp warehouses, for at least ten years. Remarkably simple, really, especially when compared with the complexity of what goes on in the casks during those ten years.

All of the above applies to malt whiskies only. The position with grain spirit is quite different. Grain whisky is a much less complex spirit than malt and it matures differently. It is a lot nicer to start with: new malt is an acquired taste, to put it mildly, while new grain is very pleasant right from the start. There are

Sherry in Jerez matures in the casks which will eventually find their way to Scotland to be refilled with whisky.

far fewer flavour congeners generally in grain and the new spirit has almost none of the nasty tastes of new malt. Grain spirit matures much more quickly and soon loses what unpleasant congeners it had. On the other hand, it does not acquire much in the way of new flavours, and may, depending on the cask, acquire some it would be better off without.

The practice of making an age statement on the bottle label as a guarantee of quality is sometimes responsible for the bottling of blended whisky containing grain spirit which is over the hill. The rules say that if you claim your whisky is ten years old, there must be no spirit in the bottle which is aged less than ten years, though there may be older. You need the ten years to bring your malts to maturity, but at that point, your grains may be well past it. Really old blended whisky owes more to the imperatives of marketing than it does to those of taste.

Old Whiskies

This is probably the most appropriate place to discuss age in whiskies. There is a popular belief that the older the whisky, the better. That belief is false. The mere fact of age in a whisky bottle is not significant: what matters is how long the spirit was in cask before it was put in bottle. Whisky does not mature at all in glass: the whisky you put in bottle today will be the same in fifty years' time, provided the bottle is not opened. If it is opened, air will get in, the spirit will begin to oxidise and the whisky to deteriorate. I mentioned in the first chapter a whisky guru who has no sense of smell: this chap has a vast collection of malt whiskies in bottle. Most have been opened and they stand with varying amounts of air above the spirit. The contents of all the opened bottles are oxidised to some extent and the value of the collection as regards the taste of whisky must be questionable. The only thing to do once you have opened a bottle of whisky is either to drink it (my preferred solution) or to treat it to a gas blanket.

Age in cask is more problematical. As a rule, malt whiskies are at their best after ten to fifteen years in cask. Beyond fifteen years, the quality of the spirit deteriorates. As time passes, the concentration of flavour components resulting from the processes described above increases. Some – esters, for example – can go on increasing for a long time without deleterious effect. Some, such as vanillin, can increase in concentration without any corresponding increase in our perception of the flavour. But many congeners are such that they improve flavour up to a certain point, but beyond that, diminish it. Think of eggs and salt: eggs with no salt are not tasty, while eggs with a little salt are very tasty; eggs with too much salt are inedible.

The moment of truth: the distillery manager checks the casks to see if the whisky is ready.

It is difficult to predict at which point maturation will peak. The newer the cask, the more rapid the extraction of flavour congeners and the more reactive the wood components, so that a cask's first fill will optimise flavour components more quickly than its second. A smaller cask will mature spirit more quickly than a large one, because more wood surface is exposed to the distillate. Whisky matures faster in a warm warehouse than it does in a cold – but the nature of the maturation is different, and the quality of the spirit will not be so good.

People differ in their tastes. Some folk appear to like the woodiness which you find in very old casks. I don't, which is one reason why I do not favour old whisky. It can be very subjective: if we have other powerful reasons for valuing a potation, we are the more likely to enjoy it. All old whiskies are very expensive: how far does that contribute to people's appreciation of them? Indubitably some people will think dear stuff is good stuff. I recall many years ago visiting a well-known London whisky merchant. He was most affable, as is his way, and suggested I might like to taste some of his stock, which is vast. Nothing loth, I nosed several drams, all of which were excellent. He then asked if I would like to try a 40-year-old Springbank, which he had just had bottled, and gave me a glass. He watched as I sniffed and then asked what I thought. I said, 'Well, it was a good whisky twenty years ago, but it's no' a good whisky now.' He said, 'Aye, but the Japanese drink it: they pay me 200 quid a bottle.'

This is nothing new. Saintsbury says, 'those who think that very old whisky is necessarily very good whisky … know little about whisky. One of those grocer-merchants, who dispense good liquor in the Northern Kingdom … once told me in confidence that he didn't himself care for any whisky that had been kept by itself in cask for more than fifteen years.' That's the rule. There are exceptions, but they are very rare.

WHY WHISKY TASTES AS IT DOES: GRAIN WHISKY

Grain whisky arises from the same beginnings as malt: it merely moved into the nineteenth century at a time when malt stayed firmly in the eighteenth as regards both technology and materials. Malt distilling is essentially a cottage industry: in materials, processes, plant, and culture. Grain whisky distilling is the same thing, but organised in terms of the industrial capitalism, which by the end of the first quarter of the nineteenth century was taking Scotland headlong into the Second Industrial Revolution. Malt and grain whisky production diverged and might have stayed divergent, had they not been brought together by a marketing imperative, as described in the next chapter.

The basic processes are the same: the enzymes in malted barley are employed to convert starch into sugars; the sugars are fermented into alcohols, and the mixture is distilled to separate the potable alcohols from the rest. The scale is different; grain distilleries are very much larger than any malt distillery, and the product is different, intended for a different purpose.

Enzymes, as we have already seen, are organic catalysts. Catalysts cause chemical reactions to take place, but are not themselves consumed in the reaction. As a result, a very small quantity of catalyst can facilitate a great deal of chemical activity. Malt enzymes are no different: the diastase in the malt is capable of catalysing the conversion of starch in quantities much greater than those found in the grain of malt. This was known from at least the eighteenth century, when malt was used to convert other starches into sugars for fermenting. Adam Smith in 1776 says that 'in what one called malt spirits, it makes but a third part of the materials; the other two-thirds being raw barley, or one-third barley and one-third wheat.' Following the end of the French wars in 1815, there was an economic recession, but by the mid-1820s demand had begun to rise. Demand for alcohol was part of that rise: alcohol as feedstock for industrial processes and alcohol as anaesthetic for the industrial workforce.

Then, as now, the cheapest and most convenient way of making fairly pure alcohol was to distil it from fermented sugars. Enormous pot-stills were originally employed, with flat bottoms exposed to the fire, which could distil large amounts of wash very rapidly. These had originated in response to crazy Excise regulations, but were put to use as proto-industrial units. They were inefficient, however, and only with the invention of the patent still, first by Stein in 1827 and later by Coffey in 1830, did the production of alcohol depart from its origins in mediaeval technology.

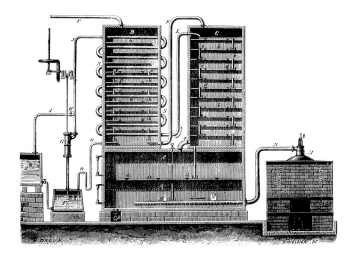

An 1870 illustration showing the inner workings of a Coffey still. As can be seen from the modern photograph overleaf, the basic design of the patent still has changed little over the years.

Grain whisky is made using a relatively small amount of malted barley together with other cereals. The barley is in the form of either an unpeated, dried malt, or a green malt which is delivered to the distillery, alive and damp from the maltings. Timing is critical in the use of green malt: if there is a delay in using it, the distiller can be left with a load of barley plants and most of the sugars consumed by the barley. The malt is ground and mixed with the other cereals, usually wheat or maize: the enzymes in the malt are sufficient to convert all of the starch present into sugars.

Not all grains are as easily malted as barley, for the starch may be inaccessible to the malt enzymes. In the case of maize, the starch in the corn grain requires a preliminary treatment to render it capable of saccharification. This is done by cooking it under pressure, which breaks down the long-chain starches into shorter chains which can then be further broken down by the malt. Thereafter the processes of mashing and brewing are very much the same as in a malt distillery.

The ale which results is less flavoursome then one made purely from malt, for the other cereals are simpler in their chemical makeup than barley grains. There are consequently fewer flavour congeners going forward into the still.

The patent still is the core of grain distilling. It is not difficult to imagine the domestic origins of even quite large pot stills, but the patent still looks like something out of an oil refinery – indeed when oil began to be refined later in the nineteenth century, also in lowland Scotland, it relied for its methods on experience with patent stills. The fractionating column which is used to separate different hydrocarbons is very similar to the rectifier of a patent still.

The patent still is one of those things which are fundamentally simple, but difficult to understand intuitively. The description of its parts as analyser and rectifier doesn't help, for the terms come out of the early technology and have no counterparts in most people's experience. What happens is this: you set up a big pipe with lots of baffles across its inside all the way from bottom to top, so that liquid poured in at the top can trickle slowly down to the bottom. The liquid you pour in is the wash you got from brewing. It is mostly water but with five or six per cent of alcohol. You blast steam in at the bottom. The steam forces its way up, past the wash which is trickling down. The wash is heated by the steam and, because alcohol evaporates at a lower temperature than water, the alcohol in the wash becomes a vapour. This vapour mixes with the steam, which carries it up to the top of the column. The water in the wash doesn't evaporate and it runs off at the bottom of the pipe.

A modern patent still at North British Distillery.

There is a tube from the top of the first column to the bottom of the second, so the steam and alcohol vapour mixture is blown into the foot of the second column. In the second column it hits pipes containing cold liquid, which cause it to condense. Since the least volatile liquids condense first, and then the others, in order of molecular weight, the column can be tapped and the potable alcohol drawn off at the appropriate point. In a neat piece of energy saving, the cold liquid used to condense the steam is the wash which is on its way to the first column.

The first patent stills were made of iron, which reacted with the acids in the spirit to produce a whisky so vile that, even by the low standards then prevailing, it could not be sold – and had to be redistilled for use as gin. Later wood and copper were used, and produced a much more acceptable spirit. It was a light spirit and described as neutral, though in fact it was nothing of the kind, since both the wood and the copper participated in distillate reactions. Modern stills are made mainly of stainless steel, but with copper pipes and sacrificial copper, in recognition of the fact that though less complex than the pot still, the patent still is nevertheless the locus of important reactions which produce flavour congeners.

The patent still produces spirit which is around 95 per cent ethyl alcohol, together with small quantities of congeners, mostly higher alcohols and a few esters. Production is continuous, since no part of the process requires to be stopped to allow another to proceed. It is possible to make very large quantities of alcohol without any sacrifice of quality, so the output can be sold much cheaper than that of a pot still. It is this which enables blended whiskies to be less expensive than malts. Some part of the production of the grain distillery is filled into casks for maturation as grain whisky. Some goes for further distillation for use as gin or vodka; some is used as industrial alcohol.

Like malt, grain whisky must be matured for three years in wood before it may be called Scotch whisky. One can understand the reasons for this, though it seems a pity, for the stuff is really very agreeable when new: much more so than malt spirit. Given a good cask, though, it can emerge at the end of its three years as a very pleasing, aromatic potation. Happily, there is a movement in the industry toward putting grain whiskies in casks of better quality than before, with consequent improvement in the quality of the mature stuff. That said, I have yet to meet a grain whisky in the mature state which I prefer to the new spirit. My colleagues and I have recently experimented with combinations of ten-year-old malt and new grain, with very palatable results. It can't be called Scotch whisky for legal reasons, but it is an agreeable and intriguing potation.

WHY WHISKY TASTES AS IT DOES: BLENDING

t is a reasonable assumption that the great majority of the readers of this book will have come to it by way of an enthusiasm for single malt Scotch whiskies. There is a contrast between people who drink malts and those who drink blended whiskies, which until now has gone unremarked, as far as I know. Malt whisky drinkers tend to want to know something about what they are drinking, whereas those who prefer blends do not ask questions, relying instead on the authority of the brand. This simple difference betrays a deep cultural split. It is a divide of mutual incomprehension which does neither side any good, so it is worth devoting some space to the subject, in the hope that by doing so, we may be able to persuade malt drinkers that many blends are worth drinking, and those who drink only blended whiskies, that they might enjoy a malt.

Blended whiskies arose from a combination of technological advance and marketing opportunity. The advance was the invention of the patent still; the opportunity the opening in 1860 of markets for whisky bottled in Scotland south of the Scottish/English Border.

By 1860, Britain was already a predominantly urban, industrial society whose values were those of the commercial middle class. Like many societies in a state of traumatic transition, its view of the world was that of a previous generation. As the great engine of empire and industry drew all into its mesh, people sought reassurance in myth. One myth ready to hand was the idea of Scotland as a romantic land of mountain and flood where pre-industrial heroic figures chased deer across the hills and fought battles which could only be – and were – compared with those of the ancient Greeks, whose literature was the staple of the educated classes. (Our own generation, accustomed to drugs and terrorism, has formed a very similar – if shorter-lived – attachment to the imagery of Braveheart.) Out of this unholy combination was born the kilted, tartan version of Scotland with which we are all so familiar. Queen Victoria declared things

Queen Victoria, seen here enjoying a picnic in her beloved Highlands, conferred a respectability on all things Scottish – whether real or imaginary – including whisky.

Scottish to be OK by buying a castle at Balmoral as her holiday cottage. Scotland became the first colony of the British Empire and the Scots its privileged servants.

Quite suddenly, things Scottish became socially acceptable to the great English market. Scotch whisky came to rival and then surpass Irish as a fashionable drink. It was greatly helped by the arrival in France of the Phylloxera plague which over the next two decades destroyed the French wine industry and with it brandy, which had been distilled from the wine. The Scotch which the Victorians drank was blended Scotch whisky, not malt, though a fair amount of single malt found its way across the Border.

But why blend? Why not malt? I confess that this is a question which bothered me for years. I used to ask it of people in the whisky industry, who generally thought I was just daft to ask the reason for a fundamental property of reality. I usually got two answers, one of which made sense to me and one of which did not. The sensible reply was to the effect that you can make grain whisky much more cheaply than malt, and therefore blends cost less in the shops than pure malts. This reply did at least have the virtue of being candid, but it did not explain why there were some very expensive blends. The other reply did not help at all: malt whiskies are too strong-tasting for most people's palates and have to be diluted by grains, which are milder. Also, malt whiskies are too variable in quality, so blending is required to ensure consistency.

Those were the official explanations and everyone believed them. Indeed, you will still get them if you ask anyone in authority. However, the more I got to know about malts, the dafter this seemed as an explanation. If malts are so strong-tasting, why do so many folk drink them? Were my forefathers – who drank Bell's – all wimps, though they sailed tall ships or died, playing the pipes, on the Somme? And if malts are so variable, why is this bottle of Glenturret just as good as the last one?

The explanations do make sense, but only if you put them into context. The context is the state of whisky at the time when blending got under way. By the middle of the nineteenth century, people still took their whisky straight from the still. There was no legal requirement to age the stuff until the Act of 1915 and the appreciation of the virtues of cask maturation was confined to those few fortunate individuals who were in a position to keep their own cask. It is against that background that we must consider the twin myths of blending, namely that malt whisky on its own is too individual to drink, and that patent-still spirit is silent, or effectively tasteless.

New malt spirit is indeed strong-tasting stuff. Even the best of it today is an acquired taste and most malts are not agreeable when young. Consider then what new malt spirit must have been like 150 years ago, when there was little demand for quality in the distillate and controls of materials and process were down to the man with the shovel. The object was to get as much alcohol as possible and foreshots and feints alike went into the cask. The spirit took its flavour from the casks which transported it – any old casks: rum casks, butter casks, tar barrels. And, in the Highlands at least, peats were the only fuel available for drying the malt. No wonder it was pretty strong-tasting stuff.

Compare with that the output of the patent still: far fewer flavour congeners and those for the most part pleasant ones. A spirit which needs little maturation, and is perfectly pleasant when new. It is little surprise that the blenders wished to mix the one with the other, or that blending came to be a highly expert business, given the huge variation in the components of the blend.

The society into which blended whisky was sold, was one in which an emergent middle class had lots of disposable income and sought to spend it – as middle classes typically do – in ways which would publicise its members' new status. It did so by strict adherence to certain social norms and an unquestioning acceptance of authority, especially as regards what today we would call its lifestyle. If you wished to be accepted into Victorian society, there were certain things you had to do and other things you must not do. Those norms were dictated by custom and were not to be questioned. The great success of the whisky blenders was in having their brands adopted as part of the system of customary values. Chaps drank whisky because that was the right thing to do. Asking what was in the whisky was not the right thing to do; indeed knowing anything about such technical matters was *déclassé*. Gentlemen did not know how to cook; their cooks did. Anyone who knew how to cook had their social status defined by that particular. American upper-class society acquired most of its norms from the British, with the result that by the end of the nineteenth century, there was a huge divergence between Anglophone and other societies as regards anything to do with food or drink. The learned judge who cooked in his spare time, like Brillat-Savarin, was unknown to the English-speaking world – or at least, if there were such, they didn't publicise the fact.

Blends were sold – as they still are – by brand-marketing techniques. There were two elements to this. First, you had to create a strong brand identity, something which people would recognise. Second, you had to get people to accept the authority of that brand. Both could be achieved by advertising to a newly-literate public through the mass media of the time. The acceptance of the brand might be achieved by reference to the quality of the whisky, but – then as now – it was more likely to be got through values which had nothing to do with quality.

That was the background to the Royal Commission of 1908. Against the big battalions of blended whisky brands, the malt distillers could bring only the small arms of their belief that malts were the authentic, original Scotch whisky and the proposition that the stuff tasted better. No wonder they lost. Malts disappeared from view for sixty years, save for a few enclaves in Scotland, in which a belief in the virtues of malts persisted as part of a *samizdat* Scottish culture. That belief was the property of a combination of the *cognoscenti* and the common people, which stands more in the European tradition than the British. The belief – and the drinking of malts which went with it – were served by distilleries such as Glenfarclas which continued to supply the local gentry with whisky in cask, as they had done for over a century, and by independent bottlers such as Gordon and MacPhail, who would deliver your malt whisky along with the groceries.

In the 1960s when malts came back into public view, they did so as part of a resurgence of Scottish culture which was to culminate in the re-establishment of the Scottish Parliament. The demand for malts in Scotland was of a piece with the recovery of traditions which had been demeaned and subverted by Scotland's colonial status within the British Empire. The stage was then set for the great malt explosion of the 1980s, in which malts were to find a world market alongside – and eventually above – cognac and armagnac.

Whisky blenders reacted variously to the malt explosion. Initially, they mostly ignored it – with a few honourable exceptions such as William Grant & Sons,

Then – as now – blends were marketed by appealing to values which had little to do with the quality of the whisky itself.

who, beginning in the 1960s, blazed a lonely but eventually much-trodden trail with their malt in the triangular Glenfiddich bottle. It was possible for blenders to ignore malts because the 1970s saw blended Scotch whisky on a seemingly endless course of expansion, propelled by brand values, with little reference to quality. The popularity of Scotch was as a popular drink: the connoisseur of distilled liquors drank brandy, mostly cognac, in a curious reversal of roles. As a digestif, Scotch was nowhere, despite the existence of so-called 'de luxe' blends.

Nothing can go up forever, and by the early 1980s, some markets for blended whiskies suffered a precipitate decline. This gave a shock to the system such as the Scotch whisky industry had not known for generations. World wars it could cope with, but a decline in peacetime demand unrelated to a general economic recession was unknown. The response was varied: amalgamations took place in a sprawling industry still operating with the management structures of dozens of family firms; there was expansion into new foreign markets and, most importantly, the quality of the blends was addressed.

By the end of the 1970s, a number of important blends had become bywords for poor practice. Materials were often poor, production slipshod and the casks for maturation long worn-out. The contrast between the quality of the single malts and that of most of the blends had become extreme, to the great detriment of the latter. There began a process which is still in train. Only major brands capable of surviving in an international market could prosper; the others would go to the wall. Most of the major brands were, and are, owned by multinational conglomerate companies. Whatever the demerits of such corporations, their managements aim to make rational decisions as regards their markets. In the case of Scotch whisky, this has shown itself in a gradual improvement in the quality of the spirits bottled as blended whiskies.

Rather oddly, this has not shown itself in the way in which blended whiskies are promoted. Sales are driven by the propagation of brand values, as they are for any other liquor. The result is that in the home market, sales of blended whiskies continue to decline, while in some countries where they know almost nothing of Scotch or Scotland, the market soars – though not, one assumes, from any response to product quality, given that the same markets have responded at other times to some pretty vile potations.

Meanwhile, the relationship between malts and blends continues to be interesting. It is curious that in Scotland, the re-evaluation of malts did not bring about a corresponding disparagement of blends. Folk who took a dram would mostly take any dram, though saving particular thanks for a fine malt. The idea that you should drink only malts was a foreign one, an invention of enthusiasts. It came when malts had escaped from Scotland and become the property of people who valued them for their excellence and distinctiveness, but had little or no apprehension of the cultural context. The proposition that cultural context is necessary to appreciation of fine liquor is the subject of the next chapter.

But at least the folk of whom I speak value their malts for the right reasons, if maybe not all of the right reasons. It remains the case, broadly speaking, that malts are the province of the discerning drinker, whereas blends are taken by those for whom brand values are important. One disturbing trend should be noted, however. A number of malt whiskies are now being sold using the brand-marketing techniques which have been applied to blends. This happens mostly, but not exclusively, in countries which have little cultural connection with Scotland, in which it can be assumed that the consumer is unable to separate the dross of the branding image from the real thing. Unhappily, however, there is so much rubbish in the traditional imagery of Scottishness, that it is not difficult to use Scottish icons for such meretricious purposes.

So where does that leave you, when faced with your glass of Johnnie Walker or Ballantine? What should you, as the truly discerning consumer, do with it? The answer, of course, is anything that pleases you – so long as the decision is yours, arrived at by consulting your own pleasure and not as the result of some glossy advertisement. If you want to mix it with apple juice, by all means do so. Indeed, it's rather nice mixed with apple juice and a little ice.

If you wish, you can treat it as if it were malt, and analyse it, as described hereafter. That said, it isn't easy, for blends are designed specifically to be resistant to analysis. The object of the blender is to produce a pleasing overall sensation, rather than one which is readily separable into its constituent aromas and tastes. It is said that there are people who can tell which malts are in a blend, though I have never met any and neither have any of the technical experts whom I have spoken to recently.

Analysis of flavours is possible, however, should that be your inclination. The techniques and the equipment are as for malts. You put the spirit in a nosing glass, add a little water, and sniff. That's about it. With most blends, especially the cheaper ones, the first thing you will get is a whiff of grain whisky. In the cheap blends, that won't be a pleasant experience, and whether it is tolerable will depend on your taste and on the malts which may mask it. In the better blended whiskies – and that today means many middle-market blends – the grains will show themselves only upon very close inspection, and not always then. How they show themselves depends on how they were matured as well as on the production values of the companies which made them. If the grain spirit is from North British or Strathclyde or Girvan or some others, it will be a light, agreeable potation, which will complement the malts, especially among the higher alcohols and esters.

If, however, the grain spirit has been put in poor-quality casks, as is all too likely, it will exhibit off-notes of various kinds, depending on how long it has been in cask. As with malts, so much depends on the cask. As I write this, I have in front of me a sample of North British grain which has been five years in a first-fill bourbon cask. It is perfectly delightful, and there are no off-notes at all. It is recognisably grain whisky – I think, though I'm far from sure – because of the cereal aromas over flowery scents. Grassy with water, then sweet-sour, then aniseed. Who said it was silent spirit? One thing I can be sure of: I would have no objection to this stuff, either mixed with a few good malts as a blend, or on its own.

The business of blending has traditionally been shrouded in mystery. It is regarded with awed respect both by consumers, who can be excused, and by most folk writing about whisky, who ought to know better. The mystery of blending is the most important element in the authority of the brand. Like most such authority, it's mainly bullshit.

Blending is very similar to the preparation of a perfume. Both have a signature scent which forms the base upon which other parts of the bouquet is built. In the case of blended whisky, this will be a malt whisky from a given distillery, of a given age and cask-maturation. The criteria for choosing the base whisky will have some regard for taste, but will be mainly to do with availability – there is no point in establishing a brand if you can't meet the demand you create.

The blender will call for samples to be drawn from the company's stock of whiskies in cask, of the required type and age. He will have a standard for each of the malts and grains in his blend: all the samples which he inspects will have to meet the standard or be rejected. The better the blend, the higher the standard.

The process of selecting the casks is not as difficult as it might seem to the uninitiated, or is implied by the silence which has traditionally surrounded the process. (It is essentially akin to the difference analysis described in How Whisky Tastes. If you have one whisky which you take as the standard, it is not too hard to acquire the skill of comparing its scent with that of any other offered.)

The malts used in a blend are generally those made in distilleries owned by the group doing the blending. (Almost all big blended whisky brands are owned by conglomerate companies.) Where a blend calls for a malt not owned by the company, it will often be acquired by an exchange agreement. Each blend is made to a formula, and once the selected malts and grains have been mixed according to the formula, the mixed spirit will be compared with a standard of the blend. If, unusually, at that stage it is judged to be lacking in some particular, it will be adjusted by the addition of one or other of the ingredients.

Having been mixed and reduced in alcoholic strength, blended whisky is usually returned to cask for a period of some months, for the components of the blend to marry. This is an important stage in blending, a purely empirical practice which only now is beginning to receive some underpinning of science. The marriage being deemed after a few months' duration to have achieved its object, the cask contents are once more emptied into mixing vats and sent for bottling.

WHY WHISKY TASTES AS IT DOES: CULTURE

WHISKY IN CONTEXT

U p to this point, in our pursuit of the true appreciation of whisky, we have been concerned solely with the individual: with how we each of us discern and evaluate what we find in the glass. We now turn to another aspect of appreciation; one which is rarely recognised, but which is none the less important: its social context.

There are three distinct cultures relevant to a knowledge of whisky: Scotland, or the culture of origin; corporate culture, or the culture of production; and drinkers' culture, or the culture of consumption. But for convenience we will treat the categories as though they were separate.

THE CULTURE OF ORIGIN: SCOTLAND

To write in general terms about the culture of any nation is to lay oneself open to criticism; to do so at less than book length requires omissions and abbreviations which will open the door to criticism – especially in a country such as Scotland, whose history is the object of so much feeling. My only apology for what follows is that the book would be incomplete without it, and that it may be of value to those for whom it is intended, namely those readers who have no special knowledge of Scottish history or society and who wish to acquire a little, the better to appreciate their whisky.

So what do you need to know about Scotland and the Scots, which is relevant to your whisky? In the most general terms: how whisky arose in the society; what sort of society it arose in; how both society and whisky changed and how each influenced the other; how we got to where we are to day; and where we are today.

When whisky first makes its appearance on the stage of documented history, in the late fifteenth century, it is to a mongrel people. Two, maybe more, waves of Celtic invaders have overrun the ancient dwellers in the land; Anglians from the south and Norsemen from the north have each contributed their genetic

The legendary martial prowess of the Highlander, here depicted at the battle of Killiecrankie, became an integral part of many a brand image

material, and the whole has been overlaid by a French-speaking aristocracy of Norman origin. Racially, they are a gangrel bunch, and they spend a lot of time killing each other, but from very early times they seem to have had a strong awareness of a common identity. This probably owed something to their neighbours, the English, who were just as mean but a lot bigger.

The Scots are a social mixture as well as a racial one. In the country of one Friar Cor, who is the first person known to have distilled malt spirit, feudalism overlay Celtic tribal society. The military aristocracy of the Norman-French incomers fitted well enough into Viking-Celtic customs, which were mostly to do with slaughter, but found it difficult to displace the social assumptions on which the latter society was based. Feudal society was a socially polarised society: a hereditary aristocracy on the one hand and serfdom on the other. The serf was legally the property of his master, who had power of pit and gallows over him. Clan society appears to have been in some respects similar: the chief was (relatively) rich and the clansman definitely poor; the clansman had the right to get subsistence from the land (or at least his womenfolk did) and in return had to give military service. The difference lay in the assumptions on which the society was based. Feudal domination came by right of conquest: the serfs were the remnants of a defeated people. The clan was more like a family: every member of the clan was believed to be descended from a common ancestor and therefore the meanest clansman was a blood relation to the chief. His allegiance was voluntary and enthusiastic; he gloried in the magnificence of his chief because it reflected upon him; an insult to his chief was an insult to him. There was a strange sort of equality and a lot of fighting.

Scotland is divided into Highlands and Lowlands. The mountains begin a little north of the Forth-Clyde valley. At the time of which we speak, there were no roads and a few tiny towns. The climate was rotten: cold and wet, and the only grains which would grow readily on the poor soils were oats and barley. When whisky first appears in the Exchequer Roll of the Scottish Court in 1492, the Lowlands are mostly Scots-speaking and feudal; the Highlands Gaelic-speaking and the land divided among many clans, who hold it by ancient custom supplemented by force of arms. The Crown resides in Linlithgow and the effectiveness of central government depends on who wears the Crown. Relations with the neighbours (the English) are mostly bad, which means war, which the English mostly win.

The whisky – or *aqua vitae*, as it is described – is made by monks, who at the time are the only group possessing the requisite technology. It is distilled in a copper alembic from ale made from bere, which was fermented by wild yeasts. It is probably used for medicinal purposes. If it is taken as a drink – there is no evidence either way – it is probably better stuff than it will be after the monasteries are dissolved in the following century. Monastic technology was far in advance of contemporary secular methods and the monks did themselves rather well – whence their downfall and replacement by the reformed kirk, a theoretically democratic theocracy, of which the less said, the better. Whisky continued to be distilled through the seventeenth century, and people evidently began to drink the stuff, though it probably was none too pleasant.

By the time whisky begins to be seen as a peculiarly Scottish thing, in the later eighteenth century, society has changed enormously, though you can discern the old ways within it. The dominant group is an educated middle class whose values and aspirations are aristocratic but whose lifestyle is not. Society is still stratified, but social mobility has become accepted and the highest ranks are open to energy and ability. Clan society has been destroyed in the wake of the '45 Rebellion. It survives, however, in the values of the people and in heroic myth.

We know that whisky was being used as a drink by the seventeenth century: the imposition of the Excise makes that clear, as do references to domestic stills in legal reports and rent rolls. We know that it was regarded by the people as their property in the eighteenth century: Duncan Forbes of Culloden has become a popular hero by having his distillery at Ferintosh burnt by the Jacobites. By way of compensation, the Government gave him exemption from duty for all whisky distilled from grain grown on his estate – an exemption but recently ended when Burns wrote: 'For loyal Forbes' chartered boast / Is ta'en awa'.'

Whisky was the drink of the common people of Scotland. The gentry drank wine and brandy. In the eighteenth century, an association between popular culture and whisky developed which has never entirely disappeared and which has been in large measure responsible for the recovery of malt whisky from obscurity in our own day. It is an association which, it has to be said, is little represented in the distillers' version of the heritage of whisky. The assumptions of fundamental equality and liberty which underlay Celtic society re-emerged as an element in the popular political radicalism of the later eighteenth century. When he wrote 'A man's a man for a' that', Burns expressed a sentiment which, while it was common to reform-minded people, found in Scotland a society to which the idea was not new, as it was, say, in France. What is more, it had its roots in popular attitudes and customs. Even in their drink, the Scots spoke of liberty. Burns again: 'Freedom and whisky gang thegither.'

The whisky of which he spoke was very different from what we drink today. Burns would have known two sorts of malt spirits, referred to as *usquebaugh* and *aqua vitae* – the 'water of life' in Gaelic and Latin respectively. *Aqua vitae* meant

In the eighteenth century, whisky would have been produced on stills such as this.

what we would today call malt whisky; *usquebaugh* was whisky flavoured with herbs. Thomas Pennant, in 1772, says that on Islay 'in old times the distillation was from thyme, mint, anise and other fragrant herbs.' The straight malt spirit was thought to be better for the health and the use of the term *usquebaugh* – or, rather, its anglicised form 'whisky' – eventually changed to mean unflavoured spirit.

Whisky was a domestic affair: every substantial house had the right to distil its own whisky for consumption by the people associated with the house. In a pre-dominantly rural society – which is how things were until halfway through the nineteenth century – the brewing of ale and its distilling into whisky was an important way of using agricultural surpluses. Grains which were unfit for consumption could be fermented and distilled, thereby converting waste into consumable foodstuffs. The people drank whisky as part of their ordinary diet; it was really only with the advent of large-scale urbanisation that drunkenness came to be seen as a serious social evil and alcoholic liquors to be stigmatised.

The later eighteenth century saw in Scotland a particularly brilliant flowering of the pan-European phenomenon known as the Enlightenment. It was essentially a middle-class matter in Scotland, though one in which, because the lower classes were literate, was not restricted by class as it was elsewhere. The result was a flowering of genius difficult to parallel in any small country save perhaps Greece of the fifth century BC. It was a most convivial age, in which hard drinking was usual among men and not uncommon among women. What today we would describe as café society was the norm in all of Scotland's towns and cities: people met in taverns to conduct their business and their pleasure. The stories are legion, of how drinking on an heroic scale was integral to the fabric of civil society: of how, for example, in the High Court in Edinburgh, the judge would mount the bench of a morning, having laid down his whisky glass a few hours before; of how he would hear pleas by legal counsel who had done likewise, and give judgment between parties to a cause, who also had been at the bottle well into the morning – sometimes all in the same tavern. What is noticeable and impressive, is that everyone conducted their business in a perfectly decorous manner.

With the nineteenth century came the rise of industrial society and a British empire in which Scotland was the foremost colony. Colonial status would have been fiercely denied by the Scots of the time, who saw themselves as partners – if not-quite equal ones – in that great enterprise. They were, however, a colonised nation by all of the usual indices of such things. Their indigenous values were subverted and replaced by others more appropriate to their colonial status. The marks of nationhood were supplanted or replaced and new icons of Scottishness usurped genuine traditions. This was the period in which were adopted many of the signs by which Scotland is recognised today: the short kilts and the clan tartans were invented and made to serve as icons of Scottishness. So was the (blended) whisky.

Scots throughout the world, having embraced an alien polity, would cling to those vestiges of identity. We find them today in North America, in Australia, in Hong Kong, in England: people who once or twice a year will dress up in what they fancy is Scottish dress, to celebrate at Burns or St Andrew's night, what they fancy is Scottish culture. And they will do it by drinking what they fancy is the authentic Scottish spirit – made and supplied by the authentically Scottish supranational conglomerate corporation.

The funny thing is that this is an authentic culture, for the simple reason that anything people do is authentic culture. It is even, in a sense, an authentically Scottish culture, for it is a culture inhabited by people who regard themselves as Scottish. Unless we are to erect some canon of what is and is not Scottish – an extremely un-Scottish thing to do – we cannot gainsay it.

The rise of British imperialism and the rise of blended whiskies went closely together. The Empire supplied the markets and the ideology; the distillers supplied the product: liquor in bottle which wouldn't go off in the hold of a ship or in a tropical climate. Colonisation involved the subversion of the values of the colonised society and their replacement by those of the colonial power. The Scots took an enthusiastic part in this, doing to the Indians and others what had been done to them a century or so before. That is why upper-class Indians today sound as though they have been to Eton and drink whisky. So, of course, do upper-class Scots.

Whisky was the British gentleman's drink in the latter half of the nineteenth century, and therefore of half the world, for the world took many of its values from the greatest imperial power. (France, Germany and the USA didn't: they were rival imperialists and their liking for whisky developed mostly after Britain had ceased to be a serious player in the imperial stakes.) The whisky was blended whisky: malt never had the prominence of the great blend brands and after 1908 it disappeared from view altogether. Everyone thought blended whisky was great because it was British, and drank it with ice and soda – so it didn't much matter whether it was good or not.

Some of it was definitely not good, and by the 1960s, whisky had ceased to be regarded as high-class liquor. Once again, chaps in their after-dinner armchairs would drink cognac from their balloons. They would put the stuff in absurdly large glasses and savour it, a treatment they would never think of according whisky. No one drank anything but blended whisky and everyone believed all the whisky experts who told people that the only sort of whisky worth drinking was blended whisky. Even the people who ran the whisky industry believed it, despite the fact that both malt and grain whiskies were very different from what they had been when blends were invented and the original rationale for blending had disappeared.

That was the state of things when in 1963 William Grant began to export Glenfiddich malt whisky. David Grant said, 'There were many in the industry who were only too happy to tell us that there was no market for malt south of the Scottish border.' Happily, they were wrong, and Glenfiddich pioneered a trail which many followed. It was a time in Scotland when a new generation, which had been brought up on the tired kilts-and-tartans imagery of their national culture, were awakening to the reality beneath the kitsch, and finding that reality much more to their liking. The main vector of this was the folk-song movement, which tapped into a popular song culture which had simply never gone away. It had its roots in mediaeval ballads; it had survived through the centuries because it came from the people and expressed their beliefs, their ideals and their desires.

*Men in funny clothes (1):
The Victorians invented customs
to fit an imaginary Highland
heritage.*

Men in funny clothes (2): Highlandry meets dress-wear hire in the service of bad whisky.

There came about a revival in Scottish culture which is still with us today and whose culmination at the end of the twentieth century is surely the re-establishment of the Scottish Parliament: a new sang for an old nation.

Whisky was part of this whole movement. From the 1960s onward, there has been a gentle movement among the people, not to embarrass those who cling to kitsch, but to replace it with an awareness of the authentic. There has been a huge explosion of the study and writing of Scottish history. History has become – as it was two hundred years ago – a national pastime. Scottish music has resurrected ancient forms – and combined them with rock. One could go on at length. The essence of the movement has been the resurrection of the real from under a century or so of pastiche. Malt whisky began to be rediscovered by the Scots in the 1960s. By the 1970s, the Glenfiddich initiative was beginning to pay off and other malt distillers had joined in. Malt began to be known beyond the Scottish border and to be valued for its own sake.

Malts have become the new icons of the new Scotland. They are a source of national self-respect: not the strutting, bombastic pride of colonial times, but something more appropriate to the dignity of a small nation which, if it is to make its way in a new century, must do so on the basis of real worth.

THE CULTURE OF PRODUCTION: THE SCOTCH WHISKY INDUSTRY

Most of what most people know about whisky is derived from advertising of one kind or another. Beyond the Scottish border, few folk have any connection with whisky except in a bottle, and most of them know nothing about Scotland. For many whisky drinkers, indeed, most of what they know about Scotland comes from whisky adverts. This is a deplorable state of affairs for, as we all know but tend to forget, the only object of an advertisement is to sell things. Therefore what most whisky drinkers get to know about whisky and its country of origin is what whoever pays for the advertising wishes them to know.

If you are to appreciate whisky, in the meaning of 'appreciate' which we have been pursuing, you must be able to separate what is true about your dram from what is false. You can do this with regard to what is said by advertisers only if you know something about the people who pay for the advertisements and why they do it. That means knowing about the whisky distillers, their marketing policies and the methods which they use to sell their product.

The first thing which you, as consumer, ought to understand, is the nature of brand marketing. In a global marketplace, very few commodities are sold on the basis of rational choices made by the consumer, in full knowledge of the costs and benefits of alternative purchasing decisions. When the science of economics began – in Scotland in the eighteenth century – it was thought that people would consciously seek their own greatest good when buying in an open market. We now know that that is not the case. Brand marketing is based on the irrationality of the consumer. Its method is to create a subconscious value which will influence choice at the moment of purchase. That is what advertising campaigns are about: to generate a good feeling about a product. It doesn't matter whether the product is any good or not; nor does it matter whether the good things in the advertisement bear any relation to the product; all that matters is that the consumer should be left with a favourable impression of the goods for sale. We all know that this is effective, because we are all subject to its influence. But we are all capable of stepping outside that influence and thinking about what we do. That is what this book is for.

Whisky brand marketing has in the past tended to split between malts and blends. Blends are sold by means of admass techniques and promotional activities which rarely make mention of what the stuff tastes like. The object is to build the brand: that is, to generate in the public mind an image favourable to the brand. Malts bring the public closer to the idea of rational choice, in that flavour is a consideration: the idea that the whisky is pleasant to drink has a place in adverts for malt whiskies.

Many malt whiskies now make a point of telling us what the contents of the bottle taste like, in the form of tasting notes. At the time of writing, Aberlour has a range of seven malts, from ten to thirty years old, whose promotional material makes extensive use of tasting notes. As regards those of the range which I have tasted, I can say that the notes are pretty accurate. The route taken by Glenmorangie, of telling us not only how the whiskies taste, but how they are matured to achieve that taste, is to be commended. Whatever your opinion of finishing as a maturation technique, the mere fact of a company's laying its wares so transparently before the consumer is laudable.

Where advertising campaigns make any reference to quality or origins, heritage and tradition are by far the most common themes. The heritage message is that Scotland is a country rich in colourful and desirable tradition and that whisky is an integral part of that tradition. That, as it happens, is true. The implication, that all Scotch whisky is made in purely traditional ways by purely traditional people,

Men in funny clothes (3):
Heritage in advertising whisky.

is not true – though as we know from previous chapters, departure from tradition does not necessarily mean less good whisky. Some of the adverts are tolerably close to the truth, and these are often the most effective. Not the ones about mermaids at Bowmore, naturally – which are bizarre and embarrassing – but Glenmorangie's Fourteen Men of Tain series, which is pretty close to the mark: the distillery is indeed run by a small number of local people, most of whom live in Tain, an ancient Royal Burgh close by. The company, on the other hand, is run from a large warehousing complex in the Lowlands, where its head offices lie – but that does not devalue the claim about the distillery.

Most of today's malt whisky brands began as small farm-based enterprises, but industrial-scale production plants for both malt and grain spirit were in use by the close of the eighteenth century. The vicissitudes of trade and the economy forced amalgamations in the nineteenth century and into the twentieth, without which there probably would not now be a Scotch whisky industry on any scale – and you would be without your favourite dram. The Scotch whisky industry today presents a picture of astonishing diversity. On the one hand, there is Diageo, the biggest liquor company on the planet, whose interest in United Distillers and Vintners (UDV) makes it responsible for more than half of all Scotch whisky produced and sold. On the other, there are companies which are owned and run by the members of a single family.

There are still three family-owned companies: Glenfarclas, Springbank and William Grant & Sons. The first two are small; the third medium-sized in whisky industry terms, which means respectably large by other, less gargantuan, standards. John Grant, managing director of Glenfarclas, reminds one of the whisky barons of a former age. Incisive, convivial and hugely energetic, he travels the world, selling his product. He does so with the conviction of a man who knows that his malt is unsurpassed for quality, and with an urgency born of knowing how many people in Ballindalloch depend on his efforts for their livelihood. Down at Springbank, the folk in Campbeltown know exactly what his problems are. They too have a small distillery which has been in the family for as long as anyone can remember. They too have to survive by making and selling malt whisky in a highly competitive environment in which the big corporations have all the advantages of scale. Both distilleries make fabulously fine whisky: malt connoisseurs the world over give thanks for their efforts and hope they may continue to thrive.

William Grant & Sons (no relation to John, save that all are descended from the great Clan Grant) own two malt distilleries: side-by-side sit the Glenfiddich and the Balvenie. Both make first-class malt, but on a scale much larger than either Glenfarclas or Springbank. William Grant went into the blended whisky business a hundred years ago with their Grant's Standfast: so successful have they been that in 1963 they were able to build Girvan grain distillery, still today the largest of the grain whisky distilleries. Grant's is by any standards a substantial concern, but two things are noticeable about it: it remains a private company, and the descendants of the founders still run the show. These things might not be surprising in Germany or Italy; they are uncommon in Britain.

Life is tough for a middle-sized whisky company, for it must compete in the same world markets as the big guys: not for it the little niches which can be occupied by Glenfarclas or Springbank. What they lack in strength in the global arena, however, they make up for in intelligent strategy. Unlike a public corporation, a family company can decide not to pay dividends and its directors have the security which gives them an incentive to invest its profits in far-sighted projects. They can also take the long view as regards product quality: not for them the quick buck necessary to meet parent-company targets or to placate institutional shareholders. Public companies of a middling size, such as Glenmorangie plc, are in possibly the most difficult position, that is, squeezed by the big guys, but without the freedom of movement of the independents.

One would imagine that the larger the company, the more it would be able to plan ahead, given its greater resources. In some respects that is certainly true: the financial muscle of the multinational corporation enables it to invest in plant and to develop markets which are well beyond the capability of most private companies. Against this, however, must be set the nature of the beast and its relationship with its people. Public companies are staffed and led by people who, in the UK at least, have as their principal objective their own advancement. Since most executives retire in their sixties – and some earlier – the programme which best serves the aims of an individual's career is not necessarily that which best promotes the welfare of the organisation. The Scotch whisky industry has had no shortage of directors of public companies whose commitment and loyalty have been as great as those of the members of a family firm. But we live in an era of vast conglomerates. The maximisation of shareholder value or the short-term demands of the market all too often results in the overnight disappearance of a brand which has taken a century to grow. Such things do not promote loyalty or vision.

Indeed, what is surprising in the circumstances, is how well the whisky industry is served by its people – the people who make the whisky and the folk in its ancillaries from barley supply to sales management. In the last few years, I have spent a lot of time going round distilleries, speaking with the managers and the stillmen, the coopers and the brewers and the blenders and the salesmen. What has struck me most forcibly has been the devotion to the product which all of these folk evince. Without exception, what they care about is making and selling really fine whisky. Whether it is a small malt distillery or a large grain plant, everyone takes the greatest pride in what he or she does. Each outfit tends to have its own ways of doing things, so there is plenty of variation, but everyone will tell you with pride what makes their plant or product unique. One cannot help but feel that the people who make Scotch whisky, and who sell it, deserve top management better than they get.

In a milieu in which heritage is the principal value, all three of the family-owned companies have a great luxury: they can afford to be truthful. They can feature their people in their promotions without straining credibility, for there is not the stratification which is found in large companies: the people who make the whisky are well known to the people who sell it and the folk who run the company. Marketing and production can therefore be integrated in a way which is uncommon in a big public company. There is no great cultural divide either, and it is not uncommon to find one of the owners of the distillery being addressed, by his first name, by a man with a shovel. I have seen this: it was done with respect but not deference and it put me in mind of nothing so much as a clansman addressing his chief.

You won't find much of that in the big corporations. In that part of the Scotch whisky industry which is owned by supranational conglomerates – UDV (which owns Johnnie Walker. J&B, the Classic Malts and half the whisky industry), Seagram (which owns Glenlivet and Chivas), Allied-Domecq (which owns Ballantine's and Laphroaig) – a separation is evident between the people who make the whisky, those who sell it and those who run the companies. What I have said about the people who make the cratur is as true of those folk who work for a conglomerate as it is of the others. Indeed, at the level of production, co-operation rather than competition is the rule, and one distillery will borrow a part from another, though their respective marketing departments are at daggers drawn. The marketing departments of big companies are staffed by people who are professionals in the matter of marketing. For them Scotland is merely a commodity value, to be exploited in any way they can. Their responsibility is to sales and sales alone; their culture is the culture of the company. Small wonder, then, that when heritage-oriented marketing campaigns go awry, they usually belong to big companies. The people who make the whisky inhabit a culture which is that of the Scottish nation: no doubt about that. But the executives of big corporations inhabit a culture which is created by the corporation. Corporations inhabit the culture of international capitalism. The last is much the most powerful and I am sorry to say that the big-company sector of the Scotch whisky industry now is dominated by it. We would find their use of heritage as a way of selling whisky more convincing if they showed any real appreciation of heritage other than as an instrument for the generation of profit.

The small and medium-sized companies are more integrally *Scottish* than any of the big ones, principally because their top management inhabit the same Scottish culture as the rest of the company. William Grant, through one or other of its brands, is the sponsor of a whole raft of initiatives and awards in Scottish public life. So is the Macallan. If you appreciate your whisky because it is Scottish, then the drams you will get from companies such as those will have a particularly fine savour.

Those of us who care about such things have been much cheered by recent events at Highland Distilleries. Highland, who own the Macallan, Highland Park and numerous other distilleries as well numerous brands such as The Famous Grouse and Black Bottle, had been vulnerable to takeover by one of the mega-corporations. Had that been the case, the company would have ceased to be meaningfully Scottish. So a lot of people raised a cheer when the new owners were announced to be a partnership between William Grant & Sons Ltd on the one hand, and the Edrington Trust on the other. That is the sort of development which can do nothing but good for Scotland and for whisky, and we hope they prosper.

THE CULTURE OF CONSUMPTION: WHISKY DRINKERS

There was a time when just about everyone in Scotland drank whisky – or at least all of what were called the common people. Elizabeth Grant describes how her aunt said to a small child who had just been offered whisky, 'My goodness, child, doesn't it *bite* you?' 'Ay, but I like the bite,' replied the creature. Whisky was a common currency, a recreation, a solace, an anaesthetic. It was the medium of celebration at weddings and of consolation at wakes. My recollection of family funerals is of funeral meats washed down with glasses of Haig. Nobody ate much of the collations, but they did justice to the Haig. I remember, in the company of various uncles and cousins, dropping my grandfather on the stair, thanks to the Haig. Since Grandfather was in his coffin at the time it did him no harm, but the incident – particularly the hilarity which accompanied it – was viewed with disfavour by some of my aunts.

My favourite account of funeral potations comes from Easter Ross. Anne Gordon tells how the Cromarty joiner, having made a coffin, set off up the glen to deliver it, together with nine mourners. They stopped on the way for a dram. Then 'he dealt with the kisting, then had supper and a dram; then attended worship and had a dram; then went out for a smoke and had another dram. He was put up for the night at a nearby house, but before settling down, had a toddy. He was up at seven o'clock the next day and when a visitor or mourner was seen approaching the house, he was brought in and everyone had a dram. Then they had breakfast and a dram, followed by another dram. They all went to the house where the body lay and had a dram, saw to things, took a walk and newsed with people coming to the funeral, then began serving out whisky, bread and cheese.' All this, notice, before the funeral. The drinking began later. And notice, too, that none of these people were what we would now call alcoholics. Whisky was part of their way of life, and they were long-lived and stalwart.

It is the despair of the distillers that the young no longer drink whisky in the British Isles. In Scotland, people under thirty are more likely to take designer drugs than they are to take whisky. In the Glasgow conurbation as in places like Fraserburgh, once-exotic drugs have replaced whisky, both in the preferences of the wayward young and in the homilies of the censorious old. The culture, however, shows admirable continuity: being young is a miserable business and if you are stuck in a dead-end housing estate or a fishing port on the grey edge of the North Sea, you ameliorate it how you can. It is all a matter of values and concepts. Bourbon, which is not so dissimilar to whisky, is undergoing a vogue in the UK at the moment – while it is in decline in the US. Images of old southern boys in dungarees are thought of as attractive to the urban youth of Scotland, being associated with blues and guitar-picking. The same images in their place of origin are regarded as merely banal. For the same reasons, guys in kilts are thought prosaic in Fraserburgh but exotic in Barcelona.

The one consolation the distillers have is that people get older and as they do, they turn to whisky. If they survive the drugs, that is. In English-speaking countries at least, whisky seems to be a drink of maturity – or at least of age. It is very rare to find anyone aged under thirty who likes even malt whisky. Yet in recent years, in France, Spain, Greece and other European countries, as well as in those on the Pacific Rim, whisky has become fashionable among the young. It may just be fashion, in both cases, though that seems a bit thin as a hypothesis.

With the growth of single malts over the last twenty years, a division has become apparent, between those who drink blended whiskies and those who prefer malts. The people who drink blends are in the great majority, around 95 per cent. If they think of malt whisky drinkers at all, which few of them probably do, it is as posy and effete. Malt whisky drinkers, on the other hand, tend to have very definite views about the majority, mostly to the effect that they are persons who have yet to receive the benefit of enlightenment which will reveal to them the true, the blushful, etc. Whether this is justified depends on what were the formative influences. Those of us brought up on popular blends in the 1960s and 1970s, have good reason for preferring malts. Those who came to their whisky later have less justification, since the blended whiskies were for the most part much improved by that time.

I have noticed that in a number of countries, there are people who, regarding themselves as connoisseurs of single malts, will refuse to drink blended whiskies. I cannot think of anyone I know in Scotland who takes such an attitude. There is clearly a cultural difference, probably to do with lifestyle choice: people seek to differentiate themselves from the mass by adopting a minority value. By drinking only malt, they declare their superiority. It's a point of view, but not one supportable by any reference to taste. It is an attitude which tends to go together with a collecting-for-the-sake-of-collecting attitude to malts. That is, one which divorces its object from its natural context and raises canons of excellence which are not found in the world. However, there's room on earth for ilka wean, as Hamish Henderson wrote, and we should meet intolerance with toleration where our favourite drink is concerned.

TASTING WHISKY

What follows is about using what you know about whisky to appreciate it. You have the information: now is the time to use what you know to acquire or develop your ability to evaluate. This chapter is a practical guide to whisky tasting. With any luck, by using it, you will enhance your ability to discriminate: between different whiskies, and among the flavours you will find within a single malt. The final chapter, Appreciations, consists of a few short essays about whiskies and whisky companies. Its aim is to bring together some disparate perceptions and evaluations into what I hope we may call appreciation.

THE TASTING SESSION

How you approach whisky, or any other liquor, depends on what you want to do. People drink whisky for a lot of different reasons and an approach which is suitable for one, won't do for another. It is my business in this book to help you get the most out of your dram, so in what follows I will try to show you how best to taste it, irrespective of why you drink the stuff. You should be warned that none of the boundaries are fixed and things are rarely black or white.

There was a time when the only people who tasted whisky were the blenders. In past times – despite the rhetoric of the adverts – a lot of blending seems to have been a pretty slap-dash business. Nowadays, though, it is very well organised. No wonder, given the capital value of successful brands. However, whisky tasting has moved out of the laboratory. Now lots of people taste whisky. Within the industry, tasting is about the assessment of spirit, whether for bottling malts or for blending. The organised tasting of whiskies for enjoyment is a thing created by amateurs, which the whisky industry took a god ten years to latch onto. (I can say this with some confidence, having been one of those responsible for the creation of whisky tasting as something done for enjoyment and instruction.)

Obviously, recreational tasting is likely to be done differently from professional tasting. In the distillery or the blending hall, tasting is about the

objective assessment of the characteristics of a batch of spirit, either with a view to its being bottled as representative of the malt, or for inclusion in a blend. The batch is measured against a standard and consistency is paramount, for the end of the process is that the customer should be unable to discern any variation between different batches: the whisky tasted under the brand name today must taste exactly the same as the bottle purchased last week.

In tasting for pleasure, there isn't usually so much concern for strict objectivity. Since pleasure is subjective, it matters not whether what the taster thinks is there, really is there: all that is required is that the tasting produces a pleasurable sensation. Since smell is so closely linked to emotion, it is quite easy to produce an agreeable sensation by suggestion – a device which has at least cheapness to recommend it. If you doubt this, I can assure you from long practice that if you tell tasters that a certain aroma is present – and if you do it with enough authority – they will smell what you describe. They won't just think they smell it, you understand, they really will smell it.

However, there are other pleasures to be got than passive enjoyment. Enjoyment allied to knowledge and understanding is what appreciation means. That is our object in the objective tasting of whiskies.

ANALYTIC AND SYNTHETIC TASTINGS

There are two quite different approaches to whisky tasting. On the one hand, analytic tasting, whose aim is an objective assessment of a sample of spirit; on the other, what I think we may call synthetic tasting, whose purpose and technique are convivial. Analytic tasting of Scotch whisky is not new. Since people began to appreciate that there was a difference between good and bad whisky – probably some time toward the end of the eighteenth century – someone had to say which was which. With the advent of blending and the mass-marketing of whisky beyond the Scottish borders in the 1860s, there was a need for some form of organised quality assurance. Blenders sought not only quality but consistency, so that the whisky taster became a person of some importance in a chain of production and consumption which, if it began in a barley field in Buchan, might end in a glass in Bengal.

Synthetic whisky tasting is of much more recent origin. It is about putting words to flavours – but in a spirit quite different from the analytic approach. If you use your imagination, you can go beyond the mere attaching of verbal labels, to descriptions which convey more complex ideas. Our language is not rich in words to do with smell and taste. To take descriptions of taste beyond the mundane, one must use metaphor. The problem with metaphorical expressions is that they can get out of hand. The flight of fancy must be restrained by the tether of discretion. (A couple of good metaphors there.) Otherwise you end up with the sort of wine connoisseurs' hyperbole which has brought tasting notes into disrepute and everyone thinks you're a poser. The whole thing started with the Scotch Malt Whisky Society, which is described in the next chapter.

The Scotch Malt Whisky Society was (and still is) basically a mail-order firm which sold single-cask bottlings of malt whisky. Because no one had done anything like that before, and because each bottling was different, we needed some way of telling prospective buyers what the whisky tasted like. So we hit on the idea of using wine tasters' terminology and writing tasting notes to guide members of the Society in their purchases.

This is where the metaphors come in. I had figured that the best way to write such notes was to have half a dozen of my pals sit round a table, taste the whisky and talk about it. The members of the group were both literate and knowledge-able about whisky, so not only did we have a good time, but the descriptions of the whiskies which emerged in the course of the evening were both accurate and illuminating, if occasionally fanciful. I took notes, and usually wrote up the tasting notes after the gang had left, while still under the influence.

From such beginnings, there grew an activity which seems to have taken on a life of its own. Whisky tasting has become *sui generis* and, for people around the world, the business of tasting whisky and describing the tastes found, has become an absorbing pastime. It has also become an important instrument for marketing malt whisky.

Tasting for fun is different from just drinking, though naturally the one may merge into the other, and often does. However, in so far as it is tasting, part of the fun lies in the interest of the liquor. So some of the conditions and the techniques applicable to analytic tasting are required. How far one goes along that road depends on what balance is required between interest and mere drinking. In what follows, I have set out the requirements for straight analytic tasting. How you adapt them is up to you. It is worth remarking, though, that many of the desiderata of analysis (such as proper glasses, good water, intelligent company, etc.) are also highly conducive to synthetic tasting.

At this point, I should perhaps make clear just why I use the term 'synthetic'. I don't mean ersatz, as opposed to real. I am thinking rather of the philosophical or dialectical sense of 'synthetic' in which synthesis is a resolution of disparate or contradictory elements into a whole which is more than the sum of its parts. Given a few bright people who like each other and enjoy each other's company, tasting whisky can be a most rewarding experience. Each brings to the tasting his own experience and ideas, each sparks off the others, and the result of the sparking and the liquor is to produce descriptions which transcend mere individuality.

Before we get around to tasting any spirit, we must look at the conditions in which the tasting takes place, for those conditions will affect how well and how accurately we shall be able to taste the whisky.

THE TASTING ROOM

We begin with the room in which the tasting is to take place. It should, as far as possible, be odour-free. That means no smells coming in through the windows, no smoke lingering from the previous occupants, and above all, no furniture polish. I remember a tasting which had been elaborately set up by an assistant, with whisky samples, glasses, spittoons, water and notepads, all on the gleaming mahogany of the boardroom table, ready and waiting for the tasters and a few important guests to taste the whisky. Unfortunately, the gleam on the tabletop had been produced by Susie, our industrious cleaner, who used a beeswax polish scented with lavender. We had to abandon the whole thing – and when the lot was transferred to a dingy, but odour-free storeroom, we found that the glasses had picked up so much of the lavender that they had to be washed.

While on the subject of extraneous odours, it is worth remarking that the tasters, too, must be devoid of odour. Personal perfumes and deodorants are banned: not only because they interfere with the perceptions of the other tasters, but the person wearing them is likely to be odour-blind in those scents which are used in the perfume. If anyone is so naturally aromatic that they really need such stuff, they must just be excluded. Smelly feet and armpits carry odours which are often to be found in whisky, and we can't have perfectly good spirit being condemned because one of the tasters resembles a rodent.

Glasses must be perfectly clean: recently washed and properly rinsed. (Most detergents are detectable even in quite low concentrations and must be excluded.) Glasses should be air dried in a place free from odours and polished with a cloth ditto.

Water must be provided: a jug for each taster. The purpose of the water is twofold: it is for diluting the whisky, and for sniffing to counter the effects of habituation. With whisky as with any other odour, the nose very quickly becomes acclimatised and must be refreshed. Doing this is quite simple: you just stick your snout into the water jug and take several deep breaths. If you haven't tried this before, you will be astonished at the difference it makes: aromas which had disappeared will once more be apparent.

The water must be still and, as far as possible, tasteless. The presence of chlorine in water does not render it unusable, for chlorine will evaporate completely if the water is left for a few hours in an open jug. However, water which needs to be chlorinated to make it safe, is probably unlikely to be the kind of water you would want to put in your whisky anyway. Chlorinated water is usually found in large urban areas: it comes from water treatment plants and has passed through the kidneys of numbers of our fellows before it gets to us. In the process, it tends to acquire detectable traces of unpleasant-tasting substances, so is unsuitable for whisky, even if it is safe. If the tap water is chlorinated, your best course is to use still, bottled water – but taste the stuff first, for the fact of its being in bottle is no guarantee of the quality of water.

A word of warning here: if you have arranged a tasting in a hotel or the like and have specified bottled water, check to make sure they have given you still water. Hotel staff often think that whisky goes only with the fizzy kind.

Best of all for diluting whisky, is water from the spring which is used to make the whisky. That, however, is perfection, and rarely attainable away from the distillery. We are fortunate in Scotland, in that almost all of our water is of very high quality, so that you can run the stuff straight from the kitchen tap into your glass. I have seen people in Scotland insist on bottled water in their drams, but this is mere affectation. At the time of writing, some friends have recently set up an Internet whisky sales operation called Scotland Direct and are selling Scottish water along with Scotch malt whisky.

The tasting room should be of equable temperature, light and airy. Ventilation should for preference be natural and if air conditioning is used, there should be no perfuming or other treatment of the air. If this seems absurdly obvious, I would say that I know of some prominent hotels whose air conditioning is such as to render serious tasting impossible. *And* the wine lists are expensive. If you are in the happy position of relying on open windows for your air, make sure nobody is going to burn garden refuse or the like. The nose can accommodate some smells, but nobody could taste through odours of the variety and pungency which result from a fire of that sort.

THE TASTERS

First, the nose. There is no point at all in setting up a tasting for people who can't smell. Asking someone who can't smell to taste whiskies is a bit like asking a blind person to judge paintings. People vary greatly in their ability to smell. I remember visiting the Macallan distillery in the days when it was led by the legendary Willie Phillips. Willie had got the tasters to test the entire staff for their olfactory ability – and found that the best nose in the company belonged not, as you might expect, to some hoary stillman, but to a 19-year-old typist.

Some people can't smell at all, and quite a lot not enough to tell the difference between one whisky and another. The condition is surprisingly common. Most folk just have very little experience of using their sense of smell, and can be taught. The main thing is that people should be prepared to reflect on what they are doing when they smell, and judge whether they do it well or not.

Second, experience. The object of tasting whisky is to identify the aromas which come from it. It is axiomatic that you can't refer to smells if you don't know what things smell like. The tasters should have a wide experience of odours. That generally means they should be people who are accustomed to using their noses – in our culture, a rare attribute, and one which is becoming rarer as our environment becomes less odorous. I once lived downwind of a tannery. If you have never smelt a tannery in full production, or a batch of festering hides as they pass the door, you probably won't appreciate quite what I'm talking about. It is an experience which leaves a strong impression, and if, a half a century later, someone says a smell is like a tannery, the sensation will come instantly to mind. But if you live in a nice house where the strongest smell is the stuff used to clean the kitchen floor, and you work in a nice office, the chances are, you won't react to the mention of a tannery in quite the same way.

You can remedy inexperience by teaching people to identify smells. When we run whisky schools, we give people smells in bottles and teach them some of the basics. This is worth doing, if you wish seriously to be able to identify aromas. You may think you know what aniseed smells like and that you can tell it from fennel, but try telling which is which blind, and you may not be quite so sure.

The only sure remedy for lack of experience is experience. If you once become accustomed to using your nose, it is surprising how often, even in today's depleted environment, you will find yourself following an invisible trail of scent. In Edinburgh you can tell which way the wind is blowing, by the smell of malt from the breweries. A century or so ago, there were dozens of distilleries, brewhouses, slaughterhouses and tanneries situated in the closes and wynds of the old town which, together with the practice of discharging of nightsoil into the streets, made for a milieu which was, to put it mildly, interesting from an olfactory point of view.

The smell-in-bottle approach works fine up to a point, however, it is very limited, especially when it comes to complex smells. We can show you what vanilla and almonds smell like, but unless you have eaten – and preferably made for yourself – fresh marzipan, you are unlikely fully to appreciate the aroma of that excellent comestible. (It's not remotely similar to shop marzipan.) One of the best whisky tasters I have known is my friend Ian Revie, who teaches French at the university in Edinburgh. French literature is not an obvious qualification for the job – but Ian is also expert in French cuisine, so he brings to tasting a wealth of experience of odours and tastes, of the most subtle sort.

Smells are – or ought to be – an essential part of living, and the best way of learning is to reflect on experience. For that, besides the experience, you need the habit of reflection. If you have those, the rest will follow.

The third requirement in a taster is to do with language. The taster needs to be literate, or witty, or in some way good with words. Tasting is about putting words to smells. If you don't know the words, you lack an essential tool. Again, we can teach you to be a more-or-less competent taster, but unless you have a feeling for words, you are unlikely to show anything more than competence. I have written earlier about the use – and misuse – of tasting notes. Anyone can come up with daft descriptions, which may amuse for a little, but in the end do nothing. A person who loves his dram, and who has the ability, will be able to transcend the banal and reach for a lyricism worthy of the spirit. I fondly recall David Daiches, presented with a sample of St Magdalene, a distillery which had been destroyed some twenty years before. David looked through his glass, sighed, and said it felt like looking at a distant star, which had exploded millions of years ago, but whose light we still could see. Not precisely a comment on the *goût* of the whisky – but lyrical. Lyrical-meaningful, that is, not lyrical-pretty, which is how some people take the term.

We can't all aspire to be like David, a great Scots scholar, no mean poet and a man to whom Scotland and whisky owe a lot. But we can learn to think in terms which are appropriate to the sublimity of a fine spirit. I would venture to say that only if we are prepared to do so, shall we bring to our drams an attitude which will allow us fully to savour them. Having said that, I should say immediately that I'm not suggesting our attitude should be one of reverence. Or even at all times, seriousness. The stuff is for drinking, after all, and it produces an elevation of spirit in which we can all have at least the impression of our own brilliance. It won't always last to the next morning, but is none the worse for that.

EQUIPMENT

You need the right tools if you are to do the job. The equipment for whisky tasting is pretty simple: whisky, glasses, covers, water jug, spittoon and, naturally, a nose. A mouth comes in handy too, so to speak.

There has been a lot of talk about the perfect glass for whisky tasting, and from time to time the marketing department of one or another whisky company comes up with a new tasting glass whose unique properties uniquely exhibit the unique character of their particular whisky. It's mostly puff, and while the glasses are generally good at doing what they are designed to do, none to my knowledge is better than the traditional nosing glass.

On the subject of traditional glasses, a brief digression may be in order here. For well over a century, the traditional whisky glass was the thing you still see in some of the adverts: a cut-glass short tumbler whose straight sides taper slightly toward the bottom. That sort of glass was used (and still is) for drinking blended whisky. It was used (and still is) by people who took their whisky with ice and mixers. It is fine for what it is intended for, and if you like your Johnnie Walker with green ginger and soda water, it is just the job. But if you want seriously to taste the whisky, that is, if you want to get beyond the general pleasant taste to the interest of the thing, it is no use at all. Any aroma which survives the ice and the soda, will quickly be lost from the open mouth of the glass.

The glass used in the whisky industry for tasting – that is, for nosing – whisky, is a variation on the Spanish sherry glass, or copita. It is a fairly small glass – the amounts needed for tasting are not large – with stem, bowl and narrow mouth. The stem is for picking it up, the bowl for making the spirit move, and the narrow mouth for retaining the whisky-saturated air in the glass. This kind of glass has been universally used for the professional nosing of both malts and blends for a very long time. It works very well, and I think we can conclude that it is best suited to the job.

Some years ago, I had a visit from Georg Riedel, the Viennese glass maker. Riedel make some of the poshest glass in the world and they really know their business. Georg had come to Scotland to look at whisky, and at the possibility of making the definitive nosing glass. We had lunch and a bottle of very good Chablis, which Herr Riedel poured into two of his tall-stemmed goblets, each of which was big enough to contain a half-bottle of wine. The glasses were paper-thin. We drank a toast and clinked our glasses: he enthusiastically, I tentatively, lest the glass should shatter. He laughed and clinked the glasses together again,

Nosing glasses: clear and – for the perfectionist – cobalt.

this time with force enough to make them bounce and ring. He explained that really fine glass, though thin, is very strong.

We set up a tasting of whisky, using one of the specially-designed Riedel glasses, a copita, a cheap copita-based glass which I had designed for everyday use at the Scotch Malt Whisky Society, a glass designed for Bowmore and one ditto for Glenmorangie. Our conclusion was that, though none too convenient for actually drinking the stuff, the copita was easily the best for nosing. There wasn't a lot of difference, though, and all of the others were pretty good.

So a copita it is. There are few things I like better to see than a row of copitas, each with a shot of malt, their colours ranging from pale straw through to dark brown. As the eye runs down the line, one forms a pleasurable expectation of the tastes to come. Now while that is very agreeable, it is exactly the opposite of what you want if there is to be any objectivity in the tasting. I wrote earlier about how the eye is the dominant sense and how what the eye sees can affect what the nose and the palate detect. That is certainly the case with whiskies, and since colour is but a poor guide to taste, it is better that the whisky be not seen at all.

A well-devised whisky tasting will not show the tasters the whiskies at all. There are various ways in which this condition can be achieved. You can do it in the dark or with blindfold tasters, neither of which is convenient. The best course – and the only one for a seriously objective tasting – is to use dark glass, through which the spirit cannot be seen. The glasses used for professional purposes are cobalt blue. They are a lovely colour and a pleasure to look at and, because blue is a colour which almost never occurs naturally in foodstuffs or drinks, they do not produce any expectation whatever.

It may be objected that all the books about whisky which have photographs of professional tasters tasting whisky show them using clear glass. That is certainly true, and clear glass is widely used in the industry. However, the circumstances of professional tasting tend to be rather different from those facing the amateur. The professional will usually taste samples from quite a large number of casks at any given session. The taster will know what sort of casks the whisky has come from, he will be looking for quite specific characteristics, and will assess against a standard. Most of the casks will tend to be similar provenance, and therefore will vary little in colour. Since the main purpose of the tasting is to identify any cask which departs from the norm, the use of clear glass is no disadvantage.

With the growing recognition of malt whiskies as liquor of the highest quality, we have seen malts take the place of brandies in restaurants, where they are

Clear glasses allow the taster to see how the cask has coloured the spirit.

often served in balloon glasses which are used for cognac. Some of these glasses are so absurdly large that a decent shot of malt barely wets the bottom. Such things should be avoided. They have no purpose other than ostentation. Unless you put half a pint in them, the vapours of the spirit cannot reach a concentration appropriate for nosing.

If you are tasting one whisky at a time, there is no need to do anything other than pour the stuff into the glass and sniff. But if a tasting is to be set up in which a number of whiskies may be considered and compared, then some means is required whereby the more volatile aromas are prevented from escaping. The glasses must be covered, and the traditional way of covering them is by using watch glasses. Watch glasses, for those who have not met them, are glass discs which are slightly bowled: the name derives from the bezels of the turnip watches which gentlemen once wore in their waistcoats. If you can't procure watch glasses, anything which can cover the glass will do. Cling film works, though it is not so convenient as a watch glass and looks a bit vulgar.

Spittoons should be provided. While most of what you need to know about a whisky can be got by the nose alone, there are some sensations originating in the mouth which it is desirable to record. In general, the spirit should not be swallowed, but spat into a suitable receptacle. This too ought to be opaque, for expectorate is not pretty to look at.

Most whisky is best tasted with the addition of water, so an open-mouthed jug for water should be provided, one for each taster. The jug can also be used for refreshing the nose when tasting dulls the sense of smell.

Pad and pen are usual where people may wish to record their impressions.

TECHNIQUE

How you approach whisky tasting depends on what you wish to achieve by it. In analytic tasting, we are trying to find out what is there. Not what we may think may be there, but what is actually, objectively, in the whisky. Since, as already discussed, nosing is such a subjective business, the tasting should be set up so as to minimise extraneous influences. Analysis requires isolation, repetition and control; synthetic tasting the reverse: communication, criticism and discussion.

Ideally, analytic tasting should be done in isolation. The taster should have no communication with his fellows and should report his findings in private. Glasses should be poured by an organiser and each glass identified only by a numeral. The taster should record his findings on a sheet against each numeral.

The procedure is generally as follows, with perceptions being recorded on a sheet of paper at each stage.

- Nose the whisky without the addition of water. Some whiskies are best approached in this way. On the whole, the alcohol will render the flavour unapproachable. However, a brief whiff will do no harm. Don't spend a lot of time with your nose in a glass of uncut whisky, though, for the nose will soon become anaesthetised.

- Add a little water and nose. In general, whisky should be inspected at a strength of about 20 per cent alcohol by volume. That means that if you are using a standard-strength whisky, you should put in almost as much water again.

- Nose again – as often as required. There are two ways you can play this. The most volatile compounds in the whisky will evaporate first, so they are the first odours you get. As the nose accommodates to the volatiles, it ceases to register them, so that you are able to see what lies beneath. So there is a case for continuing to nose the whisky continuously over a period of time, say a quarter of an hour. Alternatively, you can rely instead on the progressive evaporation of the more volatile compounds – in which case you can inspect the whisky at intervals. Both methods seem to work pretty well.

- Taste (that is, take by mouth). Only once you are satisfied that you have got all there is to get by nose, should you actually taste the spirit, for once you have done so, you will have interrupted the sequence of odours as they present themselves to the nose.

- Spit. Most decent whiskies have a pronounced aftertaste, which makes itself apparent only once you have cleared the mouth of almost all the spirit.

When nosing a wine or spirit, people tend to keep the mouth closed, the better to ensure that they draw the vapours into the nose. This is a mistake: if you keep your mouth open while nosing, the flow of air through the nasal sinuses is much improved. Try it: nose your whisky first with your mouth closed and then with it open. Open-mouthed, you will find that the flavours are much more pronounced and some may be discernible which before were not.

Spitting is not a common accomplishment these days, nor is it a pastime which meets with much approval. But if you would be a taster with class (in the American sense of the term, denoting style rather than status), then you must know how to spit. I am pleased to say that I went to the sort of elementary school in which spitting was much practised – among the pupils, anyway. I come of a long line of expert spitters, so I soon acquired the rudiments. (My father smoked black twist tobacco in his pipe; my grandfather chewed the stuff; both were spitters of elegance and accuracy.) I must say, though, I never expected to have much use for such a skill. Many years later, having been introduced to professional wine tasting by the wine correspondent of one of the big Sunday newspapers, I found myself – to my surprise – treated with some respect. My hostess explained that the casual but accurate manner of my spit, had been very well-received.

If you are tasting a number of whiskies (see How Whisky Tastes), then the order in which you taste them is important. As you know, if you taste a weak flavour after a strong one, your perception of the weak one will be affected by the contrast. You will probably have some idea of what the whiskies to be tasted are going to be like, in which case you should sort them in ascending order of strength of flavour. If you don't know this, or if you find any whisky adversely affects your nose, then the best course is to pause after each nosing and to take a sniff of your water jug. Simply inhaling the water will clear your olfactory epithelium.

In an analytic tasting, it helps to have by you a list of the flavours you may hope to find. There are hundreds of possible flavours, but the list given on page 41, is a good starting place as regards the basic elements. Each of the basic flavours may be exhibited together with one or more of the basics in a compound flavour – and there are lots of flavours other than the basic, which may show singly or in combination. It doesn't take a lot of thought to appreciate the complexity of possible combinations. It is difficult to systematise the apprehension of these, though the various flavour wheels are a starting point. However, I have serious doubts as to the efficacy of a flavour-wheel configuration and think that on the whole, the best course is to do as suggested earlier, and arm your self with as wide an experience of smells as you can.

Synthetic tasting is a lot more fun, and no less effective. If you assemble a company of lively individuals, all of whom already know a fair bit about food and drink, this can be both amusing and informative. I generally appoint one person to take notes and act as chairman, for their needs to be someone who can keep order. The bottle is handed round and everyone pours a dram. Everyone then noses it and whoever is first moved to say what he or she smells, does so. The others agree or disagree. (It is important to have independently-minded people, to counter the effects of suggestibility.) The stages are the same as for an analytic tasting, but there is a lot more discussion and – in the course of time – hilarity. The chairman's job is to write down what the others say and to try to keep the show on the rails. It isn't an easy job, but it is essential if the thing is not to degenerate into drunkenness and anarchy. Now you may think that the best course is not to have the sort of people who are liable so to deteriorate – but the best folk for a synthetic tasting are exactly the sort of people who are liable to get out of hand. It doesn't work with serious, sober folk. Believe me, I've tried it, though not for long.

APPRECIATIONS

MALT DISTILLERS: BOWMORE

I have a photograph of Bowmore on my wall. The main street of the little island town is not long: it runs down from the curious, round church with the conical roof, to the harbour and Loch Indaal: to walk it will take you all of five minutes. To the left, as you come to the harbour, is the distillery, nestling against the sea wall. On the right, the road runs between rows of plain, two-storey, stone-built, slate-roofed houses by the lochside to Bridgend. On the left-hand side, the yards of the houses back onto the sea. Over all, is a vast expanse of sky, marked only by the flight of gulls and oystercatchers, and the curls of peat smoke rising from the chimneys of the houses.

Peat is still the means of heating homes on Islay. The owners of each house have the right to cut peat on the moor. The scent of peat smoke permeates the entire village. It gets into your hair and your clothes; it flavours your food and your drink. So it comes as no great surprise that the whisky made at the distillery should reek of the stuff. They make the malt at the distillery: there is a kiln with a proper pagoda roof, with a fire beneath. The fire is coke, to begin with, but once it is going properly, the fireman throws on top of the coals great black peats, whose smoke soon rises to the malt above – and beyond that, it adds its mite to the perfume of the town.

Bowmore Distillery

153

Bowmore is an old favourite: a consistently well-made whisky, its quality was apparent when David Daiches visited the distillery thirty years ago. The whisky is as good today as it was then, and much more available. David tells the story of how he visited the distillery in 1968. He was doing research for a book which was to be published the following year under the title of *Scotch Whisky, Its Past and Present*. The book is, to my mind, the best thing that has been written about whisky. A work of love and erudition in equal proportion, it was certainly the most important book in the history of the malt revival.

In those days, no one who wasn't in the whisky trade would think of visiting a distillery, and facilities for visitors were non-existent. As a scholar of literature and whisky, David was a rare bird indeed. He was most cordially received, by the distillery owner himself, as befitted such an exotic migrant, and shown the entire process from malting to maturation. The tour ended in the distillery manager's office and of course drams were produced – of a blended whisky, whose principal malt was the Bowmore. David asked very politely whether it would be possible to taste the malt by itself. His request was received with great courtesy and some astonishment. The astonishment increased when he pronounced the single malt a most excellent potation, which provoked the owner of the distillery to ask him seriously whether he really meant that he liked the malt on its own, unblended, as a single malt. When David said yes, he thought it splendid, the owner admitted that he had never thought of drinking Bowmore by itself, unblended!

In case you haven't got the point of this story, let me spell it out. As late as the 1960s, people thought that the only whisky worth drinking was blended whisky. So dominant was this belief that even well-informed persons, whose business it was to make malt whisky, saw malt only in terms of its destiny as part of a blend.

Happily, things have changed for the better. At the time of writing, no fewer than eight different Bowmore bottlings are on offer: Bowmore Legend, which carries no age statement, but is eight years old and bottled at 40%; Bowmore 12, 15, 17, 21, 25 and 30-year-old, all bottled at 43%; and a cask-strength 12-year-old which comes out at 56% alcohol by volume. I tasted these in the company of Jim MacEwan and Tom Mackay. Tom is chief blender for Morrison Bowmore and in charge of the sample room. Jim was for many years the manager of Bowmore distillery and is now a roving ambassador for its products and those of the other whiskies in the MB stable, Auchintoshan and Glen Garioch. The day of my visit is the 36th anniversary to the day of his starting work at Bowmore,

Jim McEwan hard at work at Bowmore

as an apprentice cooper. (I have in my workshop an adze which Jim gave me years ago. I had to go back to him later to get him to show me how to sharpen it properly, and then how to use it.)

Jim is now a most eloquent expositor of the virtues of his whiskies, speaking of them with a lyricism which, if it is sometimes hard to follow, leaves one in no doubt as to his qualification for the job. The whisky industry can have seen few more appropriate appointments than Jim as ambassador.

The Bowmores are all patently part of the same family: variety is contained within a strong underlying identity. We took them – at my suggestion – in order of age. With most malt whiskies, there is an age of maturation at which the product seems most clearly to exhibit the core characteristics. In this case, for my money, the 12-year-old.

The level of peating is consistent throughout – at 20 parts per million – and so are the maturation characteristics. As you would expect, the peat is apparent to a greater extent in the younger whiskies and, while it never disappears completely, in the older bottlings is much muted.

Bowmore is matured in bourbon hogs and oloroso sherry butts, in a proportion of 60% bourbon to 40% sherry. Of the latter, approximately 10% are first-fill and 20% second-fill – the final 10% being old but still good casks. The quality of the casks is uniformly high: the level of activity is such that the youngest, the Bowmore Legend, is to my taste insufficiently mature – but it is a deficiency which is more than compensated by the quality of the distillate. I have tasted Bowmore new spirit on a number of occasions and have never seen fit to alter my first impression, which is that this is a whisky which is good enough to take straight from the still. It follows that I can have no serious objection to it at eight years of age. Indeed, looking at my notes, I see none of the comments I would make on an immature spirit. It is lightly peated and devoid of the sharpness one associates with some underage whiskies. It is sweet, mild and accessible. If it lacks, it is mainly by comparison with its elder brother – or, to use Jim's possibly more appropriate terminology, sister.

Bowmore 12-Year-Old

The 12-year-old is a great whisky. This is a hickory bull in the swelter of summer, come in its great good time to the sultry, biding herds. Bottled at 43%, it shows peat at first, but in better proportion than the younger spirit. With a little water it exhibits the full panoply of fruity flavours and acquires a pepperiness which does no harm either to one's perception of its sweetness or to one's desire to repeat the experience. I would suggest that this be taken as the benchmark against which to measure the older whiskies.

Bowmore 12-Year-Old Cask Strength

There is another 12-year-old, bottled at full cask strength, 56%. It is recognisably the same product but, as is generally the case with full-strength whiskies, easier of access and productive of greater variety of odour. My first impression, curiously, was not of the fish and tar which the peat makes so evident, but of vanilla: like eating an ice cream while up to your neck in kippers. Even so, the quality of the distillate comes through and once the nose adapts to the phenols, it shows a range of fruity flavours.

Bowmore 15-Year-Old

The 15-year-old is a more poised and classy version, using the same basic ingredients. Drinking it is, to extend the metaphor, like watching one's sister change from a dazzlingly pretty girl to a beautiful sophisticate. The qualities are the same; their presentation different.

Bowmore 17-Year-Old

With the 17-year-old, we enter different territory. The direct influence of the peat begins to diminish and the wood begins to show. We now start to see another aspect of the cask quality: at an age at which highly active or inferior casks begin to cause a downturn in quality, we perceive only improvement. This is true of the entire range, for at no point does the whisky become woody. Right up to 30 years of age, at which point it need make no excuses, the spirit shows no trace of the nastiness which for some misguided souls marks maturity. A slight astringency begins to underlie the now-familiar characteristics, and to complement them. It is mild as milk.

Bowmore 21-Year-Old; Bowmore 25-Year-Old; Bowmore 30-Year-Old

I have a problem with superlatives: like sugar, it is easy to overdo them. I thought the 21-year-old a complete star in every respect. The bonny lass of the twelve is now come of age and is an absolute stunner. More of the previous qualities, but arranged to perfection. The 25 by comparison is a disappointment: she seems to have hit a flat patch, as we all do from time to time. But if the gear is good, it is only a matter of time before things get better again. And the 30-

year-old does just that: it moves to a higher plane altogether. This is a five-star whisky. I don't often rate old whiskies highly, as I have said elsewhere, but this is superb. There are no off-notes at all. The only signs of the great age are a little tannin and a great sweetness. I am reminded again of David Daiches, and his 80th birthday party, at which we celebrated the publication of his 44th book, and his first of poetry. He quaffed Bowmore malt in quantity and discoursed with brilliance, with wit and erudition, on Scotland and whisky and Chekhov and love.

MALT DISTILLERS: MACALLAN

Easter Elchies House, spiritual home of The Macallan

The Macallan office is in a lovely early-eighteenth-century laird's house which looks down over the Spey towards Craigellachie. The distillery sprawls out behind: stillhouses and warehouses, all nearly black with age and the smoke of former times. There are lots of spirit stills, all tiny. Macallan has the shortest stills in the industry and when the company decided to expand production, they very wisely did so by increasing the number of stills, not the size. However, I have not come to view the distillery, which I have done more than once. I have come to look at the product, in company with David Robertson, the manager and Jim Robertson (no relation), who was the manager and is now in charge of materials for Highland Park.

Macallan and Highland Park are both owned by Highland Distilleries plc. When Highland bought Macallan a few years ago, there were worries, not only within the company, that the new owners might dilute the quality standards which had been built up under the admirable Willie Phillips. David tells me that Highland have sought only to improve on the Macallan strengths and have not stinted investment whose purpose was the enhancement of the quality of the whisky. At the moment the air is thick with the agreement by William Grant and the Edrington Trust jointly to take over Highland and return it from the vagaries of the stock market to being a private Scottish company. We discuss this briefly: they have concerns, but agree with me that such a move must be desirable, if only to secure in Scottish ownership two distilleries of such importance. That they are important is not in doubt. Both are great whiskies and if Highland Park is overshadowed by the Macallan, it is only because of the eminence of the latter and in no way to the discredit of the former.

The rise and rise of the Macallan over the last twenty years to its present position as the quintessential Speyside malt, has been based on an uncompromising commitment to quality in every aspect of production and maturation.

This is no advertising puff, as it might be elsewhere: it is that most powerful of promotional tools, the simple truth. The water comes off the hill from a little spring. The barley is largely Golden Promise, a variety which would probably disappear, were it not for Macallan. Of the variety's annual global production of around 5000 tons, Macallan uses 4500. David mentions that the Best Beer award this year was given to Timothy Taylor, which uses most of the rest. If you want good whisky, you must first brew good beer.

The same level of care runs through the whole operation. Tiny spirit stills produce Macallan new spirit, which is put in nothing but Spanish sherry wood. Macallan control every aspect of the maturation. They employ a Spanish firm which harvests the oak trees. The timber is air-dried and shipped to Jerez, where it is further dried, again in air. The casks are constructed and then loaned to a bodega, which uses them for one season for fermenting sherry and then fills them for two seasons with maturing dry oloroso. When the casks are emptied, they are shipped whole with some of the sherry still inside. None are sulphur-treated: it shows in the finished whisky, which has no trace of the sulphur compounds which one associates with sherry wood. When the casks arrive at Macallan, they are emptied and nosed, to check that they meet the quality standards. Those which pass (nearly all do) then have some water put in and pressurised to check for leaks. If sound, they are emptied and immediately filled with new Macallan spirit. The average cask costs Macallan £400, which is expensive. What is more, they never use a cask more than twice. As a policy it is costly, but it works, for the quality is indisputable.

David lays out for me the entire range of the Macallan, from new-make spirit to a glass whose identity he says he will disclose in due course. This is as close to bliss as a whisky drinker can get. We discuss them briefly. The malt is a mixture of Golden Promise and other barleys; four yeasts are used: two cultured distillers' yeasts and two brewers' yeasts; the stills are direct-fired, the smallest in the industry. A very narrow spirit cut is taken – 640 litres out of a 4000-litres charge, about 16%. Spirit is filled into first- and second-fill sherry casks for all of the whiskies we are to look at except the Gran Reserva, which is purely first-fill. No caramel colouring is used at all.

Macallan New-Make Spirit

You can see the quality right away: this is one of the best new spirits I have ever nosed. Most new-make whisky has rather a lot of unpleasant odours: maturation gets rid of them, so no problem. But this stuff is different: you could drink it as is. It is fruity and spicy: apples, liquorice and aniseed. You could sell this in Italy as high-class grappa.

Macallan 7-Year-Old

Light gold in colour – the wood showing already. Fruity and spicy and already showing signs of the complexity which I know characterises the Macallan. Not yet sufficiently mature, but a promising adolescent.

Macallan 10-Year-Old

This is the Macallan we all know and love. At ten years it is fully developed: vanilla, raisins, spices and lots of esters. No need to say more, a lovely whisky.

Macallan 12-Year-Old

This is the Macallan sold as the standard export bottling. My first impression is one of resentment: why only export? Two years shows a huge development in all particulars: there is more of everything. Estery fruits and flowers are up-front, unmistakable; behind them is sweetness and vanilla, ginger and cloves.

Macallan 15-Year-Old

We begin here to see some progression: it is less floral, more toffee-like. Nutty, too, and spicy. No trace of wood as yet, but an alteration in the balance of flavours such as one would expect of really fine maturation.

Macallan 18-Year-Old

The colour here begins to deepen. All the Macallans show good colour, but as it gets older, it becomes darker. Still fruity and spicy, but the balance is tipping further in the direction of the latter; the fruits now dried and crystallised. It is slightly resinous; sweet citric notes appear and the finish is very dry.

Macallan 25-Year-Old.

Bog myrtle in your face: that wildest, most delicious, most evocative of Highland smells. If you know it, I need say no more; if you don't, you cannot understand how delightful it is. Find yourself a bit of peat bog and walk across it until you crush the plant beneath your feet. You will know by the smell. Don't try to take it home, for the scent evaporates as soon as the plant is plucked. We think it must be down to the wood, but that seems a mundane explanation of something so wonderful.

Macallan 30-Year-Old

I am no admirer of old whiskies. I am also no admirer of daft gowks who pay lots of money for woody whisky just because it's old. But this is probably the best whisky of its age I have tasted. It is still fragrant, the myrtle having declined sufficiently to let us smell orange and lots of vanilla. No sign at all of woodiness.

Macallan Gran Reserva

This is mostly 18-year-old, all of it having been in first-fill oloroso casks. You can see by the colour alone (remembering that Macallan uses neither caramel nor wine-treated casks). It is dark red, the colour of Honduras mahogany. It is like the 18-year-old in the distribution of flavours, but more intense.

The Macallan Millennium Decanter

The last whisky we taste is now revealed to have been just over 50 years in cask and is Macallan's contribution to the new millennium. If anything could reconcile one to mortality, this would. Ordinarily, I would not go out of my way to taste a 50-year-old whisky. I would go a long way out for this. It is perfectly delicious and has retained a youthfulness which is totally unexpected. It is a beauty which age has not withered, though no cosmetics conceal it. Think of Katharine Hepburn at 80 and you will get the idea. It smells of lily of the valley and reminds me of my mother. There are only 900 bottles. Let's hope that few of them get into the hands of collectors and that as many as possible are drunk by folk who will appreciate them.

MALT DISTILLERS: SPRINGBANK

Springbank Distillery

Getting to Springbank isn't easy. It's over four hours by road from Edinburgh, and that's if the roads are clear. You go by way of Tarbert on Loch Lomond to Arrochar on Loch Long; then over the pass of Rest-and-be-Thankful to Inveraray and by Lochgilphead to Tarbert on Loch Fyne. Then down the Mull of Kintyre, where on a good day you can see miles of surf break on the Mull – beyond the waves lie Islay and, on the horizon, Rathlin Island. The road then turns east across the ridge and drops down to Campbeltown, which nestles between hill and harbour. As you get into the town, you slow down, and peer up alleyways. Eventually, at the end of one alley, you can, if you're quick, make out a sign which says 'Springbank'.

Not a high level of presentation for the home of perhaps the finest distilled liquor on the planet. In a world in which the makers of inferior products strive to publicise every minuscule mark of distinction, this is an oasis of modesty. You turn right through a gate and find yourself in a yard. There is a low cottage-like building facing you with some warehouses behind. On your left are some buildings of stone or green-painted corrugated iron, which house the distillery. The cottage is the office. There isn't a bell: you knock on the door. The office is of a size that no part of it is out of earshot of your knock.

This is no distillery-turned-visitor attraction, geared for the tourist as much as for the toper. No busloads of geriatrics here, seeking to alleviate their terminal tedium. This, thankfully, is the genuine article. This is the whisky drinker's Shangri-La, the last distillery in Scotland which under one roof contains the entire whisky process, from malting the barley to putting the mature spirit into bottle.

Our knock is answered by Frank McHardy, the manager. He shows us into his office, which has evidently not been altered – probably not even painted – since it was built some time last century. It has the kind of ambience which the big conglomerates pay London designers a fortune to try – and fail – to reproduce. The difference is that this is not Heritage pastiche, this is the real thing. Frank says, would we like to look at the distillery? If so, there is a lad around somewhere who will take us round. Would we like to look at some whisky? He has a few sample bottles laid out ready for us. We decide to look at the distillery first.

It isn't a long way: a few yards and we are in the malt barn: a floor malting with a steep tank. It had been disused until a few years ago, when the firm decided that, since they had it anyway, they might as well use it to malt local barley, rather than bringing tankers down the long coastal road. There is a small kiln adjacent. The malt gets six hours over peat, followed by four hours of hot air, so it is peated to a respectable degree.

The process is as with all distilleries, but shorter than most, for this is a very small distillery. I ask our guide to explain how the Springbank malt is distilled. He shows us the cast-iron mashtun which, like a reminder of mortality, has sat in the doorway for many lifetimes. Then the wooden washbacks. The still room has three small stills: one wash still and two spirit stills. The wash still is direct-fired; it has a rummager driven by an electric motor. The shaft which drives the rummager has a short chain attached and at every turn of the shaft, the chain hits a little brass bell, which rings. If the rings fail, the stillman knows his rummager has stopped and something must be done to stop the solids in the wash sticking to the still bottom and burning. This wasn't high-tech a hundred years ago.

Now we get to the difficult bit. I have tried more than once to remember just

Springbank's revitalised floor maltings

161

how Springbank run their spirit stills, and failed. This is how it goes. The wash still is charged and worked off in the usual way, with all the alcoholic low wines passing over into the receiver and thence into the spirit still. The first spirit still is then run as a wash still. That is, all of the alcoholic content – foreshots, middle cut and feints – is collected. There are separate low wines and feints receivers. The second spirit still is then charged. The charge is made up of 80% proceeds of the second distillation and 20% low wines directly from the wash still. The middle cut of this distillation is what is taken into the spirit safe at about 75% alcohol by volume. The feints receiver is cleaned twice yearly to remove deposits. There must be some interesting compounds sticking to the walls.

The only thing you can say about this bizarre arrangement is that it works. Nobody seems to know why it was adopted. That is how the Springbank has always been distilled, and, since it makes superlatively fine whisky, nobody has any motive for changing things. As is demonstrated when we move to tasting some samples. Frank explains that, being such a small concern, they have problems with continuity of supply. He has a 12-year-old to show us whose supplies will run out within the coming twelvemonth. They have supplies of 21-year-old which should last until 2003, but when it runs out, there will be a 15-year-old to follow. It would be a nightmare to market, were it not all of such superlative quality. We try the ones which are about to disappear. I refrain from describing them out of consideration for my readers, since to know of such stuff without being able to attain it, can cause nothing but grief. We look at the 12- and 21-year-old – and a couple of others, out of interest. In all of them, the peat is not readily detectable as a separate presence, being remarkably integrated into the flavour of the mature whisky.

Springbank 12-Year-Old

Dark colour from a first-fill oloroso cask. (Springbank has always been at the front of the queue for really fine casks.) It smells of vanilla, almonds, marzipan. With water, it becomes slightly salty and floral, but still smells like a Christmas cake. On the palate it is dry as a bone and the finish is clean and dry.

Springbank 21-Year-Old

A mixture of casks: some first, some second-fill sherry, a few wine-treated. (Commendable honesty here. You can afford to be honest if the stuff is as good as this and you don't have a marketing department made up of professional liars breathing down your neck.) The spirit is as dark as Navy rum. It is not woody despite its age; the nose is of treacle and plum duff and muscatels – with a little sourness as of orange zest beneath, given some water. The taste is sweet and aromatic. A lovely old whisky, but for all that not as complex as the 12-year-old.

Springbank CV

This is the product of a marriage of a number of casks, of which the youngest is seven-and-a-half years old, the rest mostly a lot older. There is no age statement on the bottle. The whisky is pale gold in colour and shows just how much age contributes to the maturation of the Springbank. The nose is aromatic and a little oily; with water it is sweet and grassy. The taste is simple, peppery and sweet.

Springbank 1966

This is ancient whisky: bottled in 1997 at 31 years old, a single-cask bottling from bourbon casks. It has a mid-gold colour and shows no sign of age at all, save for a buttery sweetness, and a savour as of salty vanilla. With water, you get the sweet spiciness of aniseed over a grassy base. The taste is dead dry, savoury and meaty, like a good Chateaubriand. It is a little smoky, like toasted brown bread. We don't ask how much it retails for, lest temptation raise its head only to be disappointed.

MALT DISTILLERS: GLENMORANGIE

Glenmorangie Distillery

One's first impression of Bill Lumsden is that he is a surprisingly young man to be in charge of all of Glenmorangie's production. Only when he begins to speak of his job – which means his whiskies – do you appreciate that the youthful looks cover immense knowledge. I was about to say, authority, for there is no doubt that he has that, but the tone of what he says is considered and tentative rather than authoritative – as befits his subject, for we are speaking of the influences on flavour in whisky. As you may have gathered, this is not a subject which lends itself readily to bald statements: it is about minuscule variation leading to barely perceptible but important differences.

Tim and I have come to ask Bill what for all but a few in the whisky industry would be very awkward questions. We want to know what things were done with the whisky and why: all stuff which almost anywhere else would be highly classified, commercially confidential information. Glenmorangie decided a long time ago that, far from keeping its light hidden, it would remove the bushel altogether and tell people how it made and matured its whisky. Given the results, in product and in sales, that must be one of the best marketing decisions in the history of the industry.

Bill Lumsden hard at work at Glenmorangie.

We inspect the firm's whiskies, and Bill explains the history and the chemistry: what was done, when and why; what have been the results.

Glenmorangie 10-Year-Old

They have laid out for us several Glenmorangie bottlings and two Ardbeg. We decide to take the Glenmorangie first. I have long been an admirer of the standard 10-year-old Glenmorangie bottling. It is a lovely, delicate whisky, which we sometimes tend to underrate, but only because we are so familiar with it. The nose is floral and flowery, strongly vanilla with an undernote of citrus; with water the fruitiness remains, but we get grassy notes, cereal and some earthy aromas. The taste is vanilla and honey; the aftertaste short and dry.

This is a well-made whisky matured in good bourbon casks. I ask Bill about it: he says that although it is designated a 10-year-old, the spirit has been ten and eleven years in cask, and some twelve. Getting the exact Glenmorangie flavour profile isn't easy: they have a nosing panel which examines the stocks and decides on the casks for bottling. They recently decided that the vanilla was becoming too pronounced, mainly because there was too much 12-year-old in the mix. They have to pay attention to the cask type as well. The present mix is 56% first-fill bourbon casks; 44% refill. (All of the refills are second-fill; there is no use of casks beyond second-fill.) The proportion of second-fill must be watched as well, for the floral top-notes comes mainly from that source.

Glenmorangie 18-Year-Old

The colour of this is darker, as you would expect. The mix is a little complicated: two-thirds of the spirit has been 18 years in bourbon casks; one third has spent 12 or 13 years in bourbon wood, and has then been transferred to sherry casks. The latter have all, in their previous incarnation, held sweet oloroso. Most of them are second-fill; a few first. As Bill says, this is more than just a finish: five or six years is enough to give a pronounced sherry-style maturation on top of the bourbon.

The result is perfectly satisfactory: nose strongly of vanilla and dried fruit, turning floral with water, some citrus. The taste is mild and sweet with, after a while some tannin. The finish, surprisingly, shows some peat and is quite dry. (Surprisingly, for Glenmorangie peats to only 2 ppm, and you would have expected that to have gone completely by 18 years of age.)

Glenmorangie Finishes

The story behind this is a lot better than I had expected. I had always assumed that putting whisky into different sorts of cask after ten years in bourbon wood was basically a marketing wheeze and a response to the shortage of sherry casks. That is undoubtedly the case with some of Glenmorangie's imitators, who shall be nameless but whose numbers grow by the day. Glenmorangie started looking at different kinds of wood back in the late 1970s, because they were worried about the quality of the bourbon wood coming out of the USA. The rise in demand for bourbon casks – the whisky industry was on a roll throughout the 1970s – had been such that American coopers had introduced a high degree of mechanisation into the production of casks. This, together with kiln-drying of the timber had resulted in poor-quality wood, and the prospects for the future looked none too bright.

Glenmorangie have addressed the problem by commissioning their own supply of new casks: all made from slow-growing oak, air-dried. These they lease to one of the bourbon producers for four years before shipping them to Scotland. Around a quarter of the Glenmorangie wood is now from that source.

However, twenty years ago, that was only a distant prospect. So the people at Tain started trying other sorts of cask, to see what effect they would have on the spirit. Sherry they knew about, and there had been various other sorts of cask floating about in the industry for a long time, but no systematic investigation of their value as maturation vessels. Glenmorangie tried putting new spirit into various wine casks, but found that the results were not what they wanted, the effects of the wine being too pronounced and obscuring the essential Glenmorangie character. Then someone had the bright idea of taking 10-year-old bourbon-wood whisky and giving it a few years in port or sherry cask. That worked, provided you got the balance right, as follows.

Glenmorangie Port Wood

I remember tasting this in New York when it was first introduced. There was a lot of razzamatazz, and all the whisky buffs were saying how great it was. I felt a bit of a curmudgeon, for I thought it was well over the top. I said so at the time, but was drowned in the chorus of approval and advertising. It turns out I wasn't the only one to think so: when first introduced, the port-wood finish had been 12 years in bourbon wood and six or seven in port. As Bill says, they now think that is too much and give it only 16 or 17 months in port wood.

The result is all one could desire: a light and delicate whisky very much in the Glenmorangie style, but with additions. The most immediately noticeable of these is the colour, which is reddish, from the ruby port. The nose is very delicate, floral but with cedar or sandalwood. It turns buttery with water, as the diacetyl and the esters emerge, as well as some grassy notes. The taste is velvety, chocolate-ish and dry; the finish clean and sweet. Good stuff.

Glenmorangie Sherry Wood

The casks for the wood finishes are all European oak: *Quercus robur* or *Quercus petraea*. The sherry casks hold oloroso sherry for 12 to 16 months. After emptying, they are sterilised with burning sulphur, hard-bunged and shipped immediately. They are filled as quickly as possible on arrival in Scotland, to preserve as much as possible of the sherry character. This they certainly do, for on the nose, the whisky shows raisins, caramel and vanilla. Some sulphur, too – as you would expect, given the provenance. With water, things don't change much, and the taste is sweet and toffee-like. It's a very good whisky if you like that sort of thing. If I have a criticism, it's that it doesn't taste to me like Glenmorangie, and as I have said before, I happen to like Glenmorangie a lot.

Glenmorangie Madeira Wood

For those who don't know, Madeira is a fortified wine made on a sub-tropical volcanic island about five hundred miles off the North African coast. The wine is aged in drums (fat, giant casks): the best of it in estufas, which are hot warehouses designed to imitate the conditions of the hold of an East Indiaman sailing round the world. The resultant wine is high in acidity and of very variable quality. The sweetest Madeira is malmsey – as in drowned in a butt of – and besides being useful for pickling Plantagenets, it is best known for its keeping qualities: it will last a hundred years in cask or bottle without deterioration. As far as I'm concerned, this is no big deal, for I don't care for the stuff at its best, let alone after a century in a stuffy loft.

However, as is so often the case, what is one man's poison is another man's maturation opportunity. Bourbon is crude stuff, by and large, but it's great for preparing whisky casks. The Glenmorangie aged in a malmsey cask has all of the virtues and none of the vices of the parent wine: it isn't sour or over the top; it smells of marmalade and burnt orange, raisins and fruit. It tastes spicy and fruity and nevertheless is dry in the finish. If folk were to stop drinking malmsey tomorrow, its continued production would be amply justified by its function in the maturation of Glenmorangie malt.

MALT DISTILLERS: ARDBEG

Islay isn't much to look at, as Hebridean islands go. It is pretty flat, and most of it is covered with peat bog. It is however a place of hidden treasures, which it will reveal to anyone who takes the trouble to look. There is a little road which runs up and down, in and out, along the rocky edge of the Sound of Jura. It is only one vehicle wide, so if someone else comes along, you must pull in to let them past. That happens rarely, so it is little inconvenience. You pass Laphroaig and then Lagavulin. Beyond that, there are two of the treasures. One is the high cross at Kildalton. It stands, as it has stood for well over a thousand years, by the little church which it seems to dwarf by its massive presence, though only ten feet high. This is monastic Christianity at its most muscular. You had to be tough to think of converting Picts to anything, let alone a religion which – bizarrely – preached peace. Columcille and his followers, when they came from Ireland in the sixth century, were the Church's heavy mob, and it shows. If you find the idea problematical, go and look at the cross at Kildalton.

If I have any virtue to the point of fault, it is a dislike of fakes. I am irritated by the ersatz, the bogus, the fraudulent. It is an attribute which, as you can imagine, has brought me into disfavour with the Scotch whisky industry from time to time. What I like about the Kildalton cross is its reality. There is a fake Celtic cross on the west side of Islay. I was unhappy about it for years, until I found it wasn't the real thing: a mere six hundred years old, it's a mediaeval counterfeit.

Treasures must be real. The other treasure down the road to Kildalton is Ardbeg distillery. I have known it for years and have visited it from time to time, when it lay, dormant, in the hands of Allied Distillers. Ardbeg may have been inactive, but there was no doubt that it was the real thing. It lay, decaying gently into the seashore from which it sprang, with stocks of whisky in the warehouse the like of which the world had not seen. Because I was picking up stray casks from every airt, I would get a glimpse of the spirit from time to time, and it was wonderful.

Ardbeg Distillery

When Allied sold Ardbeg to Glenmorangie, I confess I was apprehensive. It would get active management, which had to be a good thing, but what would they do to the place? I visited it in 1999 and I can report that little has changed, and that for the better. A bit of paint here and there, and the only demolition that which was done by the January gales. There is indeed a visitors' centre, with scones and jumpers – but the scones are the best west of Tarbert, Loch Lomond, and the jumpers, well, it seemed churlish to complain about knitwear when drinking drams of surpassing excellence, poured by a young woman whose charm and beauty are matched by her modesty and evident intelligence. She runs the visitors' centre and is married to the distillery manager. Happy the distillery manager and fortunate his company.

Ardbeg 17-Year-Old

It must be said that the sublime does not make for objectivity, so I asked Bill Lumsden (see previous) to show us the Ardbeg. (This is nothing against Bill, as I am sure he will understand.) He explains that there are supply problems. No production took place at Ardbeg from 1981 to 1989. It reopened only in 1997. There are stocks sufficient to produce a bottling which is designated as 17-year-old, though in fact it is using stock considerably older than that, mostly laid down between 1975 and 1977.

Ardbeg uses the most heavily-peated malt to be found anywhere in the whisky industry. At 50 parts per million, you would expect the spirit to taste like tar water. It does, but not so strongly as expected. This is because of its age, no doubt, and because a little Kildalton stock was used in the mix. (Kildalton is the name given to Ardbeg which is made from unpeated malt, of which they have suitably aged supplies.) It also tastes of fish and smoke and you are in no doubt as to where you stand: downwind of the fire.

Now is the time to bring habituation into play. As you nose the whisky, the olfactory organ gradually becomes accustomed to the smoke and then is revealed a whisky of great subtlety and complexity. It has sweet and cereal notes, and high levels of esters which give it a flowery nose. The spirit still has a purifier which, by returning part of the vapour for redistillation, effectively rectifies some of the spirit and produces high levels of esters. The taste is not smoky at all, though afterwards it is.

Ardbeg 1975

This is Ardbeg bottled at 23 years of age. Bill says it is his favourite. The peat smoke is even more muted and there are woody, oaky flavours. The taste is dry and tannic and a bit woody for my money. As I think I may have said elsewhere – though I hope not dogmatically – I think most whiskies are at their best from ten to fifteen years in wood. In such company and with such whisky, I willingly admit that *de gustibus non est disputandum*.

Ardbeg 10-Year-Old

People who really like peaty whiskies like them really peaty. Since the effect of peat declines with age in cask, the younger the spirit, the more strongly peated will be its flavour. I mention this to Bill and say that there has to be a market for 10-year-old or similar. He tells me that the company proposes to produce just such an article and that by the time this book reaches print, a 10-year-old will be in the shops. It is an event to which I look forward with pleasurable anticipation.

MALT DISTILLERS: WILLIAM GRANT & SONS AND GLENFIDDICH

Glenfiddich Distillery

Glenfiddich suffers from success. It was the first malt to be widely marketed in modern times. In its triangular green bottle, it is the most easily recognised of all the malts in the airport duty-free. With its light, flowery nose, it is arguably the most accessible. So malt whisky snobs – usually those who have known about malts for at least a year – look down on it, on the ground that anything that popular can't be really good. People like myself who don't like popular entertainments, tend to give Glenfiddich's visitors' centre a miss as we drive up the Dufftown road.

Which is a shame for both place and product are admirable. Just as they were the first people in modern times to market malt whisky, Glenfiddich were among the first to perceive the utility of allowing the public into the distillery where it was made. They were fortunate in their location: ease of access combined with the scenic attractions of the Fiddich glen, just off the main Spey valley. They were fortunate, too, that when William Grant and his children established the distillery and its warehouses a century ago, they built in a lovely local stone and roofed the buildings with Ballachulish slate. When the firm came to convert part of the premises into a visitors' centre, they were able to do so without straining the fabric or detracting from its natural attributes as a working distillery. It is not difficult to think of distilleries where the creation of a visitors' centre has taken the place over, creating a Disney-like atmosphere of ersatz. At Glenfiddich, you do not have the feeling of intruding on someone's workplace: there are lots of guides, who do their job with some sensitivity and not a little pride.

The place has a curious atmosphere: it does not have the intimacy of one of the little distilleries, for a lot of folk visit it in the course of a year. But neither do you get the feeling, which you do from some I could mention, but won't, of this being just a showpiece and the staff mere hirelings of a mega-corporation. You get the feeling – or at least I got the feeling – of something more familial. I think maybe that's it: visiting Glenfiddich, you feel as though you are being welcomed into a large family. Now you may think I am being sentimental here, but I don't think so. If you have read this far, you will be accustomed to the idea of thinking in terms of the perception of infinitesimals; of making distinctions among sensations which are much finer than those which you are accustomed to make, or making them in new fields. And with luck, you will have got the idea that history matters to those perceptions: that our experience has depth.

The company which the Grants began so long ago has now developed into a very substantial concern, owning besides Glenfiddich, the Balvenie distillery, the huge Girvan grain distillery, and brands which are sold worldwide. Nevertheless, it is still a private company owned by the members of the family descended from the people who started it. Not only owned by them, but actively managed by them. And because they are a private company, they are able to see their responsibilities in a frame much wider than that of those who must answer to institutional shareholders. This is apparent in the attitudes of their people, who quite clearly feel a part of the whole thing. And it can be seen in their involvement in Scottish public life: you don't find a lot of foreign-owned companies sponsoring piping competitions or funding lifeboats. Their commitment to heritage goes beyond the tokenism of brand identity, as far as the establishment of university scholarships in Scottish history

Thinking about the Grants and Glenfiddich, I had an uneasy feeling that there was an historical parallel which I couldn't quite grasp. It was only recently, and nothing to do with whisky, that I was describing to a German friend a wonderful portrait of a Highland piper from the eighteenth century, that the penny dropped. The piper, whose picture is here reproduced, is the personal piper of the chief of the Clan Grant in 1714, when Richard Waitt painted the picture. It's a great picture: he could easily be the man Elizabeth Grant refers to – or at least his ancestor, for the dates don't match – when she describes one of the retainers of her father, who was a chieftain of the Clan Grant. He was 'a piper who refused all work unconnected with whisky, for fear of spoiling the delicacy of his touch.'

The Piper of the Laird of Grant: 'a piper who refused all work unconnected with whisky, for fear of spoiling the delicacy of his touch'.

The parallel of which I speak is, in retrospect, obvious. William Grant & Sons Ltd resemble nothing quite so much as the clan from which they take their name, and on whose ancestral lands their malt distilleries lie. The hierarchical social structure, the network of mutual rights and obligations, the feeling of belonging as of right, all characterise the company, as they did the clan. If you would see a piece of real heritage, forget the kilts and the tartans and the other externalities, and consider the reality beneath the Glenfiddich. The spirit, if you like.

Now, just to show that this is not an exercise in being nice to William Grant, I am going to look at some of their whiskies – and if my descriptions are not as eulogistic as they might wish, I can claim only objectivity and honesty and the principle that if you say everything is wonderful, you have no words left for what really is.

Glenfiddich Special Reserve – No Age Statement

It is a light, fruity-sweet whisky, accessible and agreeable. There are some off-notes but not many and it well serves its market, which is that of the duty-free, first-time malt drinker. It is, none the less, welcome to the discerning.

Glenfiddich 18-Year-Old

The spirit has a fine, golden colour, got from long years in cask in a dark, stone-walled, slate-roofed, earth-floored warehouse above the river Spey. The nose is vinous, floral and smoky, like gardenias in a cigar box. It is not easily discerned, the flavours being closely integrated, but repays the effort expended in approaching it. A little diluted, it becomes green and grassy over a floral base. The floral note continues in the taste, but soon gives way to a savoury dryness, which continues long on the palate. To be taken as a digestif or with oysters.

Glenfiddich Solera Reserve

Now we come to something really interesting. In this, the Grants show two things: first, that they actually know and care about their historical position, and second, that they are of an innovative disposition as regards their whiskies. The whisky industry – or rather their marketing people – are notoriously lemming-like: nobody wants to do anything different from anyone else, but as soon as somebody does something, they all want to do it. (Look at how many have jumped on the finishes bandwagon which Glenmorangie started.) And, it seems, almost no one in the whisky industry takes an interest in or learns from the history of that industry. How else to explain the fact that Glenfiddich are the first malt distiller to do as was suggested by the excellent Saintsbury, and establish a whisky solera?

You will no doubt recall my earlier mention of George Saintsbury: literateur, connoisseur and generally good guy. In my treasured copy of the *Notes on a Cellar Book* – which I owe to my good friend Tony Edridge – Saintsbury writes in 1920:

> The more excellent way – formerly practised by all persons of some sense and some means north of the Tweed – is to establish a cask of whatever size your purse and your cellar will admit, from a butt to an octave, or an anker or even less; fill it up with good and drinkable whisky from six to eight years old, stand it up on end, tap it half-way down or even a little higher, and, when you get to or near the tap, fill it up again with whisky fit to drink, but not *too* old. You thus establish what is called in the case of sherry a 'solera', in which the constantly ageing character of the old constituents doctors the new accessions, and in which these in turn refresh and strengthen the old. 'It should be pretty good,' said a host of mine once in a country house beyond the Forth, 'it comes from a hundred-gallon cask. Which has not been empty for a hundred years.' This is the state of the blessed, to which all cannot attain. But with care and judgement it can be approached on quite a modest scale. I have done it in octaves for both Scotch and Irish whisky ... I think of their fair proportions now with unsoured fondness.

Now no one seems to have thought of following Saintsbury's advice for a very long time. I doubt whether there are many country houses north of the Forth – or south of it, for that matter – where you will find a hundred-gallon cask of good malt whisky. It is one of the many casualties of the the decline of a genuinely Scottish aristocracy over the last two hundred years, and of their custom of selling their daughters and their souls to the English establishment.

So all praise to the Grants for their Solera Reserve. They have several large oak vats at the Glenfiddich distillery, into which old, but 'not *too* old' whisky is filled. After a decent period of marrying and maturation, a part of the contents is bottled, and replaced with another batch of already partly mature whisky. The minimum age of the whiskies coming from the vat is 15 years. Obviously some will be older, and a proportion will be as old as the solera.

Grants Solera Reserve 15-Year-Old

Lots of fruity-sweet flavours, along with flowers: rich, dry, fruit-cake aromas. Savoury, too, and with a touch of sulphur at the close – sufficient to enrich but not to detract from the overall impression of luxurious plenty. With a dry, clean finish, it is top-quality stuff.

The Grants' solera vat.

GRAIN DISTILLERS: NORTH BRITISH

Visitors to Edinburgh often ask what is the nearest Scotch whisky distillery, and all the tourist guides say Glenkinchie. Glenkinchie is a very pleasant little distillery nestling in a green valley some miles east of the city. It fulfils tourists' expectations of prettiness and so-called heritage. It has a visitors' centre which stylishly combines high-tech display and lots of old artefacts.

North British Distillery

In much of what is presented as heritage, there is an undercurrent of deception. In fact the nearest Scotch whisky distillery is The North British Distillery. It isn't small and pretty and it isn't a malt distillery. It's big and handsome, and it's down Gorgie Road, behind the Tynecastle football ground. Gorgie is a part of the town not much visited by tourists, which is fine by the distillery, as it is not in the tour business anyway. It is in the business of making grain whisky, and very fine grain whisky at that.

The offices are in a fine art-deco building which stands among structures which could be part of any oil refinery. This is a modern grain distillery. It was a modern distillery when it was set up in 1885 as a co-operative venture by those blenders who were not part of the Distillers Company, to ensure themselves supplies of grain spirit for blending. Even so early, there were fears that the agglomeration of plant in the hands of one company would severely prejudice the business of the others. Fancy that.

It is now a joint venture between UDV and The Edrington Group – which means half of it is owned by the biggest conglomerate, but the other half by an organisation which operates on the basis of different considerations. It provides filling for a number of blended whiskies, of which the leading brands are Famous Grouse, J&B Rare and Cutty Sark.

I am met by a smart secretary who shows me into the office of David Rae, the managing director. I explain what I'm about: a slightly sensitive matter, given that in the past I have been known to be less than kind about some grain whiskies. I explain that I want to look at the process and if possible, the product. We look first at the intake of grain. The distillery is unusual among grain distillers in that it uses 17% barley against 83% maize. This is a higher proportion of barley by around 5% than any other grain distiller. Since most of the flavour in grain whisky comes from the barley, we will look for signs in the new-made spirit.

The maize comes from southern France and is delivered by truck from Leith docks. The starch in maize is insoluble in water, so it is cooked before mashing. The cooking is done in vast pressure cookers, after which the slurry of maize and water is mixed with green malt straight from the maltings. There are two large mashtuns

NB's old green malt pump with the new spirit storage in the background

which produce the wort, which then passes to the washbacks for fermentation. Fermentation lasts for about 72 hours, after which alcohol content is about 8%. All of the vessels are of stainless steel and the whole process is computer-controlled.

The still room contains three Coffey stills, mostly stainless steel with some red paint. What strikes one – apart from how different this is from any malt distillery – is how stylish the whole thing is. The stills are evidently of the same era as the offices: the effects of the art-deco design values are apparent and delightful. Of course, we don't talk about that: we speak of the spirit which comes off the rectifier at around 95% alcohol by volume, a much higher level of alcohol than a malt still will produce. We nose the spirit running from the still: it is fruity and aromatic and not at all the characterless silent spirit of legend.

Of the new spirit, some goes for further distillation to become very pure ethyl alcohol, for industrial use or for making into gin or vodka. But most of the production is filled directly into wooden casks, to become grain whisky. The new spirit is analysed to ensure consistent quality. As well as laboratory analysis, the spirit is subject to inspection by a panel of five noses. These are company employees chosen for their olfactory ability. None are production personnel, so that there will be no conflict of interest. Every batch of spirit must be passed by the panel prior to being filled into cask. If it does not pass, the batch is sent for redistillation. The panel retains a sample of the best batch, which it uses as a standard for comparison. When any batch surpasses the sample, it becomes the new standard, so that there is a continual racking up of the quality criterion.

The concern for quality is apparent in the attention paid to wood stock. Where in the past, the produce of grain distilleries went only into casks which had been worn out in the service of malts, some of the NB spirit is now being filled into new ex-bourbon hogs. The results are apparent in the flavour.

NB New Spirit

The liquor is colourless, as one would expect of new spirit. On the nose, it has none of the congeners one has come to expect from tasting new malt spirit. The first impression is of a flowery odour, quite free from undesirable asides. It's grassy, too. There is a buttery note to the nose, and the taste is spicy, of liquorice or aniseed. This is not, admittedly, a spirit with the complexity of a malt, but it is not without character – and that of a very pleasing sort.

NB 3-Year-Old

This is first-fill bourbon wood. Perfectly charming spirit: grassy and fruity; no off-notes at all. The taste is sweet and spicy and buttery, with a long, spicy aftertaste of which any malt would be proud.

NB 5-Year-Old

First-fill bourbon again. More of the bourbon influence evident: there is high, buttery sweetness over a grassy, cereal base. The taste is much softer than the younger version, but delicately spicy and sweet. I would have no problems about spending an evening with this.

NB 18-Year-Old

This is a special bottling of old bourbon-cask whisky, bottled for employees of the firm and for its visitors. It is a delightful whisky, which puts paid to my theories that grain spirit does not continue to benefit from maturation. The same grassy, cereal aroma which we have noted before is evidently characteristic of this grain whisky. But it is a perfectly pleasing smell; not at all the disagreeable odour which one sometimes identifies in a cheap blend as being the grain whisky component. This, if anything, is rather elegant, and its taste is delicate and sweet and spicy.

What is noticeable in this organisation is the same as I have found in all of the malt distilleries: the people care deeply about what they do and what they seek is to make the very best spirit they can. It shows, and it works.

BLENDERS: THE FAMOUS GROUSE

A generation ago, when malt whiskies were a dim presence on the edges of the drinker's consciousness, whisky meant blended whisky, and men – and some women – in Scotland drank a deadly combination known as 'a hauf an' a hauf'. This was a shot of whisky, known as a 'hauf', and a half-pint of strong beer. (Whisky chaser to those of North American dialect.) 'Hauf' is half in the old Scots tongue which then was widely spoken, and today is still the ordinary speech of a majority of the Scottish people. The origin of 'hauf' as it applies to whisky is obscure; possibly half a gill, though since that means a quarter of a pint, it seems large for a whisky measure.

Whatever it was, it was how the Scots took their drams, usually with a little water. On the bars of public houses, you would find jugs of water, for the convenience of whisky drinkers. The latter had marked preferences in the matter of their blended whiskies, and those preferences went unchanged from one generation to another. Until the rise of the Famous Grouse, that is. The makers of Grouse had realised that there might be a market for a traditional style of blended whisky which was, however, of better quality that the usual, without moving into the de luxe category. They therefore blended a whisky which had a considerably higher proportion of malts than its fellows in the middling section of the market, and introduced it quietly, as befitted so traditional a milieu, by using it to fill the bottles of their established Famous Grouse brand. Within ten years, the Grouse went from being a minor brand to one which sold over a million cases per annum and was Scotland's favourite whisky.

Its virtues spread, mainly by word of mouth. Scots drinkers, who would have disdained any drink which made a parade of its quality, were converted. Grouse became the drinker's drink in Scotland. The 'Famous' part of the name was dropped – by drinkers if not by advertisers – people said at the bar, 'I'll have a Grouse.' In marketing terms, the name was bold, for it also meant a grumble, though the addition of 'Famous' perhaps negated that. 'Grouse' became part of the Scots vocabulary; it still is. Euphemisms abound.

No book about the appreciation of whisky would be complete without a section on blended whiskies. Blends have taken a lot of stick in recent years from the aficionados of malts. Though there can be no doubt that by the 1970s a reappraisal of blended whiskies was long overdue, the pendulum has now swung too far in the other direction, and lots of malt drinkers are now under the impression that virtually no blended whisky is worth drinking. It is a proposition which the people who market blends seem unable to address. They are hogtied by the nature of brand marketing, with its concentration on the promotion of brand values and nothing else. Because brand promotion does not appeal to rational consumer choice, the owners of the big brands have been unable to state simply that their whiskies taste as nice as a malt. In some cases that is not true – though mendacity has never been a serious impediment to brand advertising – and it would be hard to make a case. However, recent years have seen the appearance of a number of malts which are poorly made and worse matured, to which any decent blend would be preferable. Grouse certainly falls into he category of a decent blend.

This judgement was confirmed by a visit to the chief blender of the Grouse, John Ramsay. John has the gravitas of his position. So does the blending room in Glasgow, to which whisky samples are taken for inspection prior to blending. With its wood-panelling and benches laden with sample bottles, it looks the part. The Famous Grouse brand is owned by Highland Distillers, so of course it uses mainly malt also owned by them. Like any blend, however, its base is grain whisky.

The grouse uses grain whisky from various grain distilleries. Its mainstay is

North British – of which more elsewhere – but there was mention of Strathclyde and Cameronbrig as well. Since Highland Distillers are partners in the NB distillery, Grouse can specify the quality of the casks to be used for its grain from that distillery, which is, mainly, first-fill bourbon, with a smaller number of refill bourbon casks.

The new grain spirit from other distillers is taken from the distillery in tanker to Grouse's warehouse at Muirhall, where it is filled into the firm's own casks. The commitment to quality is as apparent here as at any malt distillery. So is the appreciation of the importance of the cask in maturing the whisky – as one would expect from a group of companies which makes the Macallan.

The malts in the blend are mainly from distilleries owned by the group: Macallan and Tamdhu, Glen Rothes, Glenturret, Glengoyne, Bunnahabhain, Highland Park. Some others, from distilleries outwith the group are used, though in smaller quantities. We look elsewhere at the maturation of the Macallan. It does not have a monopoly of fine casks, however, for close attention is given to the maturation of all of the whiskies in the group. A little malt is filled into ex-bourbon casks, but most come from Spain. Both Spanish and American wood are used, and casks are filled for two years with dry oloroso sherry before being emptied and shipped to Scotland. The malts for use in the Grouse are matured in both types of sherry wood, in a proportion of two American white oak to three European.

The cask contents are assessed by a panel chosen from among thirty or so trained noses among the company's personnel. Each malt and each cask of grain is assessed against a standard and allocated to one of four grades for quality. Only those which pass the quality threshold are used in the blend. The proportion of each whisky which is used, and the ages, are of course a trade secret. John was, however, prepared to tell me that the whiskies range in age from five to fourteen years. Casks are assembled according to a picking list and brought to the company's blending warehouse at Drumchapel, in Glasgow. All are sampled again and any which fail to meet the standard are rejected.

The malt whiskies are then vatted in the proportion required for the blend. The grain whiskies are also sampled and vatted, either at the distillery where they lie or at Drumchapel. The final stage is to bring the malt and grain together, reduce the strength to 45% ABV, and return the mixture to the wood to marry. The blend lies in the marrying casks for at least six months, following which it is again assessed, to ensure it meets the Grouse flavour profile.

During the marrying period, the whiskies do not mature any further, but the marrying process makes a significant difference to the quality of the resultant blend. This practice is purely empirical: people know that keeping the whiskies together in cask for a bit does improve their flavour. Recent research at Strathclyde University has shed some light by suggesting a mechanism whereby flavour components embed themselves in clusters of ethanol molecules, a process which facilitates their discernment by the drinker. When whiskies are mixed, those clusters break up, and the marrying period allows them to reform.

After marrying, the whisky is assessed yet again, to ensure that there has been no diminution in its quality. The casks are emptied once again, this time into vats for bottling. The strength of the spirit is reduced at this point to the bottling strength of 40%. It is then chill-filtered. A two-stage filter is used which, together with the employment only of very coarse filters, takes as little from the whisky as is compatible with stability. In this, the Grouse can be compared with an inter-nationally-known blended whisky – which shall be nameless – which uses filters graded at 120 against the Grouse's 45. This means that the Grouse will go a little cloudy if you are daft enough to freeze it, but it also ensures that it retains much of the flavour which has so commended it to whisky drinkers in its native land.

The Famous Grouse

The mature whisky has a mid-gold colour. On the nose, it shows toffee and caramel together with the floral notes which we know from the constituent malts and grains alike. Some peat is evident, thanks to the Highland Park, but otherwise, it is not easy to separate the flavours, for the blending has been a complete success and the resultant whisky is tightly integrated. Altogether a satisfactory blend, and at a very modest price, considering what you will pay for lesser potations. All things considered, it is not surprising that the Scots have taken it to their bosoms.

PRIVATE BOTTLERS: GORDON & MACPHAIL

In the mid-eighteenth century, when a ship arrived in the Roads of Leith with a cargo of wine from France, the importer would load a barrel on a wheelbarrow, hire a man to trundle it up into the town and sell it by the jug. The Edinburgh townspeople could thereby taste the cargo and judge how much they ought to pay for it. For the most part, wines were sold young, and consumed before the effects of excessive oxidation could make themselves felt. Over the next hundred years or so, things changed slowly. Industrial-scale glass-making caused the price of bottles to fall and it became economically viable to sell wine by the bottle. Bottles, moreover, allowed wine to be stored for long periods and people came to appreciate the benefit of maturation in bottle. With the growth of the middle class, demand for bottled wine increased and to supply the new market, existing firms of wine merchants expanded. The Vaults in Leith, which had been a wine importer's warehouse since the fourteenth century, was raised from one to its present four storeys and its owners installed a bottling plant – which was later to be used for whisky.

Wine merchants were, however, relatively rare in Scotland. The source of bottled wine for most people was not the wine merchant but the licensed grocer. This was an establishment which sold general groceries, with wine as a sideline. We are familiar with the early photographs of ornate shopfronts with staff in long white aprons. Gordon & MacPhail was one such, established in Elgin in 1895, to serve the growing prosperity of Elgin's bourgeoisie as well as the needs of the landed gentry who lived on estates in the surrounding country. Visiting Elgin today, it is not too difficult to imagine how it was a century ago. Most of its Victorian town centre is still intact and the buildings speak of a prosperous and self-confident population. A licensed grocer would have been expected to supply all of a house's foodstuffs save fish and butchermeat. He also supplied its drink: beers as well as wines, for the days of domestic brewing were long gone. And he supplied whisky. Domestic distilling was a forgotten art: whisky making had become big business and the valleys which stretch into the hills above Elgin were dotted with distilleries. It was the heyday of blended whisky and people of what was called quality purchased their whisky in bottles from grocers such as Gordon & MacPhail. They still do.

This was the north-east country, in which the habit of drinking malts did not die out, as it did elsewhere. People continued to buy malt whisky. As the twentieth century progressed, they could no longer get it from distillers, but they could get it from their grocer, for Gordon & MacPhail had expanded their trade of bottling and supplying malt whisky. With the business owned by the descendants of one of the founders, they had continuity and a long perspective. They persisted in bottling malts through the long years of the ascendancy of blends. Not only that; they laid down whiskies in their own casks. Some, indeed, were the casks in which they had imported wines for the other side of the business. At the time of writing, the firm has by far the largest and best stock of whisky in cask held by anyone other than the major distillers. In the warehouse in Elgin, or lying at distilleries around Scotland, they have 75 different whiskies maturing in a total of 10,000 casks. Given such stocks, they have viewed the rise of special bottlings of malts with equanimity, knowing that none of the other bottlers were likely to be able to maintain both supply and quality sufficient to serve a substantial market.

The firm presently bottles 80 single malts, some of them at different ages. They select the casks for bottling, and because they can choose from so great a stock, are able to maintain consistency in the bottled whisky: consistency of both character and quality. They market their whiskies under various labels, of which the Connoisseurs' Choice is the best-known. All of the Connoisseurs' Choice labels bear the names of the distilleries from which the whiskies come. I asked Ian Urquhart about this – for the use of distillery names on non-distillery bottlings has long been a contentious matter, with distillers taking legal action against independent bottlers for infringement of trade mark. He said that the firm has a dialogue with various of the distillers, who are perfectly agreeable to the names of the distillery appearing on G&M bottles. Small wonder: given the quality of their casks, G&M bottlings cannot but be good advertisements for any whisky.

The firm has had many opportunities to buy distilleries, especially in times when their purchases meant the difference between survival and bankruptcy for a distillery. They resisted the temptation until 1993, when they acquired the Benromach distillery and its stocks from United Distillers. That made sense, for Benromach is on their doorstep and is small enough not to strain resources. They re-equipped the distillery completely, and re-opened it in 1998. It is a charming place, small enough for all of the equipment, from mashtun to spirit still, to be accommodated in one room. As a visitors' centre it is perfect. The new-make spirit is clean, malty and cereal-smelling and promises well for the future.

The sample room at Gordon & MacPhail is extraordinary. Not the number of samples alone: that can be found at any bender's. But the quality of the spirit in the sample bottles, well, that's another thing altogether. When I visited the firm, to taste some of the stocks, Ian Urquhart kindly invited me to take my pick. For anyone who loves malts and believes in a hereafter in which virtue is rewarded, that is a vision of paradise. We settle on four, for I have to drive home. I explain I prefer not-too-old whiskies – for there are stocks here from which we could sample wild and

G & M's extensive sample room

ancient spirits. Ian tells me that they have stocks of whisky in cask which they will never bottle because they have gone woody and the firm rightly thinks that they should not put their name on a whisky which, though it will undoubtedly sell to folk who want old whiskies, will not be of a quality such as the firm would approve. He chooses an Inverleven, an Ardmore, a Mortlach and a 15-year-old Benromach.

Inverleven Distilled 1985, bottled 1999

An Allied Distillers whisky, produced at its Lowland plant at Dumbarton. The stills have now been dismantled, so we shall not see its like again.

The spirit is pale, from a bourbon cask. It smells of flowers and peardrops and aniseed and violets and is delicate and charming. There is honey as well as other sweets, so that the taste comes as a surprise, for it is dead dry and very substantial. Absolutely first-class stuff: a demonstration, if one were needed, of the fact that virtually-unknown distilleries can produce top-drawer malts, provided decent casks are used to hold them.

Ardmore Distilled 1985, bottled 1999

Another Allied distillery, a few miles away in the valley of the river Bogie, near Huntly. It brings to mind a line from Ewan MacColl's rendition of Burns's reworking of an Aberdeenshire drinking song: 'I wouldna gie my three-girr'd cog for a' the quines in Bogie.' It's about whisky, and it's in antique Scots. 'Gie' means give. A 'cog' is a wooden drinking cup, made of separate staves which are held together by hoops, or 'girrs', like a cask. A 'quine' is a young woman and the speaker values his cog above any quine in the valley of the Bogie.

The spirit has been in refill (that is, ex-sherry, once-before-filled) casks, so it has a good colour. It is very peaty, though officially they use malt peated to only 8 ppm. We agree that it seems like a lot more. There is lots of character to go with the peat: flowers, malt, leather, a big, powerful whisky. The peat comes up first and resurfaces later, in a double blast. It tastes dry and spicy.

Mortlach Distilled 1969, bottled 1999

This is one of United Distillers' great Speyside whiskies. Ian Urquhart says the firm was importing rather a lot of oloroso sherry at the end of the 1960s, so they filled the butts with Mortlach. This has been lying in the warehouse ever since.

It is a bit on the woody side to begin with, but not excessively so. There are sweet, vanilla smells up-front, along with a slightly sour note which balances the sweetness pretty well, to give a dried-fruit aroma. The woodiness soon disappears, and the taste is delicate and spicy. The wood reappears in the finish, but not offensively. Altogether a remarkably good maturation for spirit which has been so long in so active a cask.

Benromach Distilled 1983, bottled 1998

This is from the previous incarnation of the distillery. The stills were much larger than the new ones – though Ian tells me that the new-make spirit is remarkably similar. The casks used for this are refill sherry.

The sherry is evident at the start, soon to be supplemented by heavier, grassy scents. Later, malty and spicy aromas make an appearance. The taste is dry and delicate and it lingers long. It is a very satisfactory potation indeed.

PRIVATE BOTTLERS: THE SCOTCH MALT WHISKY SOCIETY

It has been suggested to me that in a book such as this, I ought to say something about the Scotch Malt Whisky Society. I have alluded to the organisation in How Whisky Tastes and elsewhere. I have also at various points mentioned the malt revolution. Since the Scotch Malt Whisky Society was undoubtedly influential in the latter, I assume it will be of interest to readers. That was not meant to sound grudging: it is merely that since I started the society and for many years ran it, I am a little too close to judge and my objectivity in the matter may be suspect. With that caveat, I will tell you about it.

Two of my oldest friends have a little farm in deepest Aberdeenshire, where they have lived for the last thirty years. Back in the 1970s, Stan, the owner of the next farm (a much larger one), was a man of some substance, for those were good times for farming in Scotland. However, Stan showed few signs of affluence. He lived in a little farmhouse which had been built two hundred years before and drove a battered Land Rover of apparently similar antiquity. Stan allowed himself but one luxury: once a year, he drove up over the hills of the Cabrach and down the Fiddich glen to Craigellachie; then up the valley of the Spey to Ballindalloch. At Ballindalloch is the Glenfarclas distillery, owned – then as now – by John and George Grant, son and father. Each year, for as long as anyone could remember, the Grants had filled a small quantity of new Glenfarclas spirit into sherry quarters, casks of about ten gallons' capacity. Those casks lay at the distillery for ten years or so, by which time they were perfectly mature, for in a small cask, the area of wood is large in relation to the volume of spirit. The Grants had a few customers, each of whom would buy one of the casks each year. Since the number of casks filled each year did not increase, availability was hereditary.

Having collected his cask, Stan would return with it to his farmhouse and install it on a wooden cradle by his fireside. He drove a spigot through the bung and drew his drams straight from the wood. I had got to know Stan and liked him well, despite our disagreeing on just about every topic anyone could think of. Whenever Stan heard that I was visiting the McArdles, as I did a few times a year, he would come over of an evening, bearing a lemonade bottle full of dark brown liquor, and eager for combat. We would sample the malt, on whose excellence we were agreed. But that is about as far as we could go without some debate. As the level in the bottle dropped, the intensity of the discussion rose, though never beyond the bounds of mutual liking and respect.

I thought I had never tasted such whisky. I was right: I never had; nor had almost anyone else. It was quite superb. For years, I would look forward to my visits to Aberdeenshire on account of the whisky as well as the company. I told my friends in Edinburgh and all were envious. So, when there came a day that Stan said that he had spoken to George Grant and that maybe there might be a minute possibility of a cask supply becoming available, I was able to gather those friends into a syndicate to purchase such an article. (The syndicate was necessary because we were none of us wealthy and no one could afford a cask by himself.) I went up to Glenfarclas in my old Lagonda motor car, and brought back our cask. The syndicate met in the lobby of my house in Edinburgh and we drew spirit from the wood and tasted it and found it was good. We tasted it a few more times just to be sure and then divided the contents into gallon glass jars by means of a siphon. The members of the syndicate tottered out into the night, each clutching his jar. The surprising thing is that none of the jars got broken.

Which is not to say that they were not soon emptied. They were, and the members of the syndicate began asking for more. So did their friends, so we decided that we would double the size of the syndicate, and that I would seek out more whisky. Well, you can imagine how the story goes from there. Word spread, as word does among the drinking classes, and two things became apparent: first, that the whisky really was better than any of us had ever tasted, and second, there were a lot of people out there who would like to get their throats round such stuff.

We tried other whiskies, which were almost as good as the Glenfarclas, and I enquired why it was that such stuff existed and we appeared to be the only people who knew about it. There were two reasons for the quality: we had been fortunate in getting really fine casks, and we had taken our drams from the casks at full strength. At the time, practically nobody in the whisky industry paid much attention to the quality of the casks they put their malt spirit into. (There were a few exceptions, but not many. The big guys, especially, filled into good, bad and indifferent casks, and bunged them all together when they made their blended whiskies.) It was literally the case that many of the distillers did not know the quality of the whiskies in their warehouses – and did not much care, for all of it was to go into blended whiskies, where the best would mingle with the mediocre. Most distillers who bottled malts, did so at 40 per cent because that was the strength at which blends were sold. And they chill-filtered the spirit, as they did blends, to ensure stability and stop the contents of the bottle going cloudy when cold. The chill-filtration removed much of what gave the whisky its taste. If you could procure malt whisky which had been matured in a really fine cask, and have it without chill-filtration, you got a spirit which was noticeably superior to the same whisky in a proprietary bottling. The reason we were the only people who knew about it was historical – I touch on that in an earlier chapter.

It is from that time that I date my scepticism about connoisseurs. There were plenty folk who claimed to be knowledgeable about whisky; there were few who could tell me why what I had was so good. I then formed an opinion which I have never seen fit to revise, namely that connoisseurship is mainly nonsense and self-regard. There are exceptions but, in the Scots saying, 'gey few, an' the're a' deid'.

I then formed an idea which, with the help of a few friends, I pursued, namely that it ought to be possible to sell whisky of such quality in such condition. Through friends, I obtained interviews with people in the Scotch whisky industry, who could be expected to know about such things. Without exception, they replied in the negative. There was no market for such a product, nobody would want to drink it, and anyway you couldn't sell it because nobody would let you put the name of their whisky on a bottle and without names nobody would stock it. Pretty conclusive, and had I been a little more prudent, I would have gone away and done something else, and this book would never have been written.

I didn't. I called a meeting of the syndicate and put to them the proposition that we form a limited company, to which we all contribute equally, and set up in business selling cask-strength, unfiltered whisky. They agreed. I applied to the Registrar of Companies for a company to be called The Scotch Malt Whisky Society Ltd, and got it. We bought a few casks and had them bottled, and opened our doors.

The doors we opened were up a stair on a building site. I had had another good idea, which was that we purchase a building in Leith called The Vaults, which was in the process of being vacated by J. G. Thomson & Co., Scotland's oldest wine merchants. The firm had been in the building since 1705 and now thought it surplus to requirements. It was four storeys high, the upper levels having been built in 1785, though the first floor was of late mediaeval date and the vaults beneath from the thirteenth century or maybe earlier. Five of us clubbed together to buy it and restore it. As a financial speculation, it was disastrous, but we did at least ensure that the Society could have the oldest commercial building in Scotland as its base. For a year, Anne Dana ran an office which had holes in the ceiling and sometimes in the floor, and the members of the Society (there were more than a hundred of them) loved it.

The rest, as they say, is history. We bought really fine casks of whisky and bottled the contents in dark green bottles at full strength. We identified the whiskies only by number, so as to avoid trade mark problems. We didn't advertise, arguing that the stuff was so fine and so unique that, as happened with my whisky syndicate, word would spread and discerning drinkers would beat a path to our door. Our customers would be members of a society and we would treat them as such. We would communicate with them by means of a periodical newsletter, in which we would write descriptions of the whiskies we had available. They would order and we would send the cratur to them by post.

There has been a lot of whisky through the stills since then, but the Society continues to bottle malts exactly as it originally did. Its whiskies are no longer unique (though the organisation is), for there are now lots of special bottlings, both by private bottlers and by the distillers themselves. Those very distillers, who said there could be no market for such a product, are now among the most enthusiastic purveyors of it. However, what they say about imitation and flattery is true. What is also true, is that some of the distillers get up to their old tricks, and pass inferior whiskies off as absolutely fabulous, on the basis of techniques copied from the Society. Indeed, one of them went so far as to set up a copycat organisation which is still running, despite promises to the contrary.

I expect every parent has the sensation which I sometimes experience apropos the Society, of watching offspring who, rather surprisingly, are able to survive without parental support. They grow up, depart and develop an individuality of their own. Respectable people are horrified by their tearaway offspring and bohemians find, to their surprise, that their progeny have become respectable. I think I, and the members of the syndicate, fall into the latter category; we are mystified and a little dismayed.

PRIVATE DISTILLERS: THE MALT MASTERCLASS

Until a little over two hundred years ago, the whisky still was part of the domestic equipment of most houses of any size. The Excise laws permitted private distilling in stills of not more than ten gallons' capacity. So long as the whisky was consumed by the people of the house, the distilling was legal. But if you produced more whisky than you could consume, and you sold the surplus, the still became illegal. To say such things were widespread seems something of an understatement, when we consider that in 1777, Edinburgh was estimated to have more than four hundred illegal stills and eight licensed distilleries. In 1779, a new Act of Parliament was passed which restricted the size of permitted stills to two gallons and two years later, their use was prohibited altogether and legal private distilling ceased in Scotland. From then on, for more than two hundred years, nobody was allowed to distil spirits in a small still anywhere in the United Kingdom.

To pass laws is one thing, to get people to obey them is another. Despite greatly increased surveillance by HM Customs & Excise, illegal distilling flourished in Scotland. It did so because there was a market for the product of illegal stills which was, by and large, better in quality than that which came from the larger, licensed variety. Because of its quality, illegally-produced whisky commanded a premium price and this, together with the absence of duty payable, made for very attractive profit margins. Law enforcement was largely ineffectual, not least because in the Highlands at least, there was a degree of connivance between landowners (who were supposed to enforce the law) and distillers whose stills were worked on their land. It was not until the Act of 1823 reduced duty and so reduced profit margins, that illicit distilling declined.

Nevertheless, it continued here and there, its popularity proportional to the rate of Excise duty: the higher the duty, the greater the profit from illegal distilling. It is not unknown today for that very reason. A few years ago, the *Dunbartonshire Gazette* reported the conviction for illicit production of spirits of a man who, having been made redundant by his employer, invested his redundancy settlement in distilling plant. He set up, courtesy of a local enterprise board, in a building provided by his local authority. He bought quantities of sugar which he dissolved in water and fermented with bakers' yeast. This he distilled twice, to produce a liquor which was virtually tasteless and without colour, at about 65% alcohol. He was apprehended with a vanful of the stuff in Fort William, where he had been selling it to bartenders, who sold it as vodka.

When Harold Wilson's government set up the Highlands and Islands Development Board in the 1960s, they appointed as chairman Kenneth Alexander, a distinguished economist. Ken had the job of running a committee whose business it was to stimulate an economy which at the time was doing rather poorly. He was the ideal man for the job, for not only did he have clout in high places, but he never lost the common touch, or forgot that the intended beneficiaries of the Board were the ordinary people of the Highlands. Those ordinary people knew and liked Ken Alexander (he never used the title) and one of them gave him a present of a copper whisky still. The donor was an old man, who for many years had worked the still in a remote glen.

When I was chairman of the Scotch Malt Whisky Society, we held a Burns Supper once a year to which admission was by invitation only. I issued the invitations, and there was no fairness or democracy in their issue, on the very good ground that if you were fair, you would get a lot of boring people and the supper would be dull. I invited my friends and people whom I knew would be fun, and they were. The suppers became legendary. We had some of the finest of Scotland's talent – and a fair amount of disgraceful behaviour: altogether very much in the mould of the man whose life we celebrated. One year we had to eject one of our guest speakers because he got so drunk and threw bread rolls at people from the top table. I had to ad lib the Toast to the Lasses in his absence. I don't think my toast was all that great, but it got a rapturous reception from a delighted audience. I must say Michael, whom we had thrown out, never held a grudge about it.

It was our custom at the Burns Supper to award a life membership of the Society to people who we thought had made a real contribution to the lives of the Scottish people. (We purposely avoided mention of Scotland, on the ground that 'Scotland' is an abstraction which has long been hijacked by the Establishment.) One year, we awarded the prize to Ken and he in return gave us the whisky still. It is there today, sitting above the bar in Leith.

Some years after that, I was approached by Ralph Steadman, the artist and wonderful cartoonist, who some time before had become a friend over a few drams. Ralph had just finished writing and illustrating his wonderful book about whisky, *Still Life with Bottle*. We had spoken about the still and I had said that I fancied it might just be possible to persuade Customs & Excise to grant a licence, if we could think of a good enough excuse. Ralph explained that he was due to open the Cheltenham Arts Festival the following spring, and thought it would be great if we could distil whisky as part of the festival. I liked the idea and offered to approach the Excise. This I did, and somewhat to my surprise was given a special licence to distil whisky, provided that none of the distillate was drunk and that all of it was subsequently destroyed. I got Macallan to supply a gallon of low wines and we went off to Cheltenham with still, worm tub (which I had cobbled together out of a half a hogshead) and a small gas stove to heat the still. It was a huge success: everyone wanted to see what was going on and, as Ralph said, it completely upstaged his act.

The whole thing was great fun, and I was delighted. I was even more delighted by a very old gentlemen, very elegant in a pale grey suit and white hat, who enquired politely about what we were doing. I spent some time with him and in return, he gave me a little volume of poems, which he had signed. It was Laurie Lee.

Some years later, I was obliged to leave the Scotch Malt Whisky Society, a matter which was greeted with relief in some quarters and which I now think was probably for the best: I have never been content with careful management, which is what at that time was required. Besides, the Society had become respectable and I had a boat to build, and other, more amusing, things to do. I did not, however, lose my interest in whisky, and found myself in some little demand among people who wanted an outsider's view of Scotch whisky. This book is part of the response to that demand.

It appeared to me also that there was a need for information about Scotch whisky, beyond what could be met by books alone – and for information free of the partiality and special pleading which colour the accounts of anyone trying to sell you the stuff. There was a large and growing constituency of people who had discovered malt whiskies, and who wanted to know something about them. Bars were stocking large numbers of bottled malts and bartenders were being asked about them. Sommeliers were having to respond to their customers' requests on the basis of very slender knowledge. It seemed to me that there was a need for a truly independent source of information about Scotch whisky. I spoke to a few friends, some of whom were members of the Society, others who were or had been in the Scotch whisky industry. So we set up a small firm to provide expertise on matters to do with whisky. We called it the Malt Masterclass. Under that guise we have been holding whisky tastings and running classes at venues around the world. Some of the distillers don't thank us for it, but the public seems to appreciate what we do.

One of the problems we find in explaining the whisky-making process is one to which I have referred in an earlier chapter, namely the difficulty which people have in gaining an intuitive comprehension of what is going on – especially people whose education contained little or nothing about chemistry. Distilling is especially hard to grasp, for when you see it happen in a distillery, the whole thing is on so great a scale that it is difficult to see what is going on.

The obvious answer to the problem was to show people a still working, as Ralph and I did at Cheltenham. The difficulty was to get a licence from the Excise. I wrote a letter to our local Excise office, enquiring whether we could have such a licence. They gave me a prompt and definite reply – in the negative. I wrote back, very politely, asking why not. They, equally politely, said, because it was against the law, citing the act of 1781. I then said, 'But I have already had a licence', citing the Cheltenham precedent. There then followed a long silence, followed by a telephone call, in which it was explained to me that the Cheltenham distillation had actually been against the law and I shouldn't have had a licence. I said, 'How come

I got one then?' and they said, because the people in Bristol who issued the licence were English and knew nothing about whisky.

While that seemed perfectly understandable, I thought that perhaps I might prise open the chink which it provided in the otherwise impregnable armour of the Excise laws, so I persisted with a stream of letters and telephone calls – all very polite, but firmly refusing to go away. I think, to be honest, my little campaign coincided with a certain relaxation on the part of the Excise: folk who are faced with drug smuggling and VAT fraud on a gigantic scale aren't going to worry too much about some daft guy distilling a few pints of low wines. The upshot was that we got a licence to run a small still: the first private distillers (other than laboratories and the like) since 1781.

We then needed a still. Enquiries of industrial still makers showed that it was likely to be very expensive indeed. Happily my colleague Jamie mentioned it to our mutual friend Peter Darbyshire, who at the time was MD of Glenmorangie and is a really good guy. Peter said they had a great coppersmith, Norman, who might make one for us. I went up to Tain, where Norman was one of the Fourteen Men. Norman very kindly made for us a replica of one of the Glenmorangie spirit stills, complete with boil collar and tall neck. It stands a meter or so high and takes a charge of about five litres of low wines. Norman also made us a very classy copper worm tub, out of an old hot-water boiler.

It was one of those felicitous connections which I suppose happen everywhere, but seem especially common in the Highlands. Norman and I found we had people and interests in common. He had formerly been an employee of Gardners, the great Manchester engineering firm which made what were acknowledged in their day to be the finest diesel engines in the world. They were economical to run, needed few repairs and lasted virtually forever. I knew a fair bit about Gardners, having had as my instructor in such matters my old friend Walter Scott, engineer extraordinary and Gardners expert, who had died a few years before. Norman knew Walter, because he had worked for twenty years as a young man for Gardners. He also knew my motor car, which was an ancient Lagonda grand touring saloon, which Gardners had fitted with an experimental diesel back in the 1930s. It was the same Gardner which had propelled me up to Ballindalloch for my first cask of Glenfarclas; it was the same Gardner which had propelled me and Dick Pountain to Czechoslovakia when we went there with two cases of malt to celebrate the end of Communism with our Czech friend, Berty Hornung. Dick it was who first explained to me the elements of the chemistry of whisky-making and maturing.

I could go on, but I think I have come to the end.

Reading List

Atkins, P.W., *Molecules*, W.H. Freeman & Co., New York, 1987.
The best introduction to organic chemistry generally and the chemistry of flavour in particular that I have seen. An intelligible book about chemistry for those who know nothing of the subject, as well as a delight for those who do.

Barnard, Alfred, *The Whisky Distilleries of the United Kingdom*, London, 1887. Reprint by Mainstream, Edinburgh, 1987.
The original traveller's account of distilleries and still one of the best, it portrays the distilleries in the heroic age of Scotch distilling. Lots of local detail make for interest well beyond that of mere whisky.

Brillat-Savarin, Jean-Anthelme, *La Physiologie du gout*, published privately in 1825. Various editions; published in Penguin Classics as *The Physiology of Taste* in 1994.
The seminal work on gastronomy by the greatest of amateurs: judge, violinist, scientist, connoisseur and cook.

Burns, Edward, *Bad Whisky*, Balvag Books, Glasgow, 1995.
What the lower classes were served as whisky in the nineteenth century: meths, ether, glycerine, opium and worse. A welcome antidote to the heritage crap with which some distillers adulterate the history of whisky.

Cooper, Derek, *A Taste of Scotch*, Andre Deutsch, 1989.
A volume of quotations about Scotch whisky, as vast and varied as the subject and as the erudition of the author. Use it for reference, or for a flavour of the culture of Scotland and whisky.

Craig, Charles, *The Scotch Whisky Industry Review*, Norfolk, 1994.
A vast – and correspondingly expensive – tome of facts about Scotch whisky. A source book rather than a history and mainly valuable as reference.

Daiches, David, *Scotch Whisky, Its Past and Present*, Andre Deutsch, 1959; paperback edition, Birlinn, 1995.
An erudite and elegant history of Scotch whisky by a man who, as one of Scotland's leading scholars, writes from both love and knowledge. This is the book which began the malt revolution and no serious library on whisky is complete without it.

Daiches, David, *A Wee Dram*, Andre Deutsch, 1990.
The appearances of whisky in Scottish literature – and who better to choose them? Use, like the Derek Cooper, for a taste of the variety and versatility of the Scots when attending to their native liquor.

Gunn, Neil, *Whisky & Scotland: A Practical & Spiritual Survey*, Routledge, 1935.
A writer and an Exciseman, Gunn was in a great Scottish tradition. The book, the first half of which is mostly nonsense, is nevertheless historically valuable. It is a lone cry against the distillers whom Gunn rightly regarded as having deprived Scotland of her heritage of malt whisky.

Jackson, Michael, *Michael Jackson's Malt Whisky Companion*.
The best of the pocket-sized guides: brief but good introduction, comprehensive list of distilleries, tasting notes for all the main bottlings by someone who knows his business. His star rating should not be taken seriously, though: it is unclear in its intentions and misleading in its result.

Jackson, Michael, *The World Guide to Whisky*, Dorling Kindersley.
A magisterial work on whisky: Irish, American and Japanese as well as Scotch. Well-informed, elegantly written text and good illustrations. Particularly valuable coverage of whiskies other than Scotch.

MacLean, Charles, *Malt Whisky*, Mitchell Beazley.
Comprehensive and detailed treatment of its subject: where it came from, how it is made and what to do with it. The best account of flavour and tasting. Very fine design and illustrations – most of the latter specially commissioned original photographs. A work of art as well as artifice.

McNeill, F. Marian, *The Scots Kitchen*, Blackie, 1929. *The Scots Cellar*, Richard Paterson, Edinburgh, 1956.
Two companion works by a scholar of Scottish language, culture, food and drink: they give some idea of the richness and diversity which a poor country could produce – and her recipes for punches and cordials show how whisky was taken in the days when you would steep twelve pounds of cherries in three quarts of the stuff. Her recipe for Cullen Skink is arguably Scotland's greatest contribution to gastronomy.

Moss & Hume, *The Making of Scotch Whisky*, James & James, Edinburgh, 1981.
This, subtitled 'A History of the Scotch Whisky Distilling Industry', is by far the most detailed and scholarly history of Scotch. In places almost unreadable, it is nevertheless indispensable: for what it says and for its references. Long out of print and hard to find.

Murray, Jim, *Classic Blended Scotch*, Prion, 1999.
The only work which is solely about blended whiskies, and therefore valuable. From its gush, however, you would conclude that there are no bad whiskies, for even the dullest are given tasting notes as effusive as they are fanciful.

Saintsbury, George, *Notes on a Cellar-Book*, Macmillan, 1920 (many reprints).
One of the few original sources of information on whisky-drinking among the upper classes in the nineteenth century. An English scholar and connoisseur of fine liquor; headmaster of Elgin Academy and later professor of English Literature at Edinburgh University.

Suskind, Patrick, *Perfume/Das Parfum*, Zurich, 1985. English translation by John E. Woods, Penguin, 1987.
An unsatisfactory novel, but its early part is an astonishing description of mediaeval Paris in terms of smells: a dog's-nose view, so to speak. Read it and get some idea of what you are missing by not using your nose.

Wilson, Ross, *Scotch Made Easy*, Hutchinson, 1959.
Hard to find but worth the search: a literary history of drinking in general and whisky in particular. Dense and prolix, but worth digging, for there are gems for the finding.